SO-EIH-539

"Rachel and Rebekah Winters have created the Backstage Pass to the heart of God! *Behind The Music* belongs in the bedroom of every teenager (and adult).

Who hasn't stood in line waiting to meet your favorite artist, and when it's your turn to meet them, you freeze? Your well-planned questions break from your tongue in a curt, 'I like your songs.' Only later, while listening to their music, do you remember the rich questions you longed to discuss: their view of God, favorite verses, or how they began in music. Wouldn't it be great to hear their views on humility within the world of fame, leading others to a God who allows tragedy, or how Christ brought them through a very dark time? *Behind The Music* does just that.

This is not only a devotional. It is an 80 day hope-filled journey of spiritual growth, guided by the top artists on the planet. I encourage you to meet God, *Behind The Music*."

- Doug Herman
Author of *Come Clean* and *FaithQuake*, www.PureRevolution.com

"I got to personally know the hearts of Rebekah and Rachel as we 'belly-flopped' at the foot of the cross every Monday night for a year, on the floor of our sanctuary for a teen Bible study. What a blessing to know that because of their passion for the truth and love of Jesus, they are part of a devotional that will bring thousands of others to the cross. Above all ..."

- Tim Johnson
Pastor of Pfrimmer's Chapel UMC, Corydon, Indiana

"As I reflect on the most intimate moments of worship I've had throughout the course of my life, there is a common thread tying them together ... music. In *Behind The Music*, our favorite musicians reflect on how the Lord inspired the music that has touched our hearts."

- Danny Wuerffel
1996 Heisman Trophy Winner and Former NFL Quarterback
Vice President, Desire Street Ministries, www.desirestreet.org

"In *Behind The Music*, Jason Roy from Building 429 writes about humility. In the motorsports world, the measurement of a driver's accomplishments is dictated by championships, wins, and losses. As Jason points out, however, winning is more about lifting up the person or people over whom you have triumphed. Acknowledging others during your time of accomplishment is an imitation of God. There are important and meaningful lessons to be learned within *Behind The Music*."

- Sam Hornish, Jr.
2001 and 2002 IndyCar® Series champion, www.samhornish.com

What Others Are Saying About BEHIND THE MUSIC

"Behind The Music is an amazing ministry tool. Page after page, I found myself more in love with Jesus. Thank you, Rachel and Rebekah, for being obedient to God's calling."

- David Nasser
Author and Speaker, www.davidnasser.com

"This is such a cool resource for spiritual growth. I loved hearing from the artists and getting a glimpse of how Jesus is working in their heart. I love to see how the Spirit is what truly drives the music. Thanks, ladies, for being yet another guide on this journey with Christ."

- Jayson French
Youth Speaker, Director of Conferences, Christ In Youth, www.ciy.com

"All of us have favorite songs that really touch our souls. After reading how some of these artists were led of God to pen their songs, my spirit was touched in an even deeper way. Now these songs have an even deeper meaning and significance."

- Lakita Garth
Entertainer, Speaker, and Author, www.lakitagarth.com

"Behind The Music is a fresh, original look at praising God. Rachel and Rebekah have done an amazing job of reaching the hearts of our favorite musicians and bridging a connection to our own hearts."

- Dandi Daley Mackall
Author of about 400 books for children & adults, including *Winnie the Horse Gentler, Maggie's Story, Eva Underground*, www.dandibooks.com

"When God led King Jehoshaphat to march against his enemies in the Old Testament, He had the musicians at the head of the troop. Today's musicians are no different - they're on the frontlines fighting for this generation. Building 429 says in their devotion: 'This is a generation of people who are faced with more temptation, sin, and consequence than any generation before ... God has called us to challenge the youth of America ... to strive to KNOW Him.' This book is a refreshing read because we get to see deeper than the stage persona, to the passion that drives the heart of each musician."

- Dr. Lori Salierno
President & CEO of Celebrate Life International, www.CelebrateLife.org

"This book is an amazing tool. It's about having a personal relationship with our heavenly Father, who never fails to love us. I love this book."

- Heather Whitestone McCallum
Miss America 1995, Author of *Listening With My Heart* and *Heavenly Crowns*, www.heatherwhitestone.com

BEHIND THE MUSIC

a devotional

RACHEL WINTERS and
REBEKAH WINTERS

BEHIND THE MUSIC

a devotional

devotions by your favorite
Christian recording artists

RACHEL WINTERS and
REBEKAH WINTERS

FAITH
PRESS

an imprint of winters publishing
p.o. box 501 • greensburg, in 47240 • 800-457-3230
www.winterspublishing.com • www.faithpressonline.com
www.behindthemusicdevotional.com

Behind The Music - a devotional
© 2006 by Rachel Winters and Rebekah Winters

All rights reserved. No part of this publication may be reproduced, stored in a retrieval system, or transmitted in any form by any means–electronic, mechanical, photocopy, recording, or any other–without the prior permission of the publisher, except as provided by USA copyright law. The only exception is brief quotations in printed reviews. Every effort has been made to assure that this book is accurate.

Scripture quotations taken from the following sources:
The Amplified® Bible (AMP), copyright © 1954, 1958, 1962, 1964, 1965, 1987 by the Lockman Foundation. Used by permission. • The American Standard Version of the Holy Bible (ASV). • The Message (MSG) by Eugene H. Peterson, copyright © 1993, 1994, 1995, 1996, 2000, 2001, 2002. Used by permission of NavPress Publishing Group. All rights reserved. • The New American Standard Bible (NASB), copyright © 1960, 1962, 1963, 1968, 1971, 1972, 1973, 1975, 1977, 1995 by the Lockman Foundation. Used by permission. • The New Century Version® (NCV), copyright © 1987, 1988, 1991 by Thomas Nelson, Inc. All rights reserved. • The HOLY BIBLE, NEW INTERNATIONAL VERSION® (NIV), copyright © 1973, 1978, 1984 by International Bible Society. Used by permission of Zondervan. All rights reserved. • The New King James Version (NKJV®), copyright © 1979, 1980, 1982 by Thomas Nelson, Inc. Used by permission. All rights reserved. • The Holy Bible, New Living Translation (NLT), copyright © 1996. Used by permission of Tyndale House Publishers, Inc., Wheaton, Illinois 60189. All rights reserved. • New Revised Standard Version Bible (NRSV), copyright © 1989 by the Division of Christian Education of the National Council of Churches of Christ in the United States of America. Used by permission. All rights reserved. • Revised Standard Version (RSV), copyright © 1946, 1952, 1971 by the Division of Christian Education of the National Council of Churches of Christ in the United States of America. Used by permission. All rights reserved. • The World English Bible (WEB).

Published by Faith Press
An imprint of Winters Publishing, P.O. Box 501, Greensburg, IN 47240
www.faithpressonline.com • www.winterspublishing.com
www.behindthemusicdevotional.com
800-457-3230

Cover Design by Rachel Winters and Rebekah Winters

Front Cover Photos:
Jars of Clay, from Redemption Songs by David Dobson courtesy Essential Records
Newsboys, courtesy Inpop Records
Casting Crowns, courtesy Provident Label Group
Guitar, by Kevin Russ

Back Cover Photos:
Natalie Grant, by Dominick Guillemot courtesy Curb Records
Audio Adrenaline, by Kerri Stuart
Hawk Nelson, courtesy Tooth & Nail Records
Kids in the Way, by Frank Mullen courtesy Flicker Records
Building 429, by Aaron Rapoport courtesy Word Records
Todd Agnew, courtesy Ardent Records
Thousand Foot Krutch, courtesy Tooth & Nail Records
BarlowGirl, by Kristin Barlowe courtesy Fervent Records
Skillet, courtesy Ardent Records

ISBN-10 1-883651-26-3   ISBN-13 978-1-883651-26-8
Library of Congress Control Number: 2006922291

Printed in the United States of America

CONTENTS

CONTENTS

CONTENTS

Dedications

To Jesus Christ, my Lord and Savior. Without You, none of this would have been possible. Thank You for blessing me beyond reason every day of my life, and for Your love and grace.

To Mom and Dad, who are always there for me and encourage me to never give up. Thank you for all of your countless hours and sleepless nights helping us with this book! I love you both so much!

To Rebekah, for being an amazing "big sister."

And to all of the people who helped along the way, thank you!

Rachel

To God, for making all of this possible.

To my parents... I love you.

Rachel... you're already the perfect "manager," and none of this would have happened without all your hard work.

For anyone who ever sparked a revolution, because that's what I hope this book leads to.

And to each and every one of you who buys this book... thank you and keep rockin'.

Rebekah

Dedications Dedications Dedications Dedications

Our Melody Of Thanks

Thank you to all of the artists for taking the time to write the devotions and for their willingness to be a part of the project, and to those who endorsed the book.

In addition, our thanks to all of the managers, publicists, and others who helped us put this project together, including Sean Algaier, Carrie Allen, Tamara Allen, Carol Anderson, Cheryl Anteau, Misty Ascroft, Mike Atkins, Diane Audiss, Todd Baker, Amy Barker, Vince Barlow, Blair Berle, Tracy Bishir, Shawn Blackney, Rita Blumer, David Breen, Shannon Brown, Scott Bullard, Leanne Bush, Jayme Butler, Anthony Calhoun, Melissa Campbell, Steve Campbell, Nicole Carpenter, Steve Clark, Emily Cobb, Lizza Connor, Jackie Cook, Sarah Copas, Michael Corcoran, Scott Crews, Kat Davis, Kujo Davis, Teresa Davis, Kellie Delahoussaye, Chris DeTray, Tammy Deveau, Dennis Disney, Sarah Ann Drumheller, Russ Evers, Amy Fogleman, Edlyn Forero, Jason Fowler, Tim Frank, Troy Groves, Rich Guider, Sacha Guzy, Steve Hammond, Anna Hammonds, Penny Harrison, Brock Haylock, April Hefner, Jeremy Henley, Bob Hills, Chance Hoag, James Hodgin, Rick Hoganson, Van Hohe, Ryan Howard, JoAnna Illingworth, Mike Jay, Stacey Jennette, Pastor Tim Johnson, Velvet R. Kelm, Zach Kelm, Eric Kilby, Kathy King, Ryan Lampa, Josh Lanting, Jeremy Lee, Lori Lenz, Starla Lilly, Meridith Long, Tiffany Long, Amanda MacKinnon, Randy Maricle, Aleix Martinez, Claire Maurer, Corey Mayerlen, Brian Mayes, Alisha McArthur, Mike McCloskey, Marlena McClure, David McCollum, Glenda McNalley, Shawn McSpadden, Allison Moody, Jason Morey, Andy Morris, Kim Nehs, Chris Nichols, Roxanne Nichols, Roshare Norman, Tim Ottley, Tim Parker, Lance Patrick, Steve Perry, Philip Peters, Jerry Phelps, Ivonne Pineda, Alyssa Pizer, Ray Pokorny, Rachel Raju, Aislynn Rappe, Ryan Rettler, Blair Richey, Sue Ross, Beau Rotramel, Anita Rundell, Dana Salsedo, Abby Sasser, Jonathan Scarlet, Jim Scherer, Jeremy Seawell, Andy Skarda, Jacquelyn Marushka Smith, Jennifer Smith, Alexis Soelter, Diana Stancil, Jim Stennett, Valerie Summers, Angela Sumrall, Miffy Swan, Katrina Tadman, Mo Thieman, Jessie Thomas, Steve Thomas, Hywel Thomas, Anne Marie Tucker, Darren Tyler, Mark Van Meter, Gabe Vasquez, Blair Vickroy, Dave Wagner, Stephanie Waldrop, Janet Weir, Tara Wells, Courtney Wichtendahl, David Williams, Hope Williams, Nikki Wolfe, Jeff Zubeck, and everyone else who helped along the way …

BEHIND THE MUSIC

Concert Photos Concert Concert Photos Concert

Prelude • The Story Behind The Book

We've learned a lot of things in our lives. We learned how to walk, how to talk ... we learned how to "walk the talk." We've discovered things about ourselves, our friends, life, and most of all, God.

We've grown, and our interests have changed and matured, but Christian music is something that will always have a special place in our hearts. Through our love for the music, we have been blessed to have the opportunity to see a lot of these artists you are about to hear from in concert. We began to learn one of the most valuable lessons of our lives. We began to see the stardom fade, and as the lights went down, the spotlight was put on God. The artists would share from their hearts - their struggles, their stories, their passions. God put a dream in our hearts, a desire for everyone to see *behind the music*. Thousands of emails, three years of prayer, and a hundred concerts later, that dream became a reality - this devotional.

The heart of the artist desires to show you the heart of our Lord, to give Him the glory, to guide you to turn your eyes toward heaven. Instead of being caught up in the worldly idea of fame, we challenge you to put your focus behind the music. Be still, and rest in the truth of our Creator.

May you begin to fully embrace His love for you and learn to live in His blessing.

God Bless You!

Rachel and Rebekah

KUTLESS

A CHRISTLIKE LOVE

Jon Micah Sumrall

*O*ne of our main messages as Kutless has always been loving people and the love of God. I firmly believe that loving people is what turns people to Christ, saying, "Hey, there's a better way." As I go out, and I'm able to genuinely care about people's lives and what they're going through, they know I'm a Christian. I don't have to tell them that. It's amazing how **when Christ lives in you, and you're not afraid to be a Christian, He just shines out of you.** I love the saying by St. Francis of Assisi, "Preach the gospel at all times. Use words only if necessary."

The Bible talks about how it's kindness that brings men to repentance. As an American church, we've come to a place where we try to condemn people. "You're a sinner, and you need to change." I've seen situations where people who have walked away from the Lord, or aren't Christians, have been shoved away their whole life by Christianity. Some Christians have condemned them with words or by hypocritical lifestyles. These people are looking for an answer. Too often, we point at their wrongdoings instead of pointing to the Answer.

It's been really cool to see how as we've been more effective in loving people, they've listened to what we said, and people that have had walls up forever have suddenly opened up a little bit. It's been amazing how they've started asking questions and have begun to genuinely be interested, because they've realized who we are is real. They see that there's something different, and it's that something that they're looking for. It's important that we love people, and use words only when necessary. The time will come for those words to be used.

UNPLUGGED
a deeper look

Can we draw the unsaved to Christ simply by living our lives as an example of Jesus? It is important that we share the gospel, but we have to be sensitive to the Spirit as to when someone's heart is ready to receive it. I met a woman who was into Wicca and witchcraft at a music video taping. When I shared with her about Jesus or Christianity, I saw a wall shoot up. We had very different perspectives, so I asked her about her family and how she got into film, and her face lit up. She couldn't believe that I, a Christian, was interested in her life. She had been despised by other Christians who had condemned her for the way she was living. I said, "I'm sorry. Christianity is not about us pointing fingers at each other. It's about us looking to God because we've all made mistakes." She was not ready for the gospel, but I felt like that was the first time a Christian had ever cared about her. I felt like seeds were planted that night. As you go through your life, remember to love first, and that in itself will preach. I believe in the power of God's love; spread it everywhere you can.

Do we need Christian friends to hold us accountable in our walk - friends to really connect with and build one another up? The band's a lot closer now than ever, and it's really neat to see how much more effective we can be in ministry when we're unified as a group. Growing up, I played soccer. The soccer teams were known as "the biggest partiers" in school. I trained with them; we were on traveling trips together all the time. But I had two Christian friends that were my best friends in the world. I met them at church, and we hit it off. They were the two guys that were there to keep me accountable. I could hang out with my soccer team, but our lifestyles were different. I was a Christian, and they weren't. I was able to spend most of my time with my two other friends. We'd go to church together, hang out together, and do homework

together. They were there to encourage me when I was feeling down and beat up by things that were going on. It's really important to have someone by your side that can keep you solid and focused - someone who's a Christian, that you can talk to, who understands. When you get out all by yourself, it can be a really lonely place. Start by going to church and be in fellowship with other Christians. You'll find people to become friends with that will encourage you in your Christian walk.

BACKSTAGE PASS
getting to know

How did the band meet and form? We met at Warner Pacific College in Portland, Oregon, and we started out doing a worship service at our school. We were talking one night, and a few of the guys said it had really been on their hearts to be in a band and play original music. All of us looked at each other and said, "Our hearts, too. We totally want to do this." I had written a few songs, so I brought them to the band. We started playing shows, and the next thing we knew, we got signed, and on the road we went.

Do you feel God leading the band in a special direction? Right now, we're on a bit of a new horizon as a band. I am excited to see what's around the bend. It's important to play shows for Christian audiences, and to give them an alternative to listen to, but I also have a heart for the unsaved kids. I'm not sure how that will come about, but I feel like there's some new things around the corner.

How does the band plan to further its ministry in the future? One of my favorite Bible verses is Psalm 37:4 (NKJV) which says, "Delight yourself also in the LORD, and He shall give you the desires of your heart." I've found that God will put a desire in my heart, give me a vision, and I'll be like, "I really long to do this." When I had a desire to do music, I didn't know how to make it happen. I would just pray, "God, You're going to have to make it happen. Lord, I'll just delight myself in You, and if this is of Your will, then make it happen. If not,

You'll change my heart." Sometimes, He changes my heart, and says, "That's what you want to do, not what I want to do." He will just open the doors. I'm trusting the Lord for whatever He has around this bend, and the things that are on my heart will hopefully work out.

Birthdays:
Jon Micah: October 13
James: December 27
Ryan: June 11
Dave: December 18
Jeffrey: August 24

Favorite Bible Verses:
Jon Micah: Psalm 37:4
James: James 2:12
Ryan: 1 Timothy 4:12
Dave: 2 Corinthians 5:21
Jeffrey: Romans 8:35

Website: www.kutless.com

Booking Agency:
DCB Agency
615-778-9484

Fan Mail Address:
Kutless
P.O. Box 1036
Tualatin, OR 97062

Fan Email Address: fanmail@kutless.com

OUT OF EDEN

A FRIEND THAT LASTS

Andrea Kimmey Baca

I've had the same best friend for thirteen years; her name is Maggie. I met her in middle school in the eighth grade. She wasn't a Christian when I met her, but I brought her to church with me, and to any Christian activities I thought that she would like. We hung out all the time, and I knew that in order for her to understand who Jesus is, I would have to be that to her. I tried my best to be a good influence in her life, because I was the only Christian that she knew. In tenth grade, we were coming home from youth group, and she asked me a lot of questions about God. I was able to answer her questions and direct her to the Bible, and that night she got saved.

Both Maggie and I have grown a lot spiritually since then, and like the Bible says, man sharpens a man (Proverbs 27:17). That is very true of our relationship. I have given Maggie permission to hold me accountable in the way that I act and live my life, and she has allowed me to speak into her life, too. I don't always like what she says to me, but I take what she says to God in prayer. I know that she has my best interests at heart. You know, **it's not always easy to have people tell you the truth about yourself, but it's worth it**. It would be easy for me to only have people around me who say, "Yes," to everything that I do, but I wouldn't grow in the Lord that way. My best friend and I have not only a friendship, but a covenantal friendship, which means we are committed to one another. No matter what comes up in our lives and relationship, we will seek God and work it out. We have had our share of arguments and ups and downs, but I know she loves me like a sister and that we will always be there for one another. Proverbs 18:24 (NIV) says, "… there is a friend who sticks closer than a brother."

I think it is important to have friends who don't know Christ so that we have people to minister to, but I feel my closest friends need to know Christ, so that I can trust that when they speak into my life, they are guided by the Holy Spirit. God orchestrates every detail of our lives even down to the friendships that we have. I truly believe that my best friend is a gift from God.

Pray for godly friendships. If the friends that you know don't know Christ, I encourage you to pray that God will help you to be a good influence on them and lead them to Christ. There is nothing better than a true friend.

Another Verse:
Proverbs 17:17

Prayer

Lord, help me to cherish the friendships that You've given me and commit to pray for my friends. Bless me with friendships that are meaningful and will last. If I have anything against a friend, I pray that You will forgive me and teach me to love as You love. Give me opportunities to share who You are with my friends who don't know You. In Jesus' name, Amen.

UNPLUGGED
a deeper look

Out of Eden Out of Eden Out of Eden Out of Eden

Why is it important to have relationships that revolve around Christ? Godly friendships are vital to our Christian walk because they can encourage us with godly wisdom, and we can be assured that they are coming from a biblical perspective.

How can you have Christ-centered relationships while living "in the world?" It is important to seek out people who are Christians in our school, so that we have people who will stand up with us against those things we know are wrong. It makes it easier to say, "No," when we have someone standing with us. Christ lives in us, so when we meet people it is possible for them to see that. We need to let our light shine, meaning in even little things, we talk about God or make decisions that show that we know and love God. When we get to know each other we talk about ourselves, so when you talk, season your conversation with talk of God and what He means to you.

Is it important for Christians to improve relationships even with people they may not enjoy spending time with? I don't believe that it's important to be best friends with everyone, but it's also not right to have ill feelings towards anyone. We are commanded to love our neighbors as ourselves. If there is someone who really wants to be our friend, we ought to try to put our personal feelings aside and give it a good chance.

When considering a dating relationship, what "guidelines" are pointed out in the Word? The Bible tells us in 2 Corinthians 6:14 (NIV), "Do not be yoked together with unbelievers." This means that we should form close relationships with those who believe the same things we do. It's important when starting a dating relationship that we make sure that the other person shares the same morals and values that we do, and that they fear God, obey His Word, and that they have made Jesus their Lord.

BACKSTAGE PASS
getting to know

How did the group meet and form? We are all sisters, and we grew up singing with our mom in church. She saw our talent and encouraged us to sing together as a group. In 1992, we met TobyMac from dcTalk and sang for him, and he decided to sign us to his record label, Gotee.

Do you feel God leading the band in a special direction? We feel that our hymns album is introducing great worship songs to our fans who may have never heard any hymns. We also feel God calling us to continue to minister to young women, to encourage them in their walk with Christ.

How does the group plan to further its ministry in the future? We decided to retire as Out of Eden in December of 2005. We feel like God has called us to minister as individuals and to move on to the next chapter of our lives. We will still continue to be very involved in our church community. But I believe my ministry right now is to raise my kids and be with my family.

0000405

Favorite Bible Verses:
Lisa: Philippians 1:6
& Jeremiah 29:11
Andrea: Psalm 118:14
Danielle: 1 Corinthians 10:13
& 2 Corinthians 4:16

0202401

Birthdays:
Lisa: November 27
Andrea: August 17
Danielle: October 20

Fan Mail Address:
Out of Eden
c/o Chaffee Management Group
212 Forest Ridge Court
Franklin, TN 37069

MATT MORGINSKY
OF
SUPERTONES

A MOMENT
OF CLARITY

$\mathcal{I}$ don't know much, but of the few things I do know, you may find one helpful. I'll tell you about it.

Life is complicated, and the only thing more complicated is living it, no less for the Christian, probably more so. Take into consideration that there is a war inside us against the remnants of our sinful nature (Romans 7:23). We've all seen the cartoons where the little angel pops up on one shoulder and a little devil pops up on the other side; it would be so much easier if it were really like that, but we are often unable to discern which is which.

However, I think I've found a key! We've all had moments of clarity; you know what I mean - when you're at a place in your walk with God, when you're thinking His thoughts after Him and you're able to understand and receive the meaning of the Word. It's the moment when you say, "I get it! I'll do it!" This is what I call a "moment of clarity," but really, it's the illumination of the Holy Spirit, when we grasp the meaning of the Word and are ready to put it into action. An example might be, reading Matthew 25:31-46 and saying, "I want to be a missionary," or "I want to sponsor a child," or maybe you read the Great Commission and say, " I want to tell my friends and family about Jesus." Wouldn't it be great if that was the way we thought all the time? Unfortunately, we're not always walking as closely with God as we are when we receive these epiphanies, and maybe only an hour after, our sinful self-centeredness pipes in. "Do I really want to be a missionary? They don't make much money, I'll never have my dream car." Or "If I sponsor a child, that's thirty bucks a month I can't spend on CD's."

If we listen to our sin, and what's worse, take our own advice, we are rejecting the conviction and illuminating of the Holy Spirit and failing to be doers of the Word. We are like a man who looks in the mirror and forgets what he looks like as soon as he walks away (James 1:23-24).

When God gives you a moment of clarity you need to hang on to it, no matter how clever and compelling the arguments against it seem. Don't allow the Enemy to undermine the fullness of life that Jesus died to give you! Instead, **when you hear the voice of the Enemy** seducing you, cover your ears like Bunyan's pilgrim and **run to God, crying, "Life! Eternal life!"**

UNPLUGGED
a deeper look

Do teens need to do anything to prepare themselves to receive and experience the illumination of the Holy Spirit? If illumination is shining a light on something so that you see it more clearly, it's essential to have something for that light to shine on. In this case, the Holy Spirit helps us understand the Bible, so we need to read it regularly. We need to have the Word in our minds if the Holy Spirit is going to shine a light on it. Otherwise, there is nothing to light up but cobwebs.

How can we discern God's voice from the tricks of the Enemy? Tough one, I struggle with this myself. I think you further complicate it if you believe (like many people do) that you "hear God's voice" independent of Scripture. If you think that, I would ask you how you know the difference between God's voice and the Enemy's? You may say, "I can just tell," but there are a lot of people who have done some very ungodly

things because "God told them to." I think the only sure guide here is the Bible. You can't really be sure whether or not the prompting in your head is God speaking, yourself speaking, or worse. That's the main reason why God gave us His Word in writing.

BACKSTAGE PASS
getting to know

Favorite Books: *Lord of the Rings* by J.R.R. Tolkien and *Till We Have Faces* by C.S. Lewis

Musical Influences: Elvis Costello, because he's a genius with lyrics. The Clash, because they were so creative and passionate. Otis Redding - I wish I was him.

What is God teaching you now? A lot has been happening in my life - getting married, selling one house and buying another, and the band I played in for literally half of my life came to an end. I've been living in uncertainty and transition for awhile now, and I'm learning more and more to trust in God as the Unchanging, the Constant, the Anchor.

How has your family helped you in your walk with God? In my case, it's more the other way around. I didn't grow up in a Christian family. In fact, we thought religion was a waste of time. So when I became a Christian my family was accepting, but not helpful. But what's ended up happening is God has used me in bringing some members of my family to Christ. So

everybody reading this who thinks their family members are "really far away" from becoming Christians, don't doubt the power of God! It can happen.

How do you plan to expand your ministry in the future? Funny you should ask. In the immediate future, I'm speaking to young (and older) people about how to defend the Christian faith. I think we're in dire need of learning how to answer the criticisms non-Christians direct at Christianity. It gets in the way of us sharing our faith and also causes us to question our faith for invalid reasons. So I'm on a mission to train average Christians in the ways of the logical kung fu we call apologetics.

Birthday:
June 14

Favorite Bible Verse:
Job 38

Fan Email Address:
themorginskys@hotmail.com

Website:
www.myspace.com/mattmorginsky

JASON MORANT

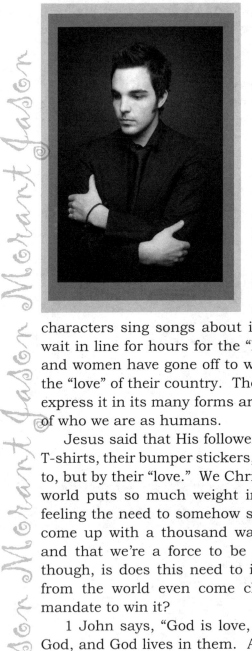

ABOVE ALL ELSE, DO I LIVE "IN LOVE?"

*L*ove ... it's a word almost every single one of us should be familiar with. Preachers preach about it, authors write books about it, movies are inspired by and made because of it, and sometimes Disney cartoon characters sing songs about it. People have been known to wait in line for hours for the "love" of a band, and many men and women have gone off to war and even lost their lives, for the "love" of their country. The need for it and the capacity to express it in its many forms are embedded into the very fabric of who we are as humans.

Jesus said that His followers would be known not by their T-shirts, their bumper stickers, or even by the music they listen to, but by their "love." We Christians, understanding that this world puts so much weight in one's identity, and ourselves feeling the need to somehow separate "us" from "them," have come up with a thousand ways to scream out who we are, and that we're a force to be reckoned with. The question, though, is does this need to identify and separate ourselves from the world even come close to the importance of our mandate to win it?

1 John says, "God is love, and all who live in love live in God, and God lives in them. And **as we live in God, our love grows more perfect**. So we will not be afraid on the day of judgment, but we can face him with confidence because we are like Christ here in this world" (1 John 4:16b-17 NLT). As I read this I have to ask myself, "Above all else, do I live 'In Love'?"

Like I mentioned before, every person in the world was created with a need for love, the need to be in love with God, Himself. The challenge then, to us as believers, is to help the world recognize that need and that it can only be fulfilled by an intimate relationship with Christ.

My wife, Brianna, and I have been married now for a little over three years, and the idea that I fell in love with her and her with me because someone simply told us that we needed to, is actually quite funny. Anyone who has fallen in love knows that's just not the way it goes down. It happens because of an encounter. And the way for people to encounter Jesus' love for them is through us. Not just by our words but through our actions. The passage in 1 John gives us the main ingredient, the key to representing Christ. His love and compassion knew no bounds and flowed from Him to everyone He came in contact with. It was proven by His actions.

As you go through your daily routine, pray and ask the Lord to show you how you can put His love into action. Ask Him to give you opportunities to be His representative, opportunities to show all those you come in contact with today what it truly means to be and to live "In Love."

UNPLUGGED
a deeper look

Do you have any advice about how we can love our enemies?
Loving one's enemies is not an easy task. I think the best way would be to change your mind-set as to who your enemies are. The truth is, in the Kingdom of God there really aren't any enemies (in the worldly sense). The only people Jesus would have called enemies of the Kingdom of God were the pseudo-religious people who thought they had unraveled the mystery of who God was. But even these He still showed compassion to on the cross. So to me, the example that was given for us as a way to battle adversity of all types is that of compassion and kindness.

Jason Morant Jason Morant Jason Morant

How can teens learn to love God with all of their heart, soul, mind, and strength? As a teen, there are many things that pull at our attention and affections. The capacity to love God with our whole being is within us, but we have to discipline ourselves to do what we can to keep that love alive. Just like any relationship needs attention and work, our relationship with God is the same way. Setting time aside daily just to spend with Him, even if for only a few minutes, is very important for keeping that connection. Ask the Lord to show you those things that are pulling on your affections more than they should. Most likely they will be innocent, normal, everyday things like sports, music, a boyfriend or girlfriend, or even religious activities. We only have so much of ourselves to give, and above anything or anyone - God deserves not only the best of us, but all of us.

The world often thinks of love as lust, rather than God's agape love. Can Christians change the world's view of love? The only way I see of changing the world's view of love is to give them an example of the real thing. We preach "Love, Love, Love," but when the world actually looks at us, all they see is division, hypocrisy, and an apathetic attitude towards anything not directly related to the Christian sub-culture we've created. No one (Christian or non-Christian) can deny when they've seen love in action, and it's our calling to be an example and lead the world to the One who showed us what true love really is through His self-sacrifice.

BACKSTAGE PASS
getting to know

Favorite Books: *The Chronicles of Narnia* by C.S. Lewis, *Provocations* by Soren Kierkegaard, *Ruthless Trust* by Brennan Manning, and *Pursuit of God* by A.W. Tozer

Musical Influences: Rita Springer, Kevin Prosch, U2, Daniel Lanois, Nick Drake, Coldplay, Duncan Sheik, and Keith Green

What is God teaching you now? With all of the recent opportunities to travel and meet new people, as well as to constantly stay busy by either touring or writing, the Lord has lately been bringing me back to the importance of silence. Whether I'm walking my dog, Emmy, or driving around in my car, I've been doing my best to take advantage of my time alone. Not just so I can hear His voice, but to simply crawl up into His arms.

How has your family helped you in your walk with God? I've been blessed to have the most supportive family in the world. From a very young age, my parents taught me the importance of following my heart. They encouraged my brother (who still plays drums with me) and me to nurture our gifts and made sure we knew that our dreams were their dreams. They always put the Lord first in our home and showed us by example what it meant to be gracious and compassionate.

Birthday:
June 12

Favorite Bible Verse:
Psalm 139

Fan Email Address:
info@jasonmorant.com

Booking Agency:
GOA, Inc.
615-790-5540
www.goa-inc.com

Fan Mail Address:
Jason Morant
c/o High Street Management
P.O. Box 1203
Franklin, TN 37065

Websites:
www.jasonmorant.com
www.myspace.com/jasonmorantmusic

JILL PHILLIPS

ALL IN GOOD TIME

"Be still in the presence of the LORD, and wait patiently for him to act. Don't worry about evil people who prosper or fret about their wicked schemes. Stop your anger! Turn from your rage! Do not envy others - it only leads to harm" (Psalm 37:7-8 NLT).

These verses aren't necessarily the most "feel good" verses in the Bible. Whenever there is a command with an exclamation point, it puts me a little on the defensive and I think, "Okay, take it easy!" But the truth is, these are extremely important verses because they get to the heart of whether or not I trust Jesus.

Jesus has promised to care for us and provide us with all that we need - not necessarily all that we want, but all that we need. He also knows what each of us needs individually, and in what time we need those things. Many of us believe this to be true, but it is so hard to remember when we watch other people succeeding in areas where we want to succeed. Maybe it is a relationship, maybe it is a job, maybe it is in sports or academics, but chances are there is someone you have looked at and thought, "It's just not fair that they have these things and I don't!" It is especially difficult when the person is someone we feel doesn't deserve to have success.

Yet **if we truly trust Him and truly believe He loves us, we can stop measuring ourselves against others to find our value**. We don't have to scramble to make things happen for ourselves or to put others in their place, we can simply sit back and trust that He will give us what we need when we need it. When someone else succeeds, it will no longer feel like it takes us down a peg, and we will be able to genuinely rejoice. When someone is prospering, but they have gotten there through "wicked schemes," we can put aside our anger, and trust Jesus that in His time He will make things clear and bring them to light. It is a constant battle to trust Him and it goes against our nature, but He will give us the grace and strength to trust Him with our lives and with others' lives if we only ask!

UNPLUGGED
a deeper look

James 1:19-20 (NIV) says, "... Everyone should be quick to listen, slow to speak and slow to become angry, for man's anger does not bring about the righteous life that God desires." Does this mean that we should never become angry when the ungodly receive earthly rewards? I don't think it is realistic to expect that we would never become angry or that anger is always wrong. I think Scripture is pointing out that when we wallow in anger and become wrapped up in what someone else has or achieves, it is harmful to us and isn't God's best for us. He desires that we trust Him to provide for us and not to find our worth by comparing our life against someone else's.

How can teens avoid measuring themselves against others with media and peer pressure suggesting they should "look this way" or "do this" to find acceptance? I think we have to combat these harmful messages with God's messages. As believers it is crucial that we read God's Word, that we are around other believers who encourage us and walk alongside us, and that we pray for strength to face these challenges. We can also take ourselves out of situations that we know are harmful to us and bring us down. Everyone struggles with these things and that is part of what it means to be human, so don't get discouraged! He will always be faithful and is bringing us on a journey to help us think a little more like Him each and every day.

BACKSTAGE PASS
getting to know

Favorite Bible Book: *Proverbs*

Musical Influences: Rich Mullins, David Wilcox, and Pierce Pettis

What is God teaching you now? I think He is trying to teach me, as always, to trust Him on deeper and deeper levels.

How has your family helped you in your walk with God? My children help me understand how vast God's love must be for His children, in a way I could not understand before becoming a parent. My husband is such a great friend and supporter, and we try to lift each other up and help when the other is weak. I think, overall, having a family has helped me realize what is really important to me.

How do you plan to expand your ministry in the future? I try to be faithful with the opportunities given to me and perform to the best of my ability, and I just pray that He does the rest. However large or small my sphere of influence ends up being, I trust that He will lead me to wherever I need to be.

Booking Agency:
The Breen Agency
615-777-2227
www.thebreenagency.com

Birthday:
February 15

Fan Email Address:
info@jillphillips.com

Website: www.jillphillips.com

KRYSTAL MEYERS

ANTICONFORMITY

"**D**o not conform any longer to the pattern of this world, but be transformed by the renewing of your mind. Then you will be able to test and approve what God's will is - his good, pleasing and perfect will" (Romans 12:2 NIV).

Anticonformity is about becoming the person that God wants you to be, and refusing to become the person that the world wants you to be. Especially at this time in our lives, being teenagers, it's a time when we're supposed to establish who we are in society. It's really easy to give in to all the push and the pull. **We all want to be accepted, but God** is there for us, and He **wants us to stay rock-solid in Him**.

In ninth grade, I had a lot of friends that were in the cool crowd, but they were into drugs and partying every weekend … and when they would ask me if I wanted to go hang out with them, I would be like, "Well, that's not really my thing. I don't think that's what God wants me to do." I was taking a major risk by saying that. Who knows what could have gotten thrown back in my face, or what rumors could have gotten started? Instead of saying, "She's 'Miss Goody-Goody'," though, they accepted that; they thought it was cool that I wasn't going to do anything for them just because I wanted to be cool. They saw that I wouldn't back down in what I believed. It ended up being a total ministry opportunity, and it was great.

It's hard to take that risk, but it all comes down to where you are in your relationship with God, and in having a relationship with Him. God is going to give you the strength to stand up. Don't worry about what the world is going to think or say of

Krystal Meyers Krystal Meyers Krystal Meyers

you. Just pursue what God has for you, His plan for you.

God doesn't call us to be quiet about our faith. He wants us to stand up in everything that we believe, in Him and His name. God wants the best for you. God *is* the best for you. If He calls you to do something, where can you go wrong? The world will pass away, but your relationship with Christ is forever.

UNPLUGGED
a deeper look

By taking a stand, how has your walk with God improved? It's been really cool. The first time that somebody asks you to take a stand with anticonformity, it's going to be really hard to do it. But it gets easier and easier every time, and that really does improve your walk with God. I've learned that I can rely on Him more and more. It really opens up your relationship with God, and you establish trust with your Creator.

When you were taking a stand at school, did you find other kids who were willing to be non-conformists? Or did you feel alone? It was a gradual thing. I felt alone at first, but as I took a stand, people figured out what I was about. They started asking questions, and there were kids that started to take a stand along with me, which was cool.

BACKSTAGE PASS
getting to know

Favorite Books: *Traveling Mercies* by Anne Lamott and *The Diary of a Teenage Girl* series by Melody Carlson

Musical Influences: Dashboard Confessional and Blindside, anything along the rock genre like those bands.

What is God teaching you now? He's really teaching me to be diligent in my devotions. It gets so hard to keep up with everything when you're out on the road, and I have to remember to set aside everyday life and spend time with Him. It's been a struggle, but God's really pulling me through, and I'm growing closer to Him.

How has your family helped you in your walk with God?
My parents are definitely inspirations - my mom's a prayer warrior, and my dad writes Bible study software. They are both very encouraging, and I can go to them with any of my biblical questions. It's awesome.

How do you plan to expand your ministry in the future?
I'm willing to do anything. I'm just waiting to see what exactly God has in store. I've made it "no strings attached," and I'm ready for whatever He wants me to do. I have no clue what it's going to be like a year from now, but I'm excited.

Birthday:
July 31

Favorite Bible Verse:
Romans 12:2

Booking Agency:
Creative Artists Agency
615-383-8787
www.caaccm.com

Website:
www.krystalmeyers.com

Fan Email Address: www.myspace.com/krystalmeyers

JOHN REUBEN

BEING COOL

Who says it's wrong to be cool and up on the times? I used to hate trends and despise the way people would buy into them - the way people would devote their personalities to something the media said was cool. Over some time, I have come to a more mature place (I say that cautiously), where I no longer hate trends, and have occasionally even participated in what was hot culturally. I have owned the trucker hats and the thrift store T-shirts. Although I would argue that I was one of the first to start sporting them ... so does everyone else who doesn't want to look like they are just following the lead. The problem with trends is that people, especially younger people (i.e. teens) don't realize that is all it is ... a trend. Something temporary, something that won't last, something that will be gone tomorrow. We end up investing so much of our time, energy and ideas into something that has a short life span. I have seen way too many folks blindly get caught up in the trap of keeping up with the Joneses ... from clothing, video games, cell phones and vehicles, to computers - all the things we are told we need to have in order to maintain a credible place in human society. This is where it becomes an issue, when we let those things define who we are. There's no problem with enjoying the material world we live in, but it must not own us. It must not guide us. Sure we participate in its developments, but **as believers we hold onto something much bigger than what the culture is telling us**. We have a relationship with the Alpha and Omega, the Beginning and the End, the Controller of everything in between - the eternal and infinite God we serve, Jesus Christ. In my opinion, this defines cool. Not clothing that will soon be outdated, not some form of music that, chances are, you will abandon in a couple of years, and certainly not some piece of electronic equipment that, as soon as you buy it, becomes "the old model." So feel free to enjoy the silly, superficial things of this world - just don't place much value in them; don't allow them to become idols ... they're just not that important. Instead, focus on being able to have an eternal effect on your culture.

More Verses:
Matthew 6:19-21

UNPLUGGED
a deeper look

How can teens remember everyday that they're living for a higher purpose, that they're living with the hope of eternal life - not just life here on earth? It's really easy to get sidetracked and forget that, so we need a reminder every day. Communicating with God through prayer and reading His Word are the best ways to help us keep perspective. It's also important to look at your influences, and whether or not people you spend time with are encouraging you to remember these things, or making it easy to forget.

What are some ways for teens to overcome the persecution they will face as they follow your Christlike definition of "cool?" When you are able to embrace a real relationship with God, "cool" will start to become less and less important in your life. At times it may seem like you are missing out on some things, but in reality you will be able to embrace life to the fullest, you will be experiencing something much more valuable, and you won't be so worried about the superficial things of this world.

BACKSTAGE PASS
getting to know

Favorite Books: *The Heavenly Man* by Paul Hattaway and *The Great Divorce* by C.S. Lewis

Musical Influences: A lot of early 90's hip-hop ... I have a wide range of influences from U2 to The Cure. I would say anything honest and authentic.

What is God teaching you now? The freedom of discipline.

How has your family helped you in your walk with God? My mom raised me to seek God on my own. She never forced anything on me, but she shared her faith and opened me up to a diverse collection of believers.

How do you plan to expand your ministry in the future? Hitting the road hard ... production ... and seeing where the Lord is taking it.

Website:
www.johnreuben.com

Booking Agency:
Third Coast Artists Agency
615-297-2021
www.tcaa.biz

Fan Mail Address:
Reuben Management
Attn: Fan Mail
P.O. Box 2457
Westerville, OH 43086

Fan Email Address:
mgmt@johnreuben.com

Birthday:
January 14

Favorite Bible Verse:
Hebrews 11:1

Natalie Grant

Being Yourself

"Anyone who intends to come with me has to let me lead. You're not in the driver's seat, I am. Don't run from suffering, embrace it. Follow me and I'll show you how. Self-help is no help at all. Self-sacrifice is the way, my way, to finding yourself, your true self. What kind of deal is it to get everything you want but lose yourself?" (Matthew 16:24-26 MSG).

These words of Jesus are important for us to digest on our journey to self-discovery. Ashamedly, I must admit, while flipping through the TV channels, I allowed myself to become engrossed in an MTV reality show called "I Want A Famous Face." Horrified, I watched as twin teenage brothers endured unimaginable pain through several surgeries, while doctors attempted to fulfill their impossible requests to turn their faces into Brad Pitt. While I respect their taste in faces (I, too, agree he's easy to look at), most disturbing to me was their deep desire to lose their identity and become someone else. They were in the driver's seat of their lives and believed they would get everything they ever wanted by recreating themselves. Of course, the end result did not give the world two more of Brad Pitt, and the Band-Aid® the boys put on their insecurities will only cause their wounds to fester and grow. While I pray none of you will go to such great lengths to find approval and acceptance, many of us attempt to recreate ourselves daily through outward appearances, personal achievements that bring awards, relationships, and so on. Our identity becomes wrapped up in trying to be what society defines as success,

Natalie Grant Natalie Grant Natalie Grant Natalie Grant

instead of what God deems successful. The world says look out for yourself. God says serve others. The world says beauty actually is skin deep. God says He looks at the heart. The world says be first in line. God says the last shall be first. It's hard for all of us to stay in the passenger seat of our lives; we want to control our destiny. I guess, to an extent, we do, because **we must choose to follow Christ**. Once we do that, letting Him lead isn't easy, but is essential to finding ourselves and fulfilling our destiny. As your insecurities and hidden fear come bubbling to the surface, don't shove them back down and cover them up with the world's temporary fixes. Embrace them, knowing that as you do, healing will come as you find yourself in Christ. Don't try to be anyone but you. There's only one Brad Pitt and there's only one you. You're an original with a God-sized destiny. So move over, because He's the only one with a license to drive your life.

UNPLUGGED
a deeper look

How can teens discover their identities in Christ and become secure in them? The only way to do that is to truly discover Christ - through prayer and His Word. No matter who you are, what your age, it's really important that you get a version of the Bible that you can clearly understand. For teenagers, *The Message Bible*, the *Revolve Bible* for girls, the *Refuel Bible* for guys. You don't have to read your parents' Bible; you can get one for yourself. Another important thing to do is shut out the things that speak negatively about you and your image. When you so desperately want to read magazines, but know that those magazines are going to make you feel inferior, feel the pressure to measure up, and speak lies to you about who you should be, instead of who you know yourself to be - put down the magazines of lies, and pick up the Book of Truth.

If we allow God to be in our "driver's seat," will our natural desire to change ourselves for acceptance fade? From my personal experience, no. In fact, I think it's a day-by-day process. I suffered from an eating disorder for five years, and I actually know these things to be true. I started to discover who I was when I really got into God's Word, and the desire to be somebody else doesn't just fade away. That's why it's important to take one day at a time, and when you wake up, to say, "Today, I choose to believe I am who God has created me to be. Today, I choose to believe that I was created in His image. *Today*, I am going to choose to live my life to glorify God, to honor Him through my thoughts and through my actions." There will still be moments when we struggle, stumble, and fall, but thank God for grace, and that His mercies are new every morning; we get another chance. When we put God first in our lives, the other things fall in the proper order. It sounds easy, but when we learn to truly honor Him with our lives, it is simple. It's a natural effect.

BACKSTAGE PASS
getting to know

Favorite Books: *Spilling Open: The Art of Becoming Yourself* by Sabrina Ward Harrison, *Blue Like Jazz* (anything by him) by Donald Miller, *The Ragamuffin Gospel* by Brennan Manning, and *The Left Behind* series by Tim LaHaye and Jerry B. Jenkins

Musical Influences: Fred Hammond, CeCe Winans, Coldplay, Commissioned, U2, Whiteheart, Mindy Smith, and Michael W. Smith's song writing

What is God teaching you now? That it's okay to be broken. For a long time I've struggled with being a people pleaser and the pressure for perfection. When God says that His strength is made perfect in weakness, it's in our weakness. In a way, He's teaching me that it's almost like we can celebrate our weaknesses. When we do, His strength is made perfect in that. In our culture, we constantly try to cover up our flaws, but God's teaching me that in brokenness, He does His best work.

How has your family helped you in your walk with God?
My parents are my heroes. I'm blessed in the fact that God gave me two parents who didn't just take me to church and expect the church to do the job of teaching me about Jesus. They understood that church was to be an extension of what I was already learning in my home. They're both very kind-natured, and from them, I've learned about the Scripture of loving your neighbor as yourself. My husband is the greatest example of Christ I have had on this earth - in the way that he treats others, through the fact that he doesn't have a critical spirit, through learning to be selfless. I've learned more about that through being married to him than anything else.

How do you plan to expand your ministry in the future?
Last year I started a foundation for human trafficking, and that's really become my passion. Music is still my love, but this is becoming the driving passion of my life. It seems to be expanding on a day to day basis, and I'm just taking it one day at a time. It's just a matter of trusting God, and knowing that if He has more for me, then I'll walk through those doors that He opens, and if He closes them, He'll give me the faith to trust Him.

Website:
www.nataliegrant.com

Birthday:
December 21

Favorite Bible Verse:
1 Peter 5:10-12

Booking Agency:
Creative Artists Agency
615-383-8787
www.caaccm.com

Fan Mail Address:
Natalie Grant
c/o Maximum Artist Management
1229 17th Ave. S.
Suite 200
Nashville, TN 37212

Fan Email Address:
info@nataliegrant.com

KIMBERLY PERRY

CARRY ON

"And what more shall I say? ... (Those) who through faith conquered kingdoms, ... who shut the mouths of lions, quenched the fury of the flames, and escaped the edge of the sword; whose weakness was turned to strength; ... Women received back their dead, raised to life again. Others were tortured and refused to be released, so that they might gain a better resurrection. ... They were stoned; they were sawed in two; they were put to death by the sword. They went about in sheepskins and goatskins, destitute, persecuted and mistreated - the world was not worthy of them ..." (Hebrews 11:32-38 NIV).

And here you and I are ... some two thousand years later ... sitting at this moment in the comfort of our bedrooms, remembering these miracle-witnessing fighters of the Bible who chose to not only give Jesus their hearts, but all of themselves, every moment of their lives. Here we are in our makeshift morning sanctuaries, one turn of the doorknob away from the world outside. In moments **we'll enter back into that world**, back into a place that's not our home, **a place that can't stand the Man we live for; where we find more bruises than battles won**, and few flickers when the flames have drowned ...

But, not all hope is lost. Sometimes peace is found only on the other side of war, and to make a change, many times you've got to stand alone. So, let your heart not be troubled ... let your heart carry on.

You were put on this planet, in this time, in your home, for an incredible, very specific purpose. God created you, first, to be His child, to love and long for Him as He loves and longs for you. Second, God crafted you to - through your words, through your lifestyle, through the things you stand for and the things you're willing to fall for - lead the creation to the Creator. That's it. Simple instructions. God wants to use *you* to change the world. So, why do so few of us ever follow through? Because there is a price to pay. Following Jesus will cost you something. That "something" may be your friends, it may be your family, it may be your comfort, it may be your plans ... following Jesus may, one day, even cost you your life ... but the life you find in return is the sweetest, most complete life and the only one worth living. Consider for a moment the price Jesus paid: He left His father and His home. He walked our streets. He chose to endure a murderous death. He paid the highest price because He wanted us to be with Him forever. You and I were worth that much to the Creator of the universe. How much is He worth to you?

One cannot answer all of the questions of those of us who live to see such times as these. Why me? Why here? Why now? Still, we must decide what to do with the time that is given to us. Keep the faith. Just as these pioneers of the Bible saw God do unspeakable things, miracles still stare *you* in the face and you'll see all impossibilities fade away.

Let your heart not be troubled ... let your heart carry on.

UNPLUGGED
a deeper look

As Christian teens, it can be difficult to risk comforts of life, such as friends and dreams, to stand up for our Creator. How can we remind ourselves of our victory in Him and live for Him anyway? It's important to remember that God never takes away without giving. What He gives is more perfect and fulfilling than anything we could ever ask Him for. God guides our dreams and desires according to His plans. He knows what is best for us even more than we do. Sometimes our friends drag us down; remember, friends are not worth compromising your relationship with Jesus. Which is more precious to you? Which will be there when the other is gone? Standing boldly for Jesus may turn off some of your friends. This is because your commitment to Jesus reminds them of their non-commitment to Him. Stay the course. Jesus will fill whatever holes a "friend" might leave. Perhaps one day, because you have shown them the difference Jesus has made in your life, they, too, will begin to live for Him. I know it's tough. He never said walking this road would be easy; He only said we'd never have to walk it alone. Jesus promises never to give us more than we can handle. If you are walking through a difficult spot in life now, be comforted in the fact that God trusts your faith in Him can withstand these troubles.

How can teens search deep inside to discover how much their Savior is worth to them? Actions speak louder than words. Get alone in your bedroom. Turn off the TV, the computer, and the radio. Be honest with yourself. What are you doing for Jesus? What is loving Him and living for Him costing you? Come up with a long list? Great. Carry on. Is your list on the short side? You may want to reevaluate *who* you're living for. Yourself? Or Your Savior? Ask yourself how *well* you are living for Him. If we, as Christians, can go to the same places and do the same things we could do before we knew Jesus and not feel convicted, then we have a serious problem ... a problem at the very core of our relationship with Jesus. Take a hard look in the mirror. Are you who they think you are? Are you who you want to be? Are you everything He imagines you can be? That is exactly how much your Savior is worth to you.

What are some practical ways for teens to lead the creation to the Creator, while fighting the war and finding peace in this "tough" world? I encourage you to use the specific gifts God has given especially to you to witness to the unsaved. Put some of *your* style into it. I'm a musician; therefore, I use music to reach the creation for the Creator. Maybe you're an artist. Create a painting that speaks deeper than words what Jesus means to you. When observers ask you about

Kimberly Perry

your inspiration, let them know Who inspires you. Maybe you're great at sports. Ever say a silent prayer before shooting a free throw? As you're giving high-fives to your teammates because you just shot the winning basket, why not just add a, "Yeah, God really pulled me through that one!" If you're shy, try writing "Jesus loves you" on your hand. Someone's bound to ask you why you wrote it. Are you a talker? All you have to do is what you do best: Share what's been happening in your life. These ideas may sound simple, but when done consistently, those around you will begin to notice something different about you, and will want to know what you've got that they don't. Give it a try. Peace is found by plugging in to the Source of peace. Seek the face of the Father. Read His Word. Talk to Him. God alone can give you contentment in this disrupted place. He alone can be your calm. You must allow Him to invade you. 2 Chronicles 16:9 (NIV) says, "For the eyes of the Lord range throughout the earth to strengthen those whose hearts are fully committed to Him." Keep your eyes focused on the call and fixed on the cross ... He'll keep His eyes fixed on you.

BACKSTAGE PASS
getting to know

Musical Influences: Christian artists have been a major influence in my life: dcTalk, Audio A, Rebecca St. James, Newsboys, Switchfoot, David Crowder Band, and Chris Tomlin. Artists that inspire me musically are: Beth Hart, Sheryl Crow, and Janis Joplin.

What is God teaching you now? Right now God is teaching me how to passionately worship Him even in the humdrum moments of life, and He's teaching me to be patient and faithful when my time frame looks different than His.

How has your family helped you in your walk with God? My family members are my best friends. My parents and two brothers, Reid and Neil, are extremely supportive and actively involved in my ministry. I've been on the road touring independently for the past six years. My family has served as my circle of accountability and has been my greatest source of encouragement. My parents have amazing godly wisdom and discernment. In many ways they've served as the "eyes" of my ministry, watching ahead and behind to protect from the vices of the Enemy. I couldn't do what I do without them. I aspire for my own walk with the Lord to be as passionate and steady as I've seen from my parents.

How do you plan to expand your ministry? I desire to stand inside the walls of the church and face out. We live in a culture driven by music. I understand that I'm competing with mainstream media for the attention and souls of listeners. I want to offer music that earns the ears and respect of the world, so that when I open my mouth and share this life I've found in Jesus with them, they'll listen. Everyday I pray for the tallest, brightest, loudest platform the world has to offer so that these words that God has burned in my heart will be heard. I don't want to limit His imagination and will walk through any doors He chooses to open.

Website:
www.kimberlyperryrocks.com

Booking Agency:
Jeff Roberts and Associates
615-859-7040
www.jeffroberts.com

Birthday:
July 12

Favorite Bible Verse:
2 Corinthians 4:16-17

Fan Mail Address:
Kimberly Perry
P.O. Box 2603
Greeneville, TN 37744-2603

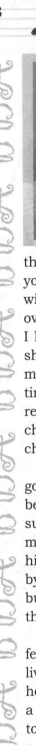

BDA

CHOOSING CHRIST

Matt Jones

*I*t's a funny thing ... how suddenly the details of life can change. Have you ever felt like that? One day you are getting comfortable with a routine you once thought you'd never grow into, and overnight something completely turns your world around? As I look back on my life, I can recount many of those sudden shifts. As a child, dealing with multiple divorces left me with a multitude of unanswered questions. Changing schools several times, without the confidence it takes to build new friendships, rendered me alone and empty. We all deal with these sudden changes that can shape the person we become as adults. Some changes can be more powerful than others.

A victim of armed robbery may have all of his life trusted the goodness of humanity, and over the course of a few moments, be forever afraid and unwilling to encounter any stranger, suspicious or not. On the flip side, a presidential candidate may fall asleep an ordinary citizen and wake up the leader of his entire nation. Granted, not all of us have been victimized by crime or had the opportunity to have our name in lights, but can you recall any sudden change in your life that altered the way you lived from then on?

For me, it's the day I met Jesus Christ. I woke up one day feeling empty and broken inside, like there was nothing left to live for, and I went to sleep knowing in my heart that I had a heavenly Father who loved me, who cared about me, who had a plan for my life. At that time in my youth, I was just starting to experiment with crime; the thrill of rebellion masked the pain I felt inside. But God's forgiveness and unconditional love suddenly captivated my heart and gave me a peace and fulfillment that no thrill or rush could ever match.

Consequently, I was saved from a long list of punishments for the things I could have done, saved from the pain I would have caused my friends and family, and most of all, saved from a life with no purpose. Whether you already know God or didn't even know it was possible to have a relationship with Him, He has a plan for your present and for your future. He loves you and accepts you just as you are, but **He wants to turn your world around for the better**. Has God made a sudden radical change in your life? He desperately wants to.

Another Verse:
2 Corinthians 5:17

Prayer

God of mercy and love, continue to change me. Make me more and more like Christ, that I would see the world as He sees it, and respond as He would. Amen.

UNPLUGGED
a deeper look

As long as we live on this earth, we must deal with change. Relationships, school, jobs, health, all things change. How can we remember God's great promises as we deal with the times of struggle in life? Scripture is filled with God's promises, and the Bible tells us to meditate on His Word day and night. Remember that these promises are absolutely true, and God never fails. Look back at the things God has brought you through already. Seeing the proof of His faithfulness in the past enables us to trust His faithfulness in the future. - Dave

Can God soften a heart that's hardened toward Him? There is a part of all of us that is hardened toward God. Even those who have been saved are being constantly softened toward the same God who seeks the lost, because He is unwilling that anyone should perish. We believe that a heart that is touched by the amazing love of Christ cannot remain unchanged. - Dave

As you said, God desperately wants to make a change in our lives as Christians. How can teens be open to these changes, and use them for His glory? To be open to God's perfectly designed changes in our lives, we must first learn to overcome the inherent human idea that we need to be in control of our own futures. Can any of us claim to have never made a mistake or bad decision in our lives? God can. He's never made a mistake in anything, so how could your plan for your life be better than His? Once we learn that God *cannot* make a mistake, it's easy to weather the changes He brings in our lives, even when they are difficult, because He is sovereign. He is the Redeemer and works all things together for the good of those who love Him and are called according to His purpose. - Dave

BACKSTAGE PASS
getting to know

How did the band meet and form? We met in 2001, our freshman year at Greenville College. Matt and I were roommates, Clint and Jake were roommates, and Ben lived just across the hall. We had our first practice in Clint and Jake's dorm room. For a year we led worship as house band for a youth group while we toured the Midwest, building a fan base. In March of 2003, we met producer Scott Williamson at a band competition in Memphis. After recording a demo with him we were signed to Creative Trust Workshop in June of 2004. - Dave

Do you feel God leading the band in a special direction? I feel like God is taking us to a place where we can continue to change lives and affect people - whether that means playing arenas or just playing for youth groups. I know that He has plans for us to just continue going through the doors He has opened for us. - Ben

How does the band plan to further its ministry in the future? Each of us is still growing in our relationship to Christ. Our desire to reach people grows and changes with that relationship. We hope to come together as a band and constantly match the desires of our heart with the needs we see around us. We also hope to pair our ministry with others already working to further the Kingdom, like we've had the opportunity to do in the past with so many friends who share this passion. - Clint

Birthdays:
Matt: January 7
Dave: March 21
Clint: April 20
Ben: November 11
Jake: October 5

Favorite Bible Verses:
Matt: Jeremiah 29:11
Dave: 1 John 4:10
Clint: Proverbs 19:21
Ben: Matthew 11:28-29
Jake: Galatians 2:20

Website:
www.bdatheband.com

Booking:
Please direct all booking inquiries to ben@bdatheband.com

Fan Mail Address:
BDA
c/o Creative Trust
2105 Elliston Place
Nashville, TN 37203

Fan Email Address: info@creativetrust.com

NATE SALLIE

CHRISTLIKE ATTITUDE

Joseph was just a 12 or 13-year-old boy, when God spoke to him in a vision one night. In this "God-sized dream," Joseph pictured his older brothers surrounding him and bowing at his feet. When Joseph awoke the next morning, he didn't think to himself, "This dream could never happen," or "I'm too young, and my brothers would never do such a thing." He had faith in the One who had given the dream, so he went directly to the field where his brothers were working to let them know what he had seen.

I would recommend praying and seeking God's will about who He would want you to share your dreams with before you spew them out, but you can't help loving Joseph's passion and boldness. That boldness is what landed him at the bottom of a deep well, and that passion is what took him to a far away land where he was separated from family and friends. At this point, I would venture to say that most of us, including me, would ask God what in the heck was going on, crying, "Please get me out of this mess!" Believe it or not, Joseph did just the opposite. He might not have been as confident and brash as he was earlier, but he continued to seek God's will in his life. He knew that if he was hungry for the things of God, he would be in the right place with the right people doing the right thing at the right time, fulfilling the prophetic assignment God had for his life.

In Genesis 39:23, it says that the Lord was with Joseph and gave him success in whatever he did. To make a long story short, Joseph became second in command only to the King of Egypt, and saved the entire region from starvation during a seven-year famine. His brothers traveled to Egypt for food and found themselves bowing at Joseph's feet, without even realizing it. At this point, Joseph could have said to his brothers, "I told you so!" Instead, he took on the attitude of Christ and chose to forgive all wrongdoings, welcoming his brothers into his palace. This was a man after God's own heart. **My prayer is that each of us would seek God's will for our lives so that we are in the right place with the right people doing the right thing at the right time!**

UNPLUGGED
a deeper look

What does a Christlike attitude mean to you? As we allow our minds to be renewed day by day through reading His Word, our attitude - or thoughts and feelings - will become more and more like that of Christ. Start the day with joy, knowing you will be meeting your heavenly Father, and used to further His Kingdom!

How do you maintain a positive, Christian outlook while you're on the road? I always try to keep in mind that I am there to serve and not be served.

What are some qualities you consider important when modeling your life after Jesus? Integrity - not just doing things the right way, but always doing the right thing; honesty, compassion, and loving the people around me.

How can teens develop a Christlike attitude? By attending church and having fellowship with other Christians. By surrounding themselves with others who are like-minded, who are going in the same direction, and have the same desires - which are to go after God and draw near to Him.

BACKSTAGE PASS
getting to know

Favorite Book: *Drawing Near* by John Bevere

Musical Influences: Michael W. Smith, dcTalk, and Harry Connick, Jr.

What is God teaching you now? That if I want vision and clarity for my life, He's there waiting to reveal it to me - if I am hungry for Him. We are hungry for what we feed on. If I crave ESPN all the time, that is because it is what I am feeding on. I want to make sure I am going after God and He is my passion.

How has your family helped you in your walk with God? They laid the foundation and planted the seed that has grown over time, as I have matured in my walk with God.

How do you plan to expand your ministry in the future? By being faithful to the process that God has laid out before me.

Birthday:
October 23

Favorite Bible Verse:
Jeremiah 29:11

Booking Agency:
GOA, Inc.
615-790-5540
www.goa-inc.com

Fan Mail Address:
VanLiere-Wilcox
Attn: Nate Allen Sallie
P.O. Box 646
Franklin, TN 37065

Websites:
www.myspace.com/natesallie
www.natesallie.com

TIM HUGHES

CONVICTION LEADS TO ACTION

What drives someone to dedicate his or her life to environmental protest? What drives someone to sell all their possessions and move to work with the poor in Calcutta? What drives somebody to deny themselves food and water to make a political point? What drives someone to be a suicide bomber? The answer? Conviction. Conviction leads to action, whatever the cost.

One of my favourite characters in the Bible is Daniel. He was a man of conviction, who whole-heartedly believed and trusted in God. Like us today, he would continually have had to resist conforming to the world, but instead, lived life as God was calling him to. Daniel served under King Darius, who at one time issued a decree insisting that all must pray and worship him exclusively for thirty days. Anyone who refused would be thrown into the lions' den (Daniel 6:6-9). You can use your imagination. Most people didn't survive very long. What would you do if faced with such a choice? I'm hugely challenged by Daniel's response.

"Now when Daniel learned that the decree had been published, he went home to his upstairs room where the windows opened towards Jerusalem. Three times a day he got down on his knees and prayed, giving thanks to his God, just as he had done before" (Daniel 6:10 NIV).

If I was in Daniel's situation I think I might have said, "Well, I'll pretend to pray and worship King Darius, but I won't really mean it. When I get home I'll close my windows and quietly hide away and pray to God. No one needs to know." Daniel would do no such thing. He so passionately believed and lived for God, that he wanted everyone to know that he would never bow the knee before King Darius. That's conviction. He stood up for what he believed, no matter the consequences. As a result, he was thrown into the lions' den. However, the story didn't end there. God, in His great mercy, intervened and saved him. If you stand up for God and honour Him, then He will honour you. **If you step out and take a risk for God, He will bless it.** We are constantly under pressure to deny our faith, to compromise and live halfheartedly for God. Making a stand for God will affect our whole lives. It means caring for the poor, loving the unlovable, being honest, living pure lives, being generous with our money, finding contentment in God and not in other earthly possessions. This, at times, may seem weird to people who don't know God. At school, by not swearing or drinking heavily, by not excluding someone, it may mean that you get ridiculed, or even excluded, yourself. Although most of us won't have our faith pushed to the extremes like Daniel did, life can be tough. As we see in Daniel's life, God is faithful to all who put Him first and stand up for the truth. Our Savior is looking for a people who will live a life of true conviction. It's a challenge to all.

More Verses:
Daniel 6:1-23

Prayer

Dear God, I ask You to give me the conviction of Daniel - that in every situation I may stand up for the truth of Your gospel. Give me the courage and the strength to put You first. Thank You that You are a faithful God. I choose to live my life for You. Amen.

UNPLUGGED
a deeper look

Sometimes we have faults in our character and actions that only those close to us notice. How can we take godly criticism from our friends and family without getting angry and with conviction to change? No one is perfect. We all have faults and can act selfishly. I've so appreciated family and friends who have pointed out things in me that needed to change - perhaps an attitude, a mind-set, or a pattern of behaviour. No one likes to be confronted, but taking criticism on board is a key to change. Sometimes we need to choose to humble ourselves and admit that we are not perfect. If you are desperate to become more Christlike, then you will welcome the input of those closest to you. They know you and want the best for you. Rather than taking criticism as a personal attack, receive it as a chance to grow in character.

Are there any important things teens should be aware of when they ask God to convict them? To ask God to convict you is a wonderful, but dangerous prayer. When you ask God to do these things, He will give you a passion for His heart. You will start to see the world as He sees it. There is so much pain and injustice in this world and it breaks God's heart. When your eyes have been opened to see this, you can't watch and do nothing. You have to act. There is nothing more exciting than walking with God day by day, but it does involve us putting God first and loving those around us. At times, God may highlight wrong attitudes in us - selfishness, pride, anger, lust, or jealousy. When He does, we need to say sorry and start afresh. We can't ask God to convict us and then do nothing about it.

How do you know if God is convicting you to do something or if your calling is coming from something you want to do? Understanding what God is calling you to do can be a really hard thing. Sometimes, as humans, we make it even

harder. We get confused - is this God, is this me? God has given us gifts and passions that He wants to use for His glory. What do you love doing? What are you gifted at? If you can't play soccer well, then God probably isn't calling you to be a professional soccer player. If you have trouble with your eyes - maybe God isn't calling you to be a pilot. What gifts do other people identify in you? Sometimes we are desperate to be good at something, but the reality is, it's just not our gifting. When I was growing up, I spent hours in my room worshipping God through song. I was passionate about it. After awhile, an opportunity came up for me to lead a bit of worship at my home church. I loved the experience. I felt so alive and excited to be leading God's people. More doors opened along the way, and friends and family identified that there was a gifting and a calling. For me, that's how I worked out I was called to be a worship leader. There was no writing on the wall. There was a passion in my heart and an open door to walk through. If God is calling you to do something, no matter how crazy it may seem - if it's His will, it will happen. If it's just something you want to do, over time it will become obvious. Then you have to humble yourself and choose to do what God is calling you to.

BACKSTAGE PASS
getting to know

Favorite Books: *Long Walk to Freedom* by Nelson Mandela, *What's So Amazing About Grace* by Philip Yancey, and *The Celebration of Discipline* by Richard Foster

Musical Influences: I've been massively influenced by bands such as U2, Coldplay, and The Beatles. Their music has incredible depth and involves lyrics and melodies that hugely inspire.

What is God teaching you now? God is teaching me the importance of trusting Him and choosing to do things His way. It can be hard to trust with everything, but it's a vital lesson to learn. Whatever God calls me to do - I want to fully obey Him.

How has your family helped you in your walk with God?
My family has helped me in many ways in my walk with God.
They are always there for me, they love me unconditionally,
and they are quick to challenge me when I'm out of order.
Practically, my wife and I pray and read the Bible together.
It really helps to have someone alongside, who will push and
encourage you to get stuck into God's Word. I've also found
it's helped me so much to have someone to pray with.

How do you plan to expand your ministry in the future?
I love the words of John the Baptist, "He must become greater;
I must become less" (John 3:30 NIV). I've tried to make that
my goal in life. In whatever I do, big or small, I want to see
Jesus become greater. I want to live to build Jesus' ministry.

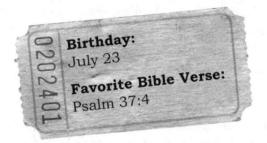

Birthday:
July 23

Favorite Bible Verse:
Psalm 37:4

Booking:
Tim Hughes

Fan Mail Address:
Tim Hughes
c/o EMI CMG
101 Winners Circle
Brentwood, TN 37027

Website: www.timhughesmusic.com

MONK & NEAGLE

DANCING WITH THE ANGELS

Michael Neagle

*I*t's one of the hardest things that we will ever have to face in our lives - dealing with the loss of a loved one. As God's creation, we must come to terms with the fact that everyone has an appointed time to be born and to pass away on this earth. I know that does not make anyone's loss easier to deal with, but a relationship with Christ will.

When I lost my father to cancer in 2002, it was truly the hardest thing that I have ever walked through in my life. He was only 47 years old, and an awesome father and friend. Why would such an amazing person die and be taken away from me? He loved Jesus and inspired many, including myself, to love Jesus more. It was in this that I was able to trust the Lord and find peace with the passing of my dad.

"For My thoughts are not your thoughts, nor are your ways My ways,' says the Lord. 'For as the heavens are higher than the earth, so are My ways higher than your ways, and My thoughts than your thoughts'" (Isaiah 55:8-9 NKJV).

Though we don't understand why certain things happen in our lives, a relationship with Jesus changes everything. Why? Because **with Jesus we have a promise**. Not just a promise that we will be okay in this life, but that we will have life and life abundantly. We have a promise that we will be with Him for eternity, and that we will see our loved ones in Christ again in heaven! You see, when we have a relationship with Christ, it takes the emphasis and burden off of us to grieve. How can we grieve for someone who is standing in the presence of the King of Kings? How can we feel sad about our loved ones dancing with the angels of heaven? Knowing that we will be with them again someday just makes it all the more joyful.

Trent and I have learned through our experiences of loss that it is okay to be sad. Sadness is actually a healthy emotion, but we have to recognize that we are not sad for our loved ones; we are sad that we temporarily can't be with them. The important thing is not to let grief set in and control our lives. We must find a place of rest and peace in the situation. Jesus offers this to us in Matthew 11:28-30 (NKJV), "'Come to Me, all you who labor and are heavy laden, and I will give you rest. Take My yoke upon you and learn from Me, for I am gentle and lowly in heart, and you will find rest for your souls. For My yoke is easy and My burden is light'."

Walking through experiences like dealing with loss always point me to Christ. I have learned that He truly does have great plans for all of us, and it challenges me to seek Him and His understanding. It also challenges me to pray for my friends and family who don't know Jesus. We never know when our appointed time is, so it is vitally important that they have every opportunity to know Him before time is gone. I hope you will pray for your friends and family as well, and may the peace of the Lord be with you.

Another Verse:
Philippians 1:21

Prayer

Lord, my prayer is that everyone who reads this will understand the importance of having Christ at the center of their lives. With You, there is no reason to fear death for us or our loved ones who know You, because of the promise that You have given us of eternity. Please comfort those who are in the midst of dealing with loss, and prepare those who in the future will lose someone. You are such a loving God, and I know that You have a plan through it all to bring them to a greater understanding of You. I ask this in Jesus' name, Amen.

Monk & Neagle Monk & Neagle

UNPLUGGED
a deeper look

How can teens witness to unbelievers in hopes of helping them make a choice for Christ before time on earth runs out? I think that unbelievers need to hear the gospel in a real and practical way. The gospel is plain and simple. People need to meet Jesus that way. We are firm believers that a lifestyle of dedication to Christ and following His voice are the best witness. People don't need a bunch of clichés and religion crammed down their throats; they need Jesus in a real and tangible way. They need to hear that, without Christ, there is no promise of anything. God will bless and use those that represent Him in that way.

Is turning loss over to God important in healing and restoration? Having both dealt with loss, we can absolutely confirm that without Christ there would have been no way to overcome the grief and pain of losing our loved ones. Healing comes through Jesus, and Him alone. There is no other way to have those deep wounds and that intense pain soothed. Though it is very hard and will be harder at times, by trusting in the Lord, you give Him the power to carry you through those times.

BACKSTAGE PASS
getting to know

How did the two of you meet and begin performing together? Trent and I met as college leaders in our youth group, and both had recently come from difficult experiences in our walks with the Lord. We had a great local church to plug into in our hometown of Amarillo, Texas. We immediately became friends and started attempting to play guitars and join our worship band. We began to lead worship at church and jokingly dreamed about someday doing music full-time together. It was only after being apart for five years and pursuing different careers, that we ended up back together again in Amarillo, and everything just fell into place by God's design.

Do you feel God leading your musical career in a special direction? Absolutely. I don't think we would have ever stepped out in faith to pursue what we are doing if we didn't believe that the Lord was leading us. Trent and I, along with our wives, sort of put everything on hold in order to do this. I think we both feel that the doors that have opened for us have been both a confirmation and a challenge to seek Him even more for the future. There are so many people out there that need to hear the message of a God who loves them, and about the beauty of marriage, and I think Trent and I have been blessed to carry that in some small, but significant way.

How do you plan to further your ministry in the future? We really want to reach people outside the walls of the church. Whether it comes through people hearing good music and then taking note of the message behind it, or by the Lord opening up different opportunities for us, we really want to affect this generation in some way. I think this will involve us being open to all sorts of new ideas musically, lyrically, and spiritually. Ultimately, we trust the Lord to direct our paths according to His plan for us.

Birthdays:
Trent: May 7
Michael: April 7

0202402

Favorite Bible Verses:
Trent: Philippians 4:13
Michael: Romans 12:1-2

0202401

Booking Agency:
Third Coast Artists Agency
615-297-2021
www.tcaa.biz

Websites:
www.monkandneagle.com
www.myspace.com/monkandneagle

Charlie Hall Charlie Hall Charlie Hall Charlie Hall Charlie

CHARLIE HALL

DEEPER IN LOVE

"Praise the LORD, O my soul; all my inmost being, praise his holy name" (Psalm 103:1 NIV).

Arousing your heart to love: David gives a great example in this passage as he begins to arouse his soul to love God. We are encouraged that no matter how we wake up we should say to our soul, "Soul, rise up to worship your King today. Jesus, awaken my heart to love You. Holy Spirit, open me up to hear Your voice." In so doing, we begin our day arousing and awakening ourselves to God. Just as we wake up physically by stepping out of bed, **we have to awaken spiritually**, too.

Reminding: David begins to awaken and arouse himself toward God by reminding himself of God's benefits toward him. We can see David saying to God, "You forgive sins, and You heal my diseases." Then he would stop and lift his hands in surrender to the memory of that beautiful benefit. He would go on to say, "God, you redeemed my life from the pit ... and Father, not only that, but You crown me with Your passionate love. Even now, as I say that, Your love and compassion are wrapping around me; You are satisfying me in the deepest places of my heart, making me fly again." It's the same with us. As we prompt our minds with truth and the reminders of what God has done, our heart and soul fall into line and release affection toward God. David speaks out with a bit more boldness and volume as his heart is coming alive again toward his God - of His attributes he says to God, "You make Your ways and deeds known. You are compassionate and patient with me as I stumble and stand again. You overflow with love. You don't treat me like I deserve to be treated, but

You are forgiving." We have to see David, not just spouting off words to be impressive to God, but relishing each line as he speaks it to God, believing every word, his heart warming each step of the way. As David is remembering God's benefits and attributes, he begins to remember who man is ... who he is. This is a great reminder for us. As David reminds himself of who he is, he becomes all the more grateful to God. He cries, "Like a father You are compassionate with me, God. I don't have you fooled, Father, but You know I am made of dust and that my days are like grass that does not last. God, I am like a flower that flourishes and then blows away with the wind. But always, God, You are in love with me. You love me as I learn to fear you. You will even be with my kid's kids as I hang with your covenants and walk in your precepts." God wants us to remember Him, His benefits, His attributes, and who we are. Doing so releases praise in us.

Proclaiming: This passage ends so "rad," as David is so stirred up inside for His awesome God that he bursts into praise, calling everyone and everything to join and unite in this anthem. He speaks out, "Look at the King. He has set up an unshakable throne in heaven and His Kingdom rules everything. Everything. Everything!! Angels, those who serve God and do His desires, heavenly hosts, everyone in God's dominion, and even my own soul - "Praise Him, Praise Him, Praise Him!!!" As we arouse our own souls to love and worship, remind ourselves of God's attributes and benefits, and remember who we are, we burst ... calling all around to love and praise Him. "You've got to see this beauty; it demands praise. Even as you just glance at Him, it enfolds you! Praise the Lord, oh my soul, praise the Lord!"

Prayer

Praise the Lord, oh my soul, praise the Lord! Awaken to today, remove the sleep, and fall deeper in love with your God. Help us to awake to You each day and think on all Your benefits to us.

UNPLUGGED
a deeper look

When we remind ourselves of God's attributes and benefits, what will begin to happen inside of us? When we remind ourselves of God's attributes and benefits, the truths of God (that are very real and powerful) get inside of us. They change the way we think. They change the way we see. As we look through the scope of God, and the Scriptures and the truths of God, things do look and feel differently. They can change from dark to light. Over time of giving yourself to truths, reminding yourself of who God is, how He is, what He gives, and what He's offered you, it starts to change the way you see. When you start to see differently, you start to feel differently.

Will we experience the fullness of God without completing the routine of "waking up" our souls? That's a big question. The complete fullness of God comes when we're in heaven, when we're with Him and we become perfect. The fullness of God on earth is when we give ourselves to Him at our greatest capacity every single day that we can, and in that way of living, He meets us all the time. I wouldn't say to anyone, "You have to have this routine to experience the fullness of God." I would say that giving and surrendering yourself to God, every day that you can, will definitely awaken you.

BACKSTAGE PASS
getting to know

Favorite Books: *Into Thin Air* by Jon Krakauer and *Soul Survivor* by Philip Yancey

Musical Influences: Rich Mullins, Keith Green, Toad the Wet Sprocket, Pete Yorn, Richard Ashcroft, Delirious, Matt Redman, and a gazillion independent singer/songwriter guys that are "Jesus guys."

What is God teaching you now? God is teaching me the power of the gospel, and that can sound really small to say, because it's something we were supposed to have learned when we first got saved, but these days - I am with a lot of people that don't know God. As I'm befriending these people and loving them, I'm seeing the power of the gospel - why the world around us needs it. He is also teaching me about Psalm 46 - how He is closer than my trouble; He's a refuge for me, and when everything is crazy, He keeps reminding me, "I am closer than the things that are crazy," which is hard to believe. He's closer than a friend. He is the closest thing to me and you. He is in our space, He fills our lives, He is around us, He is above us, and He's in other people that connect with us. He's everywhere, yet He makes His home in me, to speak to me and to guide me through my life.

How has your family helped you in your walk with God?
Their honesty and consistent pursuit of God through ups and downs of life inspire me.

How do you plan to expand your ministry in the future?
I plan to plod along simply with what I have now.

Birthday:
May 30

Favorite Bible Verse:
Psalm 27

Booking:
www.charliehall.com
info@charliehall.com

Fan Mail Address:
Charlie Hall
c/o sixstepsrecords
P.O. Box 5
Roswell, GA 30077

Website:
www.charliehall.com

SCOTT KRIPPAYNE

DEEPER STILL

My kids love the beach. They like to look for shells, dig in the sand, and play in the waves. When I say play in the waves, I mean the ones that are breaking at the shore. My children, not yet great swimmers, prefer the shallower water. If I promise to stay with them, I might be able to coax them out a little further, but they aren't big fans of the vast and deep Pacific. The shallow water is safer. It's familiar and comfortable. They know what to expect. They like being able to see the bottom.

I, on the other hand, love to get out away from the shore. I like the feeling of being surrounded by the water and carried by the waves. Sometimes it's a bit overwhelming, when I think of just how huge the ocean is and what a tiny speck I am. But there's also a sort of freedom that I feel when I'm out in the water. I know it sounds a little goofy, but it's true.

Funny thing is, in my relationship with God, I tend to be more like my kids. I'm tempted to just skim the surface. I'm tempted to stay in the places I'm comfortable. But I believe God desires more for us. **He wants to make us more and more like Him.** And if we are to be like Him, we must get to know Him. If we really want to know God, to grow in our relationship with Him, we must venture into deeper water - into the unknown. Sometimes it's scary - to be truly honest about who we are, to allow God to show us how much we really need Him. He may reveal things about us that are hard to take. He may reveal things about Himself that are difficult to understand. But He will be with us all the way.

I long to see other people the way that God sees them. I long to love the way God loves me. I desire to comprehend the amazing grace by which I am saved. I want to know what it really means to trust Him completely, but I'm not going to get there standing on the shore. I've got to dive in, swim out, and rely on the One who promises to never leave or forsake us.

May we find the life and the freedom that the Lord of the universe desires for us. May we not be content to just skim the surface, but with everything we have, and all that we are, may we plunge into an ever-deepening relationship with a God that loves us perfectly.

Prayer

Father, I want to get to know You better. Help me to trust You to lead me today. Take me deeper into relationship with You. Teach me more about who You are and show me the areas of my need. Thank You for your mercy and for loving me so well.

UNPLUGGED
a deeper look

What are some actions you've taken that have helped you go deeper in your walk with Christ? I think the biggest thing is spending time with Him. The friends we spend the most time with are generally the ones we know the best. When I'm spending good time with God, I can see that relationship play out in the way that I live. I'm a big proponent of a daily quiet time - a time that's just for you and God. Spending some time reading Scripture, praying and listening - just to be still. For some people, mornings work best; for others it might be midday or evening. If you can find a consistent time that works, it's easier to do it daily.

God instilled a passion to go deeper in many people we read about in the Bible. Does God still inspire Christians to want more of Him? I believe it still happens. All I have to do is look at my own life. I am selfish by nature, so any desire I have to know God more must come from Him. He desires to be in relationship with us, so much so, that He sent His Son here to walk this earth, talk with us, and eventually die so that we might be able to be in relationship with our heavenly Father. The more I get to know God, the more I see His faithfulness, time and time again. He is trustworthy, and my hope is to continually be striving to know Him more, to know Him better, to deny myself and follow Him.

How can teenagers stay focused on deepening their faith with all of the other distractions in life? It's not easy - our culture today is full of distractions, for teenagers, kids, and adults. Again, I think it comes back to spending time with God. When I'm actively reading His Word, it bears fruit in my life. When I am praying for others, I'm less focused on myself. I also would encourage teens and adults to pay attention to what you read, watch, and listen to; what we put into our minds tends to come out in one way or another. Simply be aware that what we watch and listen to has an effect on us - good and bad.

BACKSTAGE PASS
getting to know

Favorite Books: *Blue Like Jazz* and *Searching For God Knows What* by Donald Miller, *Mere Christianity* and *The Screwtape Letters* by C.S. Lewis

Musical Influences: Billy Joel, The Beatles, Michael W. Smith, and Steven Curtis Chapman

What is God teaching you now? Time management.

How has your family helped you in your walk with God? I tend to learn a lot from my kids - from the way they look at life. Even when I'm disciplining them for something, I can see how I've disobeyed God in the same way. Also, my wife is incredible. She's honest, and not afraid to tell me the truth. She helps me get pointed in the right direction and focus on the things that matter.

How do you plan to expand your ministry in the future? I simply hope to pursue God, do the best I can, and let Him take it where He wants to.

Birthday:
July 23

Favorite Bible Verses:
Psalm 139 and Zephaniah 3:17

Booking Agency:
The Breen Agency
615-777-2227
www.thebreenagency.com

Fan Email Address:
www.scottkrippayne.com
(contact from site)

Websites:
www.scottkrippayne.com
www.imnotcool.com

Scott Krippayne Scott Krippayne

DENVER & THE MILE HIGH ORCHESTRA

DEPENDING ON GOD

Denver Bierman

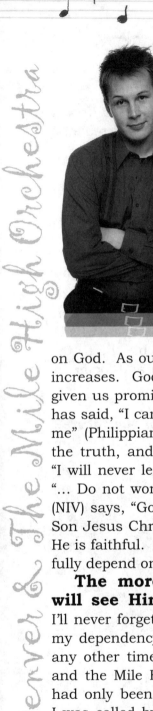

*A*s we grow in our spiritual lives, we will be challenged to grow in our faith. Our faith (Hebrews 11:1) is directly linked to our dependence on God. As our faith increases, our dependence on God also increases. God has told us in His Word who He is. He has given us promises to lean on, to count on, to depend on. He has said, "I can do all things through Christ who strengthens me" (Philippians 4:13 WEB). He said, "Then you will know the truth, and the truth will set you free" (John 8:32 NIV). "I will never leave you or forsake you" (Joshua 1:5 NIV) and "... Do not worry ..." (Matthew 6:25 NIV). 1 Corinthians 1:9 (NIV) says, "God, who has called you into fellowship with his Son Jesus Christ our Lord, is faithful." God has proven that He is faithful. He loves us more than we can fathom. We can fully depend on Him.

The more we depend on God, the more we will see Him do the unimaginable in our lives! I'll never forget one of the toughest seasons of my life, when my dependency and faith in God grew almost more than at any other time. I was 20 years old, and my band, Denver and the Mile High Orchestra, was just getting started. We had only been around for about four months, when I knew I was called by God to lead this group in full-time ministry. In a time of prayer, I knew the Lord was asking me a tough question, "If I tell you, '*Yes*,' and everyone in your life, even those most dear to you tell you, '*No*,' will you still follow Me?"

Talk about depending on God! I told God that to the best of my ability, I would follow Him. In the months that followed, the Mile High Orchestra was offered a very nice record deal. After much prayer, and many months of negotiations, the big record company went bankrupt, and went out of business. All of a sudden, all my hopes and dreams were crashing in front of me! I had no job, no money, no more opportunity, and I had just gotten engaged to be married! I still heard God saying, "Yes! You're doing the right thing! Keep going with perseverance! I'm going to bless the Mile High Orchestra!" At this point in my life most everyone around me was telling me, "No! This isn't working! There is *no* future in this!" Even the lawyer I was *paying* told me that I should find a different line of work for my life, because my band had no chance.

Those were some of the hardest, yet most rewarding, days of my life. And now, God has taken Denver and the Mile High Orchestra all over the world, playing for hundreds of thousands of people, and the love and hope of Jesus Christ has been shared, planting seeds, reaping harvests, and helping build the Kingdom of God. I attribute where I am today only because of the miraculous and amazing power of our God. I do know that God asked me a question, and how I answered that question radically affected the rest of my life. When God says, "Yes," and everyone around you says, "No," which way will you go? It starts in the little decisions we make every single day. Those turn into bigger decisions, that turn into the lifestyle we live, that turn into the reputation we have, that turn into the legacy we will one day leave on this planet. In all your ways acknowledge Him, and lean not on your own understanding (Proverbs 3:5-6). As you depend on God more and more, He will do things in and through you that you never imagined!

UNPLUGGED
a deeper look

Is there a way to be too dependent upon God? No! God tells us in His Word that there is incomparably great power for those of us who believe in Him. God also says that His ways are not our ways, and that His ways are much better! (Isaiah

55:8-9) "And we know that in all things God works for the good of those who love Him, who have been called according to His purpose" (Romans 8:28 NIV). If we don't depend on God, who else is there to depend upon?

When life is hard it seems easy to call on God for help - does He expect to hear from us in the good times, too? Jesus gave His all, His very life on the cross, for us to be reconciled to God. He desires to have an intimate relationship through all the good and the bad of our lives. In the Old Testament, we saw the Israelites wandering in the desert, crying out to God when life got hard. God helped them during those tough times, but they never even got to enter God's Promised Land, because of their lack of faith. I believe their relationship with God was severely lacking. Many times, they viewed God as a "genie in a bottle," to bail them out of trouble. When that is our view of God, we see Him for so much *less* than He really is, and we experience *less* of God than the full life in Christ, to which we have been called. Life has good, and life has bad ... call upon your Savior, and your best friend through all of life.

BACKSTAGE PASS
getting to know

Favorite Books: *No Compromise: The Life Story of Keith Green* by Melody Green and David Hazard and *Rich Mullins: An Arrow Pointing to Heaven* by James Bryan Smith

Musical Influences: Frank Sinatra, Harry Connick, Jr., Harry James, Brian Setzer, Earth, Wind and Fire, Michael W. Smith, Rich Mullins, and Travis Cottrell

What is God teaching you now? That no matter what I've done in my past, or in my present condition, His love and acceptance of me never changes. My life is more victorious in Christ than ever before, knowing that God loves me just the way I am ... as a believer in Christ.

Denver & The Mile High Orchestra

How has your family helped you in your walk with God?
My wife is a constant source of strength in my life. She encourages me, and challenges me to always go deeper with the Lord. My little son, Boston, has truly allowed me to have a clearer picture of a father's unconditional love for his children. Thanks to Boston, my walk with my Savior and Lord Jesus will never be the same!

How do you plan to expand your ministry in the future?
However the Lord leads. I live life one day at a time, and try not to fit God into my little box of my own personal plans and goals.

020240 1

Birthday:
April 10

Favorite Bible Verse:
Philippians 2:1-11

Website:
www.denvermho.com

Booking Agency:
Premiere Artists Group
615-260-6204

5c U.S.POSTAGE

Fan Mail Address:
Denver & the MHO
c/o Premiere Artists Group
8416 Terry Lane
Hermitage, TN 37076

Fan Email Address:
denver@denvermho.com

Denver & The Mile High Orchestra

PAUL COLMAN

DO I WANT THE SAFE JESUS OR THE REAL JESUS?

"The Passion of the Christ" scared the living daylights out of me. The film's violence has haunted my dreams and its brutal images are tattooed into every recess of my soul. Nothing has ever made Jesus' words, "pick up your cross and follow Me," more potent and permanent in my heart and mind (Matthew 16:23-25).

Most of the talk surrounding Jesus that I grew up with talked about safety, blessing and prosperity. I didn't hear a lot about dying, heartache and sacrifice. Jesus just isn't nearly as safe as I thought He was!

I began to wonder who it was that painted and endorsed the sanitized and Anglicized portraits of Him that I remember in my youth. Have you seen the pictures of the blonde-haired, blue-eyed, straight-nosed, pale-faced Messiah? He looks more like an American evangelist in a nativity play than a first-century Palestinian Jew born to an unwed, underprivileged teenager in the Third World.

I started to feel a little uneasier about all my boasts to follow Jesus wherever He went. I started to relate more with Judas, Thomas and the Peter we see after Jesus' arrest. I am a betrayer, a doubter and a denier. I started to wonder if I really understood Jesus of Nazareth at all!

I felt like hiding in an upper room and locking the door. I wanted to escape to 'safety'. I cowered as I heard the filthy voice of the prince of darkness and felt fear creep out of the shadows and into my heart. I have talked a lot about Jesus. I've led people to Him. I've written songs about Him. But do I really know Him?

Paul Colman Paul Colman Paul Colman Paul Colman Paul Colman Paul Colman Paul Colman

He asks me to let go of my life and fall to the ground and die. This, He says, is the only way to gain life (John 12:24). So once again, I heard Him say to me, "Follow Me!" (John 21:18-20 NIV). I closed my eyes, let out my nervous breath, and loudly whispered, "Yes, Lord." Is there any other like Him? In all of history, is there anyone who spoke like He did? Is there a single one who carried a love so pure? Is there a more selfless act than for God, Himself, to become us and be murdered by His own creation just to win us over?

I may be afraid, but where else can I go? Only Jesus of Nazareth has the way, the truth, and the life (John 14:5-7). I am afraid to follow Him, but I am more afraid not to.

I have walked on my own for most of my life. I have cheated and manipulated my way through. I have been drunk on my own self-importance, and I have done it all to gain life. But all I have been left with are the rags of my own emotional and spiritual poverty.

Jesus came and lifted me up with His own precious, nail-pierced hands - **hands that took my selfishness into them, and with every lash and blow defeated death and gave me life**. He is my champion and my Saviour. I do not know the future, and my body may not be safe, but being without Him is a greater loss than any other.

Prayer

Jesus, I am sorry that I have let fear control my life. Please show me the REAL You. I believe You are the way, the truth, and the life. Come and fill me with Yourself and set me free from my own burden. Let me live for You and know You. Teach me to do Your will and not be a slave to my own. I love You. Amen.

UNPLUGGED
a deeper look

"The Passion" showed a side of Christ that many teens are unfamiliar with. Do you advise this generation to rise up and "rebel" against worldly teachings as Jesus did, speaking the truth even when we don't feel safe? I don't advise rebellion as the initial action. If Jesus' actions were seen as rebellious or counter-culture, then it was as a result of doing what His Father told Him to, rather than trying to be rebellious or revolutionary. Listen to God and do what He says. Sometimes that will mean keeping the peace, and other times it will mean going completely against the grain. Obey God's voice. The Scripture is clear that Jesus did not do anything other than what His Father told Him to do. Speaking the truth is only possible when you are speaking God's words.

Jesus does bless us and give us safety, but as you said, we also experience heartache and sacrifice as His followers. How can saved teenagers expose the truth to non-Christians without making it "marshmallowy," or too harsh? Jesus said that as we love one another, the world will know that we are His disciples. If, as believers, we love each other and practice conflict resolution, mediation, and honesty - when it comes time to share that with others, we will be equipped. The sad fact is that we don't often do this, then we are sharp with others and yet we expect them to see great value in our relationships. In the end, the Scripture is clear that we need discipleship, and then to hear God's voice and simply say what He asks us to.

As you say, there is nowhere else to go, but to Jesus. How can we reach out to those who try other ways to ease their pain? Our relationships are meant to be a net that others swim into. Relationships in Jesus are the safest, most radical and complete expression of our faith that is possible. We reach out together. As we love each other, people are attracted to Jesus. Jesus said that as we lift Him up, people are drawn to Him. There is no program, conference, book, CD, or church service that replaces a group of believers loving each other in Jesus' love. It is the most attractive thing on the planet.

BACKSTAGE PASS
getting to know

Favorite Books: *Lord of the Rings* by J.R.R. Tolkien, *Webster's Rhyming Dictionary*, *U2 - At the End of the World* by Bill Flanagan, *What's So Amazing About Grace* by Philip Yancey, and *As Sure As The Dawn* (trilogy) by Francine Rivers

Musical Influences: Neil Finn, Midnight Oil, U2, Richard Ashcroft, Larry Norman, Bruce Springsteen, Keith Green, Steve Taylor, and Robert Colman

What is God teaching you now? To let Him control my life, to surrender.

How has your family helped you in your walk with God? Without them, I would be dead or not far from it.

How do you plan to expand your ministry in the future? By following Jesus.

Birthday:
August 22

Favorite Bible Verse:
Isaiah 53

Favorite Bible Book:
Jeremiah

Booking Agency:
William Morris Agency
615-963-3000
www.wmaccm.com

Website:
www.PaulColman.com

PILLAR

DON'T BE DEFEATED

Kalel

𝓘've had it on my heart lately to learn as much about my faith as possible. My brother-in-law was raised Catholic. He's a history major, and he's really knowledgeable in ancient history. Catholicism has been around for a long time; it's one of the longest standing religions there is. Nowadays, though, he believes that the Christian faith was compiled from different religions. He was quoting historical facts and people, and when he was saying this, I just kept my mouth shut. I knew the Scripture, but what is the good of quoting the Scripture to a guy that believes it was all made up? He didn't think, "You have to have faith," was an answer. I went home and started researching things - starting with my Bible, because he had a lot of specific questions. I found what I knew to be the answer, and conveyed that to him. I looked at non-biased online encyclopedias - just historical facts. There are Roman texts that still exist that mention Jesus. With what I learned from reading on my own - I gave him enough doubt that he couldn't prove his arguments. He's got enough reasonable doubt now to make him question what he believes.

You need to be able to stand your ground and not be defeated.

"Finally, be strong in the Lord and in his mighty power. Put on the full armor of God so that you can take your stand against the devil's schemes. For our struggle is not against flesh and blood, but against the rulers, against the authorities, against the powers of this dark world and against the spiritual forces of evil in the heavenly realms. Therefore, put on the full armor of God, so that when the day of evil comes, you may be able to stand your ground, and after you have done everything, to stand" (Ephesians 6:10-13 NIV).

UNPLUGGED
a deeper look

How can we be more prepared to answer questions about our faith? I encourage people to really research their faith - take time and actually read your Bible, take time to look outside of your Bible at other texts, take time to learn more about your faith, so if people ask you questions, you can actually answer them. Use references and get a study Bible that has a lot of background information. There is so much you can dig into, so when someone approaches you with these questions, you can have some knowledge.

A lot of teens today are faced with other religions. What are some of the basics of a few of those beliefs, and why is it important to know about them? People might approach you about other religions. Take time to learn about *your* faith. Mormonism was founded in 1830 by Joseph Smith. Scientology was started in 1954 by L. Ron Hubbard, a science fiction writer. Islam began with Muhammad, about 610 A.D. Muslims believe that Jesus, Moses, and Muhammad were prophets. I've read a little bit about the Muslim faith, because I had no idea what it was and what it consisted of. It's helped me appreciate Christianity a lot more.

BACKSTAGE PASS
getting to know

How did the band meet and form? We've gone through some member changes throughout the last few years, but the original group started in Hays, Kansas. We were going to college at Fort Hays State University, started the band, and started playing all throughout the state. As the years went on, we picked up Noah and Lester, and just kept going.

Do you feel God leading the band in a special direction? Right now, we're working on some new music. So far, the atmosphere's been really positive, and we're really excited. He's encouraging us to write the best music we can.

How does the band plan to further its ministry in the future? As far as the direction of career, we just take that one day at a time - whatever opportunities He gives us. It's hard to tell because a lot of those decisions aren't really up to us. We write the best music we can, and then, a mainstream label might call, or a movie might call, or someone who wants to do a Christian tour might call. All the paths just come to us. We just write the music and see what happens with it.

Birthdays:
Rob: August 20
Kalel: August 21
Noah: April 18
Lester: April 28

Favorite Bible Verses and Books:
Rob: Titus
Kalel: Revelation 20:10 & Psalm 22
Noah: 1 Timothy 4:12
Lester: 2 Corinthians 5:17

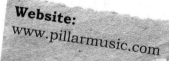

Website:
www.pillarmusic.com

Booking Agency:
Creative Artists Agency
615-383-8787
www.caaccm.com

Fan Mail Address:
Pillar
P.O. Box 700603
Tulsa, OK 74170

CASTING CROWNS

DON'T WORRY ABOUT YOUR LIFE

Melodee DeVevo

I grew up in a Christian home and was at church every time the doors were open, but I really didn't learn to depend on the Lord for everything until I was married, at the age of 23. Juan and I had been married for only three months; I was a music teacher at an elementary school, and Juan was a flight instructor. On another ordinary day in January, everything I read in my quiet time, in our Sunday School lesson for the next week, and also in *My Utmost for His Highest,* talked about trusting God with every little thing in my life. I felt God was almost speaking audibly to me. My eyes seemed to be opened, and I realized I was depending on myself for everything. All of a sudden, I was miserable! The Lord was just hammering me with Matthew 6:24-34. In a few months, God led me to quit my job, even though I knew we would not make enough money to pay our bills. I'm not saying I learned this lesson right away. It took two years of successes and failures before I knew I was depending on Him for everything. I truly believe that if I had not taken that first step, Juan and I would not be in Casting Crowns, and I would not be the person I am today. My encouragement to you is posed in this question - God loves you so much more than the birds and the flowers, and if He provides for their every need, will He not provide for yours even more? If you don't talk to Him and listen to Him speak through His Word, how will you ever know the amazing life He has for you? This life of **following Jesus Christ is our only reality**. There is nothing else.

Prayer

Jesus, thank You for everything You have provided for me. I am truly grateful for everything, but most importantly, for my salvation. I want to be truly Yours, so I ask You now to help me trust You with everything in my life. I love You. Amen.

UNPLUGGED
a deeper look

By depending on God for everything, will we be better able to live our lives according to His will? Yes, Juan and I would not live in Atlanta, and probably not be in Casting Crowns, if I had not first taken these steps of faith.

As you mentioned, depending on God alone and not ourselves, may strike fear in our hearts. As Christians, how can we deal with change without feeling that emotion? You must stand on God's Word. There are so many things He wants to say to us that would give us the strength and courage to keep going, if we would only read it.

Do you believe God will always keep His promises if we fully trust Him? God always keeps His promises. Sometimes maybe not in the ways we want Him to, but He does it in the best way possible.

BACKSTAGE PASS
getting to know

How did the band meet and form? Casting Crowns began as a student worship band in Daytona Beach, in 1999. After two years of serving at First Baptist Daytona Beach, God called Mark Hall (lead vocals), Juan DeVevo (guitar and vocals), Melodee DeVevo (vocals and violin), Hector Cervantes (guitar and vocals), and Darren Hughes (production manager) to Eagle's Landing First Baptist Church in McDonough, Georgia, in October of 2001. After arriving there, the Lord led Chris Huffman (bass guitar), a former student from FBC, Daytona, and Megan Garrett (keyboard, vocals, accordion) to join the band immediately. Then about a year later, Andy Williams (drummer) joined the group.

Do you feel God leading the band in a special direction? Our ministry started as a resource for small church youth pastors, and as praise and worship for our youth group. Jumpstartresources.com is something that we feel led to provide for youth pastors who have the vision, but maybe not the tools. We have been trying to do it since the Daytona days, but it is just now getting rolling. It is a free resource and will remain free for those who need it!

How does the band plan to further its ministry in the future? We really don't know where God is taking us in the future. All we know is that He put us in this position for now to speak to the church mostly, but also to tell people that Jesus is not religion and God is not just a book, and that He has a ministry for every person in the church. He has given us gifts that we are to use specifically for our ministry. We just take it day by day and go where God leads.

Favorite Bible Verses:
Andy: Romans 8:11
Chris: James 4:7
Hector: Psalm 119:11
Juan: Colossians 2:14
Mark: Psalm 1
Melodee: Philippians 4:8
Megan: Psalm 63:3

Birthdays:
Andy: May 13
Chris: November 12
Hector: September 13
Juan: September 24
Mark: September 14
Melodee: July 2
Megan: August 27

Website:
www.castingcrowns.com

Booking Agency:
Jeff Roberts & Associates
615-859-7040
www.jeffroberts.com

Fan Email Addresses:
andy@castingcrowns.com
chris@castingcrowns.com
hector@castingcrowns.com
juan@castingcrowns.com
mark@castingcrowns.com
melodee@castingcrowns.com
megan@castingcrowns.com

Fan Mail Address:
Casting Crowns
P.O. Box 150867
Nashville, TN 37215

Casting Crowns Casting Crowns Casting Crowns

PALISADE

DRAWING NEAR

Ashley Jett

"Draw near to God and He will draw near to you ..." (James 4:8 NKJV).

I don't know about you, but I find that amazing. What a promise! It is guaranteed that if we, you and I, take the first steps towards Him, He will come near to us. In my prayer life, I must admit, I find a battle going on. I am constantly asking Him to do all the work: "God give me a passion, compassion, move in me, awaken me ..." Does God love and honor my prayer? Yes. But if that is ALL I ever do, without putting any responsibility upon myself, then I'm not going to see much progress. It's like wanting to get in shape. You go out, buy all the right equipment, video tapes, food, and vitamins. Then you go home, eat all the food, and sit on the couch while watching the work-out video, and never participate. If that is your plan for living a healthy life, then you will end up frustrated and in no better shape than when you began. Loving God is a relationship, and it involves communication. Communication is a two-way street. He desires intimacy with us above and beyond anything else in this world. **Intimacy with Him is why we were created.** It's why we exist. If you are not experiencing intimacy in your relationship with Him, then you are missing out on what you were created for. You and I are created in the image of God. You are here for a specific purpose: To "... love the Lord your God with all your heart and with all your soul and with all your mind" (Matthew 22:37 NIV). The Father loves the pursuit of His children. Seek Him and watch Him show and tell you " ... great and unsearchable things you do not know" (Jeremiah 33:3 NIV).

Prayer

Lord, I lift up my brothers and sisters in Christ that come across this book. Burn a fire within their heart. May their eyes be opened to the realization that nothing can satisfy them but You. Our days are crazy and loud, and filled with anything but You. Help us to see how desperately we need You. May we run full speed in pursuit of You. In knowing You, we will discover who we are and who we are meant to be.

UNPLUGGED
a deeper look

How can teenagers take that difficult first step toward God and begin communicating with Him? Teenagers are slammed with activities, friends, school, church, sports, so much is going on. Being a teenager was the hardest job I ever experienced. I went from 7:00 A.M. to almost 1:00 A.M. every day without stopping. The thing we all need to realize, even as adults, is that we don't serve a religion. We have a relationship. We can go all day, and talk to God while we do our daily duties, but there is something about getting away for a few moments and just talking to Him - maybe not even talking, but just being still. Every relationship grows and becomes deeper the more time you spend together talking and just hanging out. Remember that God can't wait to talk to you and hear from you.

With all that goes on in kids' lives today, how can they find the motivation to take responsibility for spiritual growth? The more time we spend in the Word, praying and just talking to God on a daily basis, will actually give us motivation. Reading a few verses at night before bed, or in the morning before school will start to make you desire more of what God has to say. There is a place inside all of us that only God can fill. Teenage years are about finding out who you are, and about limits. No matter what we try to fill that "place" with, we will always come up empty. That is God's way of saying, "I want to spend time with you." The motivation comes from knowing that God gave us everything He had and then some - all for the sake of getting to know us.

BACKSTAGE PASS
getting to know

How did the band meet and form? Jeremy and I met at Kentucky Christian College, in 1999. Once we met, we both knew we had a passion for singing and song writing. After deciding to form a group, we wanted a girl to join us. I placed an ad on a Christian Music website and Ashley answered the ad, sent us her demo, and the rest was history. - Brandon

Do you feel God leading the band in a special direction? I think that God is leading us as a group into more of a specific ministry ... and that ministry is just one of love. We have always tried to show Christ's love to everyone we come in contact with, but I think now, more than ever, God has put a burden on our hearts to be out there showing people what He has done in our lives, and what He's capable of doing in theirs. In so many of the churches we go into, we sense a desperate need in people for something more, and we just pray that God uses us to show them that "something more" is Him, and a deep relationship with Him. That's what we're wanting to see happen. - Jeremy

How does the band plan to further its ministry in the future? We plan to continue making albums, continually growing, musically and creatively. We continue to have dates and go wherever God opens the door. We will keep at it as long as God allows us to keep going or until He says otherwise. - Ashley

0202401

Birthdays:
Ashley: January 29
Brandon: November 7
Jeremy: June 24

0202402

Favorite Bible Verses:
Ashley: Psalm 63:3
Brandon: Luke 9:23-24
Jeremy: Psalm 139

Website:
www.palisademusic.com

Booking:
Melissa Plamann
melplamann@yahoo.com

Fan Mail Address:
Palisade
P.O. Box 128245
Nashville, TN 37212

Fan Email Address: palisade_4@yahoo.com

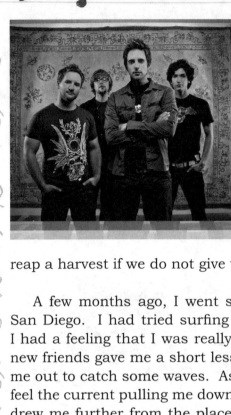

SANCTUS REAL

FIGHT THE TIDE

Matt Hammitt

"*L*et us not become weary in doing good, for at the proper time we will reap a harvest if we do not give up" (Galatians 6:9 NIV).

A few months ago, I went surfing with a family I met in San Diego. I had tried surfing a couple of times before, but I had a feeling that I was really going to get it this time. My new friends gave me a short lesson in the sand and then sent me out to catch some waves. As the ocean got deeper, I could feel the current pulling me down the coastline, and every wave drew me further from the place that I had started. I quickly realized that I was spending more time paddling against the waves than riding them. Even though learning how to work through the tide was a little uncomfortable, it was my only way to the pay off ... and that's what I got. Riding waves was even more exciting than I thought it would be!

What I learned about surfing that day helped me put some things about life into perspective. Just like the ocean, life has its own tides that are always working against us. These tides are spiritual, emotional, and physical. They are the experiences that shape us, draw out our strengths and weaknesses, and ultimately lead us to deny or rely upon our Creator.

It's our outlook and attitude that determine the course of our lives. Some people are just along for the ride and only experience momentary pleasures. Others face tremendous struggles and credit their victories to hard work and human strength. But for those of us who have spiritual vision, whose hearts beat with God's purpose, there is no true life apart from our Creator. We expect more than human rewards, because we understand that **a life in pursuit of God holds eternal rewards**.

Don't give up! Keep fighting the tide! I promise you that it will be worth it in the end.

More Verses:
Philippians 3:12-14

UNPLUGGED
a deeper look

If we are faithful servants, will God control our "tides of life" for the better? I've learned that we'll never understand why certain things happen to us. I had a conversation with a friend the other day, and some really bad things had happened to him. I've been dealing with that in my life, too. Someone might say, "Well, it's God's will," but I don't know if that's true. I think it's the fact that we live in an evil world, and because of sin, bad things happen. God promises that when bad things happen, He will work good for the believer. God may not necessarily control the tides of our life, in the sense that bad things *will* happen, but He will grieve with us and allow good to come out of those bad things in His sovereignty.

How can teens overcome life's tides and allow the Father to shape our strengths and weaknesses? God gives us strengths as a gift, to allow us to share His love with other people. Each person has a gift that is, hopefully, used to further the kingdom of God. Instead of allowing our weaknesses to eat at us, I would hope that students would understand that they do have a purpose, allow God to use them for His purpose, and find and work on their strengths. Don't be overcome with sadness about your weaknesses. Embrace them, because those are the things that allow us to become better people.

Something Brennan Manning talks about is how when we can understand God's love for us, then we can love ourselves, and we can be free to love other people. Let God sharpen your strengths, but also embrace your weaknesses. Let God show you that He can use you, despite you.

BACKSTAGE PASS
getting to know

How did the band meet and form? Chris and I were playing in chapel band together in Toledo Christian School, in 1996. We decided to start a real band - got together on weekends, ate pretzels and Cheez Whiz®, and ordered pizza from Papa John's, where Mark worked. In November 1996, we played our first show, and the rest is history.

Do you feel God leading the band in a special direction? We were feeling burnt out at the beginning of this year, but God's led us even stronger to the vision that He has for us. I've been blown away by the good that God is doing in our lives, despite all of the bad. God's leading us in our vision to reach youth. We're writing songs that are more emotional than ever, that are geared toward the personality of Christ, and how that intertwines with our struggles. If we can help other people overcome their struggles, and see the face of Christ, even in the darkness - that's our goal.

How does the band plan to further its ministry in the future? We want people to relate to us, and we're working really hard to expand our fan base, who can help us reach people with our music. We want to keep growing. The idea is mass exposure, so the message can reach mass amounts of people.

Favorite Bible Verses:
Matt: Philippians 2
Mark: Psalm 37:4
Chris: 1 John 3:18
Dan: 2 Corinthians 8:12

0202402

Birthdays:
Matt: October 19
Mark: February 13
Chris: June 16
Dan: December 17

0202401

Booking Agency:
Third Coast Artists Agency
615-297-2021
www.tcaa.biz

Fan Email Address:
sanctusreal@sanctusreal.com

Website: www.sanctusreal.com

DETOUR180

FIGHTING FOR YOU

Adrian Robertson

Every so often we find ourselves in situations that seem hopeless - those moments when the walls around us look way too high to climb. Our closest friends and family just don't understand, and may even be disappointed if they knew what we were struggling with.

It's not hard to feel like we have to deal with those situations all by ourselves. That's exactly how our Enemy wants us to feel - singled out, lonely, and tired - attempting to survive alone, to fix ourselves, by ourselves. But every time we take this road we are going to fail - not just because we aren't strong enough, but because we will never be strong enough on our own. **God has already fought so often on our behalf - it even cost Him Jesus' life.** He continues to fight for us everyday, so that one day we will finish this race and meet Him face to face.

Sometimes our pride makes us forget that we were actually created to have a relationship with Him, and not to walk alone. The Bible tells us, time and time again, how much God loves us and will never leave us. He needs to be our source of strength, because that's how it's meant to be ... that's how we are made!

David wrote, "God is our refuge and strength, an ever-present help in trouble. Therefore we will not fear, though the earth give way and the mountains fall into the heart of the sea" (Psalm 46:1-2 NIV).

Paul wrote, "The Lord will rescue me from every evil attack and will bring me safely to his heavenly kingdom ..." (2 Timothy 4:18 NIV).

Detour180 Detour180 Detour180 Detour180

"Christ Jesus ... is at the right hand of God, and is also interceding for us. Who shall separate us from the love of Christ?" (Romans 8:34-35 NIV).

Isn't it an incredible concept? The God who created the entire universe is our personal Defender, sticking up for us even when no one else seems to be. It's so easy in those hopeless situations to forget that we have a friend who will always have our back. Take a moment today to remember that God is and always will be "for you."

" ... If God is for us, who can be against us?" (Romans 8:31 NIV).

UNPLUGGED
a deeper look

Is reading the Psalms a good defense against doubt and fear? The Psalms paint an amazing picture of a God who, time and again, meets us in our hour of greatest need. Take Psalm 22 as an example, where the psalmist begins by expressing fear, doubt, and suffering - but you'll see that by the end of the Psalm, the words have changed to ones of praise. Reading the Psalms not only reminds us that other people have endured some pretty low times in their lives, but also, that God is consistently there for us in those times.

How can teens overcome their pride and accept what a sacrifice God made so He could meet us one day in heaven? Pride can be a difficult thing to get clear of, but I think serving others is a great way to overcome it. God gave us the most amazing example of a life spent serving other people, in the life of Jesus Christ. Try opening your eyes to the practical needs of people around you and offering them your help. By being a servant to others, we stop pride in its tracks.

Romans 8:31 (NIV) says, "If God is for us, who can be against us?" Why, then, do we have enemies, and how can teenagers deal with those who persecute them? The Bible teaches us to love our enemies, and to pray for those who persecute us. Often, it's our enemies in life that end up teaching us some very godly characteristics. They rub off some of the rough edges. We need to pray that God will help us to show love to those who seem to hate us, and help us to see them the way that He does - with grace and compassion.

BACKSTAGE PASS
getting to know

How did the band meet and form? Most of the band met at a Christian performing arts school, called Excel, in New Zealand. We trained and toured together, and then a couple of years later, we formed Detour180 as a way to combine our love of music with our passion for God. - Cain

Do you feel God leading the band in a special direction? Absolutely. One direction that God has been leading us is in being a really "serving-focused" band. It's easy for bands to be quite self-promoting, but God calls us to serve others - not to be self-serving. We see all of our opportunities as a chance to share the hope that God gives us, and also as a chance to serve the ministries of the churches and youth outreaches we play at. - Morgan

How does the band plan to further its ministry in the future? We're working together with World Vision on future tours that will encourage people to sponsor kids that are in great need. We see this partnership as a way to show God's love in a real, practical way. We're also developing some online "stuff" that will allow us to keep in touch with people we meet after concerts. This will give us an opportunity to talk with them about problems they are facing, things they are going through, and hopefully, we can share with them some of what God has been teaching us. - Neill

Birthdays:
Adrian: March 28
Neill: October 30
Morgan: November 5
Dan: June 27
Cain: November 22

Favorite Bible Verses:
Adrian: Psalm 28:7
Neill: Luke 23:46
Morgan: Psalm 51:17
Dan: Proverbs 3:5
Cain: Hebrews 13:5

Fan Email Address:
info@detour180.com

Booking Agency:
Verge Artist Agency
615-844-3322
www.vergeartistagency.com

Fan Mail Address:
Detour180
c/o Verge Artist Agency
3201 Cobble Street
Nashville, TN 37211

Websites:
www.detour180.com   or
www.vergeartistagency.com

JEFF ANDERSON

FINDING CONTENTMENT

"*F*or I have learned to be content whatever the circumstances. I know what it is to be in need, and I know what it is to have plenty. I have learned the secret of being content in any and every situation, whether well fed or hungry, whether living in plenty or in want. I can do everything through him who gives me strength" (Philippians 4:11b-13 NIV).

Friends of God,

Why is it that we feel the need to spend our entire life searching for "our calling?" What does this word really mean? What was it that we were created for? It feels almost impossible to answer these questions, doesn't it?

We were not created for career, marriage, or even ministry, for that matter. We were simply created because we were loved. All our Creator wants is to be loved in return, and to be King over every part of our life. We were made for relationship, "made for heaven." The God I serve cares more about my heart than my ministry. This brings us to the thought of contentment. What does it mean to be content? Paul searched his whole life to find contentment. Through wealth and through poverty, through imprisonment and freedom, through feast and through famine, he came to this conclusion: "I can do everything through him that gives me strength" (v. 13). He found **there is nothing this world has to offer that compares to the power and love of Jesus**.

In October of 2003, my wife and I found out we were going to have a baby. We were overjoyed! What we had wanted and prayed for was finally in our grasp. We told everyone; everyone rejoiced, and we were so proud. Eight weeks into Carriane's pregnancy, we were given devastating news. We lost our baby. We wept together. People brought food and comfort, and I took back a bit of the trust I gave to my Savior.

On a lonely night in November, still bitter and jaded, I felt in the pit of my heart it was time to release this baby, along with my trust, back to Jesus. I began to pray, and as I prayed, I felt peace - not surface peace - the peace that surpasses all understanding. I frantically grabbed my guitar and began to write a track for my album - "I'm Made for Heaven." God started bringing my heart back into the reality that we are made for more than this life. We were made to forever be with the King who shed His blood so that we could have freedom - what a perfect mystery!

Later that night as I dreamed, I found myself in my mom and dad's living room with my grandfather, who had passed away a year prior to this incident. We began to talk about heaven. I was awakened suddenly and became furious. I forgot to ask him about my child. Then the Lord allowed me to fall asleep again. My granddaddy was waiting for me. I then asked him, "Have you seen my baby?" To which he replied, "I've been playing with him."

God gave me a fresh understanding of the word "content." He showed me that His love immeasurably surpasses anything we could hope for or imagine. Being content in this life simply means to lay all dreams, goals, aspirations, and ambitions at the foot of the cross, being thankful, and rejoicing that you are loved by the King of Kings. Being content is trusting in Jesus that He knows what His best is for you.

Prayer

My Jesus, my King, it is only because of Your grace and mercy that I live and breathe. God, grant me wisdom so that I might understand what it means to be content in You. Help me not to question your direction, but trust You in all Your ways. Teach me how to love You without condition, so that I might please Your heart. Today, I surrender my heart to You again so that You might have Your way with me. I choose to love You today, Lord, and I choose to follow Your guidance. Show me mercy in the journey. Amen.

UNPLUGGED
a deeper look

Do you believe our ministry becomes more important to us and is more effective once we are content? Absolutely! When our heart can say, louder than our mind, "Whatever you want, Lord," or "I choose whatever is God's best for me," we can fully appreciate the path. God wants to use those who can submit their will fully to His will. John the Baptist said it best, You must increase and I must decrease (John 3:30).

While most Christian teens have probably heard a statement like, "There is nothing this world has to offer that compares to the power and love of Jesus," it is hard to grasp the meaning when their hearts are searching for contentment during a tough time. What advice do you have for them? Just like the promise, "I will never leave you or forsake you" (Hebrews 13:5 NRSV) says, we know that we can trust God, understanding that the Lord is gracious and compassionate, slow to anger, and rich in love (Psalm 145).

The word compassion means to suffer with. Isn't it comforting to know that we serve a God who weeps with us, experiences pain with us, and rejoices with us? I wrote "Love Never Fails Me" with feelings of doubt, confusion, and inadequacy, realizing the truth - that I am nothing without the power of God's Spirit. His Spirit alone can guide me through those feelings if I can only trust Him.

There is often one thing we want to hang onto in our lives, but true contentment is only found when we lay everything we are, everything we're going through, and everything we want to be at the feet of Jesus. How can teens give up that last thing to Him so they can have freedom and rejoice in their King? For me, the thing I had to give was spending this life with my baby. It was so difficult for me to give my child to Jesus. I simply had to be willing to trust Him and His timing and purpose, in order to please my Father's heart and allow Him to use the situation for His glory. I believe that if we can truly say we will be content, despite our personal agenda, in anything He would have us do - then He will draw us into what we are made to accomplish through this short lifetime. Be willing and obedient to be used by God, and trust that He is guiding you in what He is calling you to do.

BACKSTAGE PASS
getting to know

Favorite Books: *Practicing His Presence* by Brother Lawrence & Frank Laubach, *The Heavenly Man* by Paul Hattaway, *The Imitation of Christ* by Thomas á Kempis, *The Knowledge of the Holy* by A.W. Tozer, *Mere Christianity* by C.S. Lewis, and *The Celebration of Discipline* by Richard Foster

Musical Influences: Delirious, Coldplay, Radiohead, Sunny Day Real Estate, Muse, Nada Surf, Switchfoot, Elbow, The Beatles (because all of music is), and I can go on and on and on.

What is God teaching you right now? God has been teaching me the need to eliminate competition and comparison in my

Jeff Anderson Jeff Anderson Jeff Anderson Jeff Anderson

life, respecting and encouraging others in their gifting, and to seek only His approval.

How has your family helped you in your walk with God?
My father's words at the end of most conversations are, "Stay the course." My family is such an encouragement to me. In my insecurity they always seem to bring security. My wife, however, is my backbone. Carriane is my biggest encouragement. Her conviction is so strong and her wisdom is even stronger. She is the definition of helpmate. I cannot imagine I would be where I am today without her.

How do you plan to expand your ministry in the future?
I guess I will put one foot in front of the other and give Jesus the freedom to do with me what He wants. I am not really sure how to answer that. Logically, I want to set goals without expectation and try to reach them.

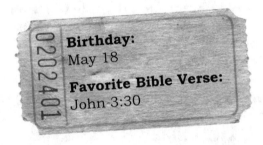

020240T

Birthday:
May 18

Favorite Bible Verse:
John 3:30

0000405

Fan Email Address:
info@jeffandersonmusic.com

Website:
www.jeffandersonmusic.com

THE DARINS

FINDING JOY THROUGH THE TRIALS

Rachelle Darin

Have you ever wondered why God has allowed you to go through a trial? I know I have. It was at the age of 7 when I asked that question for the first time. I remember having a conversation with my father and asking him why God was punishing me. You see, I was diagnosed with epilepsy at the young age of 7. Since I was the only one of my three sisters who had anything "wrong" with them, I felt very scared and alone. I wondered if I had done something wrong. Was God mad and was this His way of punishing me? As I went through my junior high and high school years, there was an ever present feeling that I was different than everyone else around me. There were times when I wasn't able to drive; I was constantly taking medication, and always fearful of the next seizure. I was too young to understand what God would, eventually, reveal to me later on in my life. I truly didn't understand God's unconditional love and compassion for me, and I hadn't come to realize that God had created me just the way that I am. I couldn't grasp that He had a purpose for my life and my seizure disorder.

As my journey with epilepsy continued, I began to see God's plan for my life unfold. I finally got the answer to the question I had asked my dad so long ago. "For I know the plans I have for you says the LORD, plans to prosper you and not to harm you, plans to give you hope and a future" (Jeremiah 29:11 NIV). Like myself, you will face a trial at some point in your life. As you journey through your trial, always remember that God will never leave you or forsake you, and that **He will never give you more than you can handle**. As I reflect on the past five years of my ministry with The Darins, I believe that I understand exactly why I have had to go through this trial.

For the last twenty years, God has been using my epilepsy to draw me near to Him so I could be at the place where He could use me. He used something that I had always seen as very negative in my life, to offer hope to others who are struggling with epilepsy, or just any trial in general. I realized that God sometimes uses us in ways that we would never imagine. I would not change anything that I have gone through in my life, to be at the place where I am today in my relationship with my heavenly Father.

More Verses:
James 1:2
1 Peter 1:6-7

Prayer

Lord, thank You today for the trials that we have to endure in our lives. There are many times that we don't like the situation that we are in and we don't understand, but help us to realize that You do. You love us more than we could imagine, and You will walk with us through the trial that we are facing. Teach us to grow closer to You through the good times and the bad. Thank You for always being with us. In Jesus' name, Amen.

UNPLUGGED
a deeper look

Some teens turn from God in times of trial. How do you advise teenagers to stay close to Him, even in difficult periods? I know when I face difficult times, I have to turn to God. He knows what I am going through, and He cares deeply for me. I lean on Him for strength and hope. You might have the tendency to blame God, but always remember He is a gracious God who created you and would never harm you. He allows things in our lives to happen so our faith can be strengthened. We come out of the trial a stronger person and a better Christian. "Your righteousness reaches to the skies, O God, you who have done great things. Who, O God, is like you? Though you have made me see troubles, many and bitter, you will restore my life again; from the depths of the earth you will again bring me up. You will increase my honor and comfort me once again" (Psalm 71:19-21 NIV). - Krista

Some teens don't feel comfortable sharing tough situations with others. Is it important to share your struggles with a godly person, or should you go directly to God? My advice to someone struggling through any trial is to share their struggle with someone who loves them and who will offer them counsel and advice based on Scripture. Often, while in the deepest part of our struggle, we don't see things as clearly as someone on the outside would. If you are dealing with a difficult situation, please find someone that you can trust, a God-fearing teacher, parent, Sunday school leader, or friend, and let them know you are seeking help. You can't get through it alone. That is why God has put these people into your life. But you need to go to the Lord, as well. True healing comes when the Lord heals your heart. We need Him. Always remember that He loves you, and when you are hurting, He is hurting. He wants you to live your life abundantly - so grow closer to Him and let Him teach you and bless you through your trial. "As iron sharpens iron, so one man sharpens another" (Proverbs 27:17 NIV). - Stacy

How can teens trust that God is only allowing them to go through what they can handle, and know that He will provide for them when they're struggling to make it through a difficult time? I don't know if it's a matter of knowing that God is only going to give you what you can handle, rather than knowing who to rely on while you are actually facing the difficult situation. It's important to know that as we face the hard times, we serve an awesome God - who desires for us to cry out to Him, and allow Him to sweep us up and carry us through the storm. Feed off of the strength of our precious Lord. "I can do all things through Christ who strengthens me" (Philippians 4:13 NKJV). I know at times it may feel as though you have been placed in the midst of a storm and you will never get out. But throughout God's Word, He continues to reveal His promise to us of how He will never leave us. Hold on strong to the following verses: "The LORD himself goes before you and will be with you; he will never leave you nor forsake you" (Deuteronomy 31:8 NIV). "Rejoice in the Lord always; again I will say rejoice!" (Philippians 4:4 NKJV). - Rachelle

How can teenagers look for what God is doing in them and through them because of their trial? Speaking from experience, it is not always easy to see God at work in the midst of our trials. It's after you actually go through the trial that you are able to see the joy and learn the lesson that God has designed for you. "We live by faith, not by sight" (2 Corinthians 5:7 NIV). Part of faith is believing in what you cannot see, and being able to trust and know that God has orchestrated for you to travel down that path and to take that journey with you, as in Jeremiah 29:11. Rest assured that God will reveal the answer in His time. - Heather

BACKSTAGE PASS
getting to know

How did the group meet and form? We are sisters, and grew up together playing sports and singing, so it came pretty naturally when we decided to start a group. We are very close in age. Only five years separate the oldest and the youngest, so we have a blast together. We are truly all best friends.

How does the group plan to further its ministry in the future? We take it one day at a time. We never know what the future holds, but we trust that whatever He has in store for us, it will be revealed. We enjoy being together as a family and ministering to people all over the country.

Birthdays:
Krista: April 20
Stacy: July 18
Rachelle: May 6
Heather: July 1

Favorite Bible Verses:
Krista: Philippians 4:13
Stacy: Colossians 3:23
Rachelle: Jeremiah 29:11
Heather: Romans 8:28

Website:
www.thedarins.com

Booking Agency:
StudioLord Management
and Booking
studiolord@comcast.net

Fan Mail Address:
The Darins
P.O. Box 681071
Franklin, TN 37064

Fan Email Address: darinsisters@yahoo.com

TODD AGNEW

FIXING OUR EYES

You know those pictures that you're supposed to stare at for a really long time, then let your eyes go out of focus, and you'll finally start to see something? Yeah, I hate those. I can never see anything. I've always thought that maybe it was just a joke that some guy was playing on the gullible people of the world, to make them waste their lives staring at a meaningless image. But you know, that's the way I actually live a lot of my life - staring at stuff that's completely meaningless, trying to find something deeper. Looking at movies, gazing at "successful" people, staring at a fallen world trying to find God. Why do we say we want to be like Christ, not the world, and yet stare at it as if it holds all the answers?

"Let us fix our eyes on Jesus, the author and perfecter of our faith, who for the joy set before him endured the cross, scorning its shame, and sat down at the right hand of the throne of God" (Hebrews 12:2 NIV). For most of my life, I knew this verse and agreed that I should focus more on Jesus, but I woke up one day and realized that I had no idea how to do it. I'm not going to give you a perfect step-by-step plan, just a couple of things that have helped me focus in a practical way.

First, find the things that stir your affections for God and do them. One of my things is running. It's a great focused prayer time for me. I do it so much that it has become routine. As soon as my feet hit the pavement, I start praying. Another one of mine is leaving my Bible by my bed. When I wake up, I open it and quickly memorize a verse - not to memorize forever, just so that as I wake up, take a shower, eat breakfast, my thoughts are first directed towards Christ. I find things that cause me to love God and try to incorporate them into my life on a more regular basis. Second, find the things that distract you from God, that lessen or steal your affections, and stop doing them. Most of us want to say we love the Lord, but we want to live on our own terms. For me, I had to pull back on the movies. I had to question the way I dated. I had to be careful what I put in my head before I got in the van for a ride, where my mind could easily wander to these subjects. To be really honest, I had to stop playing video games for awhile. That may seem strange, but I realized that, while I may not have been bringing evil destruction upon the world by playing video games, I was numbing out and losing multiple hours of my life during which God could have been moving my heart towards Him. Of course, the greatest distraction is girls ... well, relationships. I decided that I want a girl that stirs my affections for Christ, and if she doesn't, well, I guess she's out. None of these things are inherently evil, but anything in your life that gets in front of your love for Christ is a sin. It's a hard way to live, but I think He deserves it.

The more you love something, the more you look at it. The longer you gaze at something beautiful, the more you fall in love. It's kind of a circle. It works the same spiritually. The more we gaze at our Savior, the more He will redefine our concept of beauty. **The more we get to know Him, the more we will love Him.** And the more we love Him, the more we want to focus upon Him. So try Him out; taste and see. Fix your eyes and let Him show you true beauty.

UNPLUGGED
a deeper look

Does everyone have something that stirs their affections for God? How can we, with the busy lives we have today, find time to do those things and make them habits? Everyone definitely has something that stirs their affections for God. God creates us in a way that we naturally have longings for Him, and we always want to fulfill that. We've found the things that make us happy, and we've learned to do those. You do what's important to you. If loving the Lord is

not that important to you, then you won't make time for Him. Once you fall in love with the perfect God who loves you, and become consistent, that love is only going to grow. It starts getting easier and easier. You'll probably find out that falling in love with Him is much more important than just stirring your affections for Him.

How can teens begin to stop doing the things they do in place of spending time with their Father, in order to focus more on Him? That was a hard one for me. It didn't ever occur to me that I might do things that distract me from the Lord. Satan's easiest deception in our lives is, "Don't spend time thinking about what's in your life. As long as you don't analyze it, then it's gonna' be fine." Sometimes we just have to sit down and say, "This part of my life - does that have to do with the Lord? Is He a part of that? Is He honored by that? Or is that something I do that doesn't have anything to do with God?" Video games were the thing for me. I would settle in and just play. Did that mean that video games were evil? No, not at all. It just meant that I used them as an escape from life. Our rule on the bus is that to play X-Box, you can't bring a single player game. I don't think God's going to be honored by me staying in front of the television and sitting down and not talking to anybody. X-Box is for fellowship - for us to hang out together, relax together, and enjoy being brothers in Christ.

Does true beauty come only through Christ? That's such a great question for me right now. God's been teaching me that the world has redefined beauty, so that it can sell things. Do I really think that when God makes someone in His image, He doesn't find them attractive? That's a strange thing. When we say that God is loving and beautiful, what do we mean? We mean that He's pure and holy. Is that what we're attracted to in a person? Not necessarily. God's been asking me to find beauty. What I've been finding is that true beauty can only come from Christ. It can only be found in Him, but we are all reflections of that - as created beings and as His children. Some of that beauty is found in us, but it's not just what the world calls beauty.

BACKSTAGE PASS
getting to know

Favorite Books: *The Bible, The Imitation of Christ* by Thomas á Kempis, anything by Ted Dekker, and anything by C.S. Lewis.

Musical Influences: Rich Mullins, Charlie Peacock, Michael W. Smith, and Michael Card were the writers that really impacted me on the Christian side of things. I look at a whole lot of different things mainstream-wise: blues, rock, gospel, jazz, classical - you start stirring all of that stuff together, and become who I am as a musician.

What is God teaching you now? That what we think of as beautiful is not necessarily what God thinks of as beautiful.

How has your family helped you in your walk with God? My family is everything. I'm adopted, so at the end of the day, when I look back on my life, who I am is because I was chosen by my family. More importantly, my family members are great, godly people, with an attitude that taught me the Bible and took me to church. That's why I am who I am, where I am.

How do you plan to expand your ministry in the future? That's something I've really left in the hands of the Lord. What I've found is that when you plug into what God is doing, then that's where you're supposed to be, because you don't have to worry about your plans anymore. Even right now with all of the success we're having, we're trying to keep our hands off of it and say, "God, we're still asking Your blessing. We're gonna' obey whatever You say. If in a few months this Christian music thing is done, and we're gonna' go be missionaries, then that's cool." Right now, it's like this is where He wants us to be. We're going to do our everything here, trying to make a difference.

Favorite Bible Verse:
I kinda' like the whole book,
but Isaiah 6 and Isaiah 58.

Birthday:
March 15

Booking Agency:
GOA, Inc.
615-790-5540
www.goa-inc.com

Fan Email Address:
fans@toddagnew.com

Websites:
www.toddagnew.com
www.gracelikerain.com

Fan Mail Address:
VanLiere-Wilcox
Attn: Todd Agnew
P.O. Box 646
Franklin, TN 37065

DONNIE LEWIS

FORGIVENESS

I grew up in a single parent Christian home, to a young mother who was very involved in church. She was on the praise and worship team, in the choir, and if the church had anything else going on, we were there. Growing up, I saw my mother depend on God no matter what hardships came our way. My mother tried her best to protect and provide, but even in the midst of all of the praying and church going, I was molested. Yes, by a family member that was picking me up from school. Once my mother found out, I was too young to understand what all of the mumbling and whispering was about, but I knew my mother would turn to God in prayer, and the situation would change.

As I grew older, I started to see the subject on talk shows, in movies, and hear about it in school. People started trying to tell me how I should feel. I started wondering if I was supposed to be mad at him and hate him for the rest of my life. I could blame him for all of my problems. Was he the reason I became a sexually active teenager, or started having trouble in school? Was he the reason I had a hard time being comfortable around guys, no matter what their intentions, or the reason I became a teenage mom? If everybody else can blame their problems on someone else, *then why can't I?* Then God started to reveal things to me about myself, and why I was unhappy, holding onto anger toward someone who had probably gone on with his life. The fact does remain that he did wrong, but an even bigger fact is that **God heals, no matter what the situation**. Matthew 6:14-15 (NKJV) says, "If you forgive men their trespasses, your heavenly Father will also forgive you. But if you do not forgive men their trespasses neither will your Father forgive your trespasses." Even after growing up in the church and knowing God's Word is true, I still want to see things my way. How can someone do me wrong and I have to forgive them? Then I realized that God didn't do anything to me, but how many times have I taken advantage of His love and grace? Yet He has still, time after time, forgiven me.

God has given me the opportunity to go into schools and churches to share with young people in the same situation or even worse. If I was still that angry, bitter person that kept everything bottled up inside, I wouldn't have the chance to give someone else words of comfort, or strength to move on. I like the new me, the forgiving me, that allows God to have control of my life, to heal my wounds, and as it says in Psalm 55:22 (NKJV), "Cast your burden on the Lord, and He shall sustain you; He shall never permit the righteous to be moved."

Another Verse:
Isaiah 53:5

Prayer

Lord, I thank You for comforting us and bringing us through the hard times. We pray that You guide us and direct our steps. Help us to become more like You in all areas. Just as You have forgiven us, help us learn to forgive others. We stand firmly on Your Word today and everyday, so that we can be molded by You. Thank You for all that You have done and for all You're going to do. We love You and thank You in advance. Amen.

Donnie Lewis Donnie Lewis Donnie Lewis Donnie

UNPLUGGED
a deeper look

How can teenagers forgive themselves when they feel really guilty about something they've done? Read Jeremiah 6:15 - Feeling guilty not only means you know right from wrong, but that you have the Holy Spirit dwelling in you and encouraging you to make both the situation right and the right decisions. Just remember that we all make mistakes, and Jesus died on the cross long before you were born, long before you made the mistake, because He knew that no man would be perfect.

Does forgiveness from God ever have conditions? How can we apply this kind of forgiveness to others? Read Acts 13:38-39 - Yes, it comes with one condition. You have to believe in God and His promises. By Him everyone who believes is justified by the law of Moses (v. 39). Remember that when someone wrongs you, even if you haven't wronged them, you still need forgiveness.

What does the gift of God's forgiveness mean to us as Christians? "For you, Lord, are good and ready to forgive, and abundant in mercy to all those who call upon you" (Psalm 86:5 NKJV). His forgiveness takes us in as we are and loves us as if we had never sinned, and His forgiveness saves us from the depths of hell.

BACKSTAGE PASS
getting to know

Favorite Book: *The Bible,* because there is always something you can learn.

Musical Influences: CeCe Winans, Fred Hammond, Patti LaBelle and Commissioned

What is God teaching you now? To not lose faith, because everything doesn't happen in a matter of moments. I have to

Donnie Lewis Donnie Lewis Donnie Lewis Donnie

be patient and wait until His timing, because He knows when I am actually ready to enter into the next level of my calling.

How has your family helped you in your walk with God?
My mother is always someone I can call for advice, and she will be honest with me and keep it scriptural, even if it's not what I want to hear.

How do you plan to expand your ministry in the future?
I plan on focusing on those things that God tells me to focus on, not what's cool or what is working for someone else - because my path is for me and if He expands it, that will be wonderful. If He doesn't, I'll continue to follow Christ and enjoy whatever else He has planned.

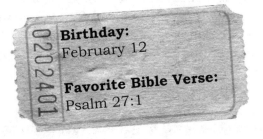

Birthday:
February 12

Favorite Bible Verse:
Psalm 27:1

Booking Agency:
Paradigm Management
615-599-2062

Fan Email Address:
donnieonline@hotmail.com

Website: donnieonline.com

JAMES CLAY

GETTING IN THE WORD

J was raised in a Christian home, so I had always heard the Word. I learned my Scripture verses in Sunday school, but never really got into reading and knowing the Word for myself. When I was 10 years old, my mother left and divorced my father. My whole life was drastically changed. I was living an entirely different life, in a new place, without my friends, and absent a father. My mother's reason for leaving Dad was conviction of the Word, so as a young man, I quickly turned to the same Word. Agreement or disagreement with my mother was not the issue. The issue was what happened in my life as a result of studying God's Word. Maybe I wanted to change her mind, even prove her wrong. Instead, I was studying the Word in depth; I got the Word very deep in my heart, and it changed my life.

Romans 10:17 (NKJV) promises, "So then faith comes by hearing and hearing by the word of God." I experienced the truth of this Scripture in a very real way. As I read and studied the Word, the world around me started to change. It wasn't that all of my problems disappeared, but that what I saw, felt, and thought began to be filtered through what I knew about God and His Word. Through "hearing and hearing," I had built my faith. That is not to say I have never slipped or fallen in my walk. All of us face trials; what you have to remember is once you get the Word in your heart and coming out your mouth, it only does good things. **God's Word is bigger than a book.** John 1:1 (NIV) says, "In the beginning was the Word, and the Word was with God and the Word was God." Studying, learning, and memorizing the Word is getting to know who God is.

I want to encourage you to let Jesus, the Word of God, be a lamp unto your feet and a light unto your path (Psalm 119:105). Hide it in your heart and watch your world change.

UNPLUGGED
a deeper look

The Bible's such a big book! Where do you start? Most Bibles have a concordance in the back. You can look up subjects; you can look up chapter and verse. If there's a particular issue, and you'd like to find out what God thinks about it, that great big book is a great place to start.

Do you have any favorite things that you do in your Bible study that might also be helpful to teens? Before I study the Word, I tend to try to be quiet and clear myself of all the distractions - turn off the television, turn off the radio. One thing I'd recommend *not* doing when trying to hear from God through His Word is multi-tasking.

What does the Word do to our perspective of others and of our circumstances? It completely changes the way that we see other people. Our natural flesh is going to want to do unto others as they've done unto us. It wants to use others for our gain, to take advantage of every situation that we can. What we learn through the Word, and through what Jesus taught when He was here on earth, is that we are to love our neighbors as we love ourselves. I think that's a drastic change in perspective.

BACKSTAGE PASS
getting to know

Favorite Books: *The Pilgrim's Progress* and *The Holy War* by John Bunyan, *Lord of the Rings: The Trilogy* series and *The Silmarillion* by J.R.R. Tolkien, *The Screwtape Letters* and *The Chronicles of Narnia* by C.S. Lewis

Musical Influences: Bob Dylan, Rich Mullins, Otis Redding, Van Morrison, Mylon LeFevre, and Larry Norman

What is God teaching you now? Patience, and how to walk on the sea in the middle of the storm.

How has your family helped you in your walk with God? Having children and being a father has completely opened up my eyes to how God sees me. As a human, I would give my life for my children, and I can't even imagine how much further God's love is to us. My family has absolutely drawn me closer to God, and given me insight into how He feels about us, and how I should feel about Him.

How do you plan to expand your ministry in the future? I think that it's God who's doing the work. If I truly am in ministry, which I believe, then it's Him who's ministering. I just happen to be the vessel for that.

Birthday: March 19

Favorite Bible Verse: 1 Corinthians 13

Booking Agency: Cinder Entertainment
615-456-1123
www.cinderent.com

Websites:
www.jamesclayband.com
www.purevolume.com/jamesclay

Fan Email Addresses:
James@jamesclayband.com
info@tenentertainment.com

WARREN BARFIELD

GOD, ARE YOU LISTENING?

Do you ever feel like God isn't listening to you? Do you wonder if He is ever going to answer your prayers? I imagine that right now you can name something that you've been praying about, that it seems like God is not hearing at all. I know that most of you, if you're honest, can name something. I can. Grab the nearest Bible. Open it to nearly any book. It will not take you long to find someone, somewhere, shouting to the top of their lungs, "Oh God, can you hear me? Do you see me here? Where are You?" Their shouts echo in us today.

Recently, during youth group at my church in Charlotte, North Carolina, I was talking to my teens about praying. I shared with them that we could talk directly to God about the needs in our lives, and He would hear us.

"That is why we have a great High Priest who has gone to heaven, Jesus the Son of God. Let us cling to him and never stop trusting him. This High Priest of ours understands our weaknesses, for he faced all of the same temptations we do, yet he did not sin. So let us come boldly to the throne of our gracious God. There we will receive his mercy, and we will find grace to help us when we need it" (Hebrews 4:14-16 NLT).

One of the most faithful guys in my group, who doesn't speak up very often, said, "God never answers my prayers." My brain automatically began sifting through the files of biblical comebacks that I have compiled over the years of being a pastor's son. With both of my feet set firmly on the ground, and my shoulders squared, my mouth opened, and the words surprised me. I didn't quote any Scripture, or tell him he lacked faith, or that he should pray louder and longer. What I said was, "Sometimes I feel the same way."

Don't you? Haven't you felt like God just isn't answering your prayers? Maybe He never will answer it, at least not in the way you're expecting Him to. Paul prayed three different times for God to take away the weakness that tormented him, but God never did. "Three different times I begged the Lord to take it away. Each time He said, 'My gracious favor is all you need. My power works best in your weakness'" (2 Corinthians 12:8-9 NLT). Who of us can explain God? Why He chooses to answer some prayers so obviously, in what seems like an instant, while others seem to go unheard.

I believe the challenge is to realize that Christ is our strength. Whether He chooses to answer our prayers in the way we are expecting, or if He chooses His higher ways that are beyond our understanding. After night after night of tears and cries to God of, "Can You hear me? Do You see me here? Where are You?" - the peace is in knowing that **He is the very reason we have the strength to cry out at all**.

Sometimes the answers to our prayers come disguised in the strength needed to get us through another day. Often it takes weeks, months, and even years before we are able to look back and see the truth in it all. God can hear us. He does see us. Wherever we are, He is. Whatever our situation is, His grace is sufficient. His strength is perfect in our weaknesses. Begin your prayer time today by reading Philippians 4:12-13, and know that Christ will give you the strength you need to face whatever situation might be awaiting you.

Don't ever give up.

Prayer

Father in heaven, You are a sovereign, Holy God. You are my God. Lord, I want Your will to be done in my life. If that requires You painfully ripping me from all I cling to in this world, then so be it. I am not living for this world, but for heaven. I know You will not put more on me than I can bear. Provide me with what I need to face today. I am in desperate need of Your grace for myself and others. Keep me close to You. You are all I need in this world and the one to come. Amen.

UNPLUGGED
a deeper look

Will God provide for and comfort us as we're waiting and crying out for an answer to our prayer? God never stops providing for or comforting us, whether we are asking for it or not. The "HOW" is the big question. We might feel like He's nowhere around, because we are not seeing what we want to see. I believe that it is in looking back that we begin to make sense of how God was there for us in past times of need, and our faith is increased for the times of need that we must yet go through.

Can strength to persevere be more important than answers when we're going through "valleys?" I think that godly wisdom and understanding are just as important as strength when we are venturing through the "valleys" of life. Maybe we should spend less time crying out for God to haul us up to the mountaintop, and a little more time seeking out what could draw us closer to God and equip us to help others. (This statement is directed at myself; if by some chance it applies to you, as well, it is by mere coincidence.)

How can we have faith that God is there, taking care of us, watching over us as we struggle to find the answers to our prayers? "For it is by grace you have been saved, through faith - and this is not from yourselves, it is the gift of God -" (Ephesians 2:8 NIV). God will give us the faith we need. Stop for just a second, close your eyes, and just be quiet. Can't you feel Him? In the middle of all the pain, doubt, confusion, anger, and fear, deep down there seems to be something that resembles peace. Eternity is ours. This life is a raindrop in the ocean of what is the life to come. I believe you know it's true. No matter how many times you tell yourself that you don't understand, I believe you have caught a glimpse of that peace. God has given you a gift. You've pulled the ribbon off of it and you are starting to pull back the paper. Wait ... could it be? ... just what I needed ... FAITH!

BACKSTAGE PASS
getting to know

Favorite Books: *What's So Amazing About Grace* by Philip Yancey, *Messy Spirituality* by Mike Yaconnelli, *Requiem Of Love* and *The Singer* by Calvin Miller, and *Ruthless Trust* by Brennan Manning

Musical Influences: My mom and dad; Singer-Songwriters from James Taylor and Stevie Wonder to Sting and Phil Collins. Way too many to list here. Every piece of music I have ever heard has influenced me in some way.

What is God teaching you now? My goal is not to see how much I can gain here on earth. I should be living for something more. He is constantly redefining what success means to me.

How has your family helped you in your walk with God? Every good thing about my life - the things that I love most about waking up - all of them, with very little effort, can be traced back to my mom and dad, my sisters, my brother and their families, my amazing wife and her family. I am blessed.

How do you plan to expand your ministry in the future?
By following Christ wherever He leads me. Sounds like an easy answer, but it's easier said than done, because God's idea of expanding my ministry might not be what I want. It could have nothing to do with reaching millions of people through my music. It might be caring for the sick in some country I've never heard of. The first will be last and the last will be first. Man, that's hard to swallow.

Birthday:
May 4

Favorite Bible Verse:
Psalm 139

Website:
www.warrenbarfield.com

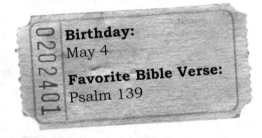

Booking Agency:
Third Coast Artists Agency
615-297-2021
www.tcaa.biz

Fan Mail Address:
Warren Barfield
c/o Dryve Artist Management
256 Seaboard Lane, C-103
Franklin, TN 37067

Fan Email Address: info@warrenbarfield.com

Alathea

God In Nature

Cristi Johnson

When I was in high school, my youth group traveled out to a retreat center every fall - we called it the boonies - our extreme plunge into nature. Always, at least one of us would fall into the river, or in love, break an ankle, or someone's heart, get lost in the woods, or finally get found.

There, with the absence of phones, TV's, CD's, movies, school, classes, and curfews, life somehow became quieter, the volume turned down. At the same time, our awareness was somehow turned up a little - we would see a sunset for the first time in months, or sit next to a blazing fire with the wind cold on our backs, or catch an insect from the shower, maybe name him and set him free out the back door.

Way back in the day, it was just possible to hear God's voice from a donkey, a burning bush, or a soft blowing breeze, or to see Him walking on water, standing in a fire, or calming a storm. Not that any of those ways are the only way, or even sure ways. Once when I was in college, I wanted so desperately to hear from God that I thought I would be like Zacchaeus, and climb up in the sycamore tree in my mom's backyard until He spoke to me. I'm not exactly sure what I expected, but the only thing that came from the heavens was drop after drop of rain, falling faster and faster until I finally climbed down, soaked and wet, and went inside. Not until I was drying off did my long-awaited conversation with God finally begin, first with my frustration, and then with laughter. My heart needed a little melting, a little softening, a little rainfall.

So when my world gets loud and chaotic and I can't seem to hear myself think, I try to find a boonies, my own little sycamore tree - which may be nothing more than my bedroom window or a walk out the back door, realizing that **the God who**, in the beginning created the stars and the sunsets, who **speaks through blazing bushes**, storms and the rainbows that follow, **is the One who knows my name**, who has chosen to make His home in me, forever creating me into His image.

UNPLUGGED
a deeper look

Can we use the miracle of God's creation to present Him to the unsaved? Since I've been part of Alathea, Mandee's seen dozens of shooting stars that I always seem to miss, and Carrie's named every shade of sunset (she's one of those artists) - they help me to pay attention, to get quiet and listen. I'm finding that God is always presenting Himself to all of us through His creation - if we'll only notice and point it out to each other.

The Bible says even the rocks should praise Him. What does this mean to you about how we should respond to God? Though we are created in God's image - as the smartest and brightest of all of His creation - we are sometimes the slowest to do what we were made to do. We forget what we were created for, and the rocks and trees are left to do our work.

Do you find sanctuary in the beauty of nature? David did. Sometimes it seems David's world was so much different, maybe even irrelevant - but when I walk out past the roads and sidewalks, into the thick of the world that God made, I find the sanctuary that David found in the wilderness, safe from his oppressors, a safe place for me to rest my hectic spirit. If God takes care of the lilies of the field and the bears of the forest, then surely He is taking care of us. And if He knows even the number of hairs on our head, then I know I'm safe to trust Him with anything. Everyday, miracles happen. Nature helps teach us how to pay attention to the miracle of God's presence all around us.

Alathea means truth. Can the truth of God's existence be made real to us while spending time outdoors in his creation? When Jesus stands before Pilate, Pilate asks Jesus, "What is truth?" A few years earlier, Jesus said, "I am the way and the truth and the life" (John 14:6 NIV). And now, Jesus just stands there in response to Pilate's question - *He* is the truth. Knowing the truth is more than learning, understanding, and memorizing. Truth is knowing Jesus. Just as we learn something about an artist by seeing his paintings or about a writer by reading her story, we learn about God by spending time in the middle of all that He has made. Our surroundings help to shape not only our songs, but who we are becoming.

BACKSTAGE PASS
getting to know

How did the band meet and form? While in college, we all volunteered with a ministry to high school students. We were sitting around in our hotel room during a leadership/planning retreat, and Mandee pulled out her guitar. Carrie and I started singing along. A few hours later, we were calling this pass-time the "harmony game," and a few weeks later, we were spending all of our free time playing it. A few months later, we were playing at any place that invited us, and a few years later we're here, talking to you.

Do you feel God leading the band in a special direction? Authenticity - being honest. Not being afraid of what we don't know, but trusting the One we do know. Not being forced to look, act, sound like everyone else, but relaxing in who God has made us to be. Not measuring success by money or popularity, but by how well we're loving and caring for the people in our lives, and by how well we communicate that love through our music. Not settling for being "okay" at what we do, but working really hard (on our instruments, our songs, our music) at always becoming better, so that even the chords and the melodies are pointing to God.

How does the band plan to further its ministry in the future? We just want to do justice, love mercy, and walk humbly next to God (Micah 6:8) and then commit our way to Him (Psalm 37:5-8), so that it is up to God to use us however He sees best - in big or small ways.

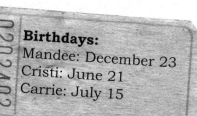

Birthdays:
Mandee: December 23
Cristi: June 21
Carrie: July 15

Favorite Bible Verses:
Mandee: Micah 6:6-8
Cristi: Isaiah 30:15-26
Carrie: Psalm 37:5-8

Website: www.alathea.com

Booking Agency:
Street Level Agency
574-269-3413
www.streetlevelagency.com

Fan Mail Address:
Alathea
P.O. Box 356
Unicoi, TN 37692

Fan Email Address: alathea@alathea.com

THE MYRIAD

GOD INTERRUPTED

Jonathan Young

Early one dark winter morning, I found myself walking quickly to work. Checking my watch to see how I was doing on time, I realized I was gaining on a rather tall man who was also heading to work. As he passed under one of the street lamps I noticed he was wearing rather short, high-water pants. So short, in fact, that the top of his hiking boots and white tube socks were exposed before the cuff of his pants began. I kind of rolled my eyes and thought this guy looked awfully funny - tall, gangly, and he didn't have the sense to wear proper length pants to an office setting. Right then, God interrupted my thoughts and spoke to me.

"Jon, what are you looking at?" He asked.
"That man up ahead," I replied.
"Are you really looking at him or just his clothes? Go ahead and look again ..."

As I looked up and watched from behind, I noticed the man walked with a bounce in his step as he gazed up at the sky. His gaze moved to a tree and then to something else - I couldn't tell what. It looked as if this man was enjoying the walk and the start of a new day. He looked like a kind and jolly person, the kind that would greet you with a friendly hello, ask about your weekend, and actually take the time to sit and really listen.

"Now, what do you look like?" God asked.

I looked down and noticed that I was walking hurriedly, only focused on getting to work early. I felt pompous and judgmental. As I entered the door to work and took the elevator up, **I felt humbled and yet glad that God had interrupted my thoughts**. It was needed, for my pride was taking over.

Once at my desk, I pulled my Bible from my bag, took hold of the ribbon and opened up to the place I had left off the day before. I was reading through the book of James and that morning in chapter 4 (NIV) I read, "...'God opposes the proud but gives grace to the humble.' Submit yourselves, then, to God. Resist the devil, and he will flee from you. Come near to God and he will come near to you ..." I thanked the Lord for interrupting me.

UNPLUGGED
a deeper look

Will God always "interrupt" our thoughts if they are prideful or ungodly, or do we have to be listening and in tune first? How can teens make sure they are ready to listen when God's ready to speak? I feel that God is always trying to interrupt our thoughts ... we can get so wrapped up in our own little world that we forget about the bigger picture, and more importantly, the Creator and Conductor behind it all. Whether we are in tune with Him, in a prideful moment, in deep crisis, in deep sorrow, brimming over with joy, I believe He is still trying to get our attention to make sure we always turn our focus back to Him. That is the beauty of this relationship ... He is always there, always faithful and seeks us first. The bigger question is, are we always listening? The answer, sadly, is no. I have been working on listening to Him for years, and it does take discipline and purpose - discipline to spend that quality time with Him just as you would with any close relationship - sharing your deepest thoughts, joys, and pains. We also need to be purposeful in our thoughts, trying to always give them over to God. Paul certainly wasn't seeking God's presence, but Christ interrupted his travel to Damascus. Peter also easily heard from God on the rooftop when he made the time, and was purposeful about seeking His presence. - Jonathan

Can we see the good in others, and possibly the weaknesses of ourselves, on our own, or is it only through God that we can see these things? Since we are made in His image, I believe we can only see the weaknesses of ourselves, as well as the good in others, through God alone. Even if a person does not have a personal relationship with God, I still think they view the world through the lens of God's perspective, because they are made in His image. We are tainted by sin, so we do not see everything clearly. The more closely we seek Him in our lives, the more we are privy to understanding the weaknesses in ourselves and the goodness in others. - Jonathan

BACKSTAGE PASS
getting to know

How did the band meet and form? A few of the members had been playing together off and on in their home town of Redding, California. There was a decision to change artistic directions, really focus, and move to Seattle. Once in Seattle, Jeremy and John met up with former band mate, Jonathan, and began rehearsing. Jeremy was working at a studio and met Steven, who was interning there. They quickly realized that they had similar musical influences, and Steven started playing with the band almost immediately. Most recently, Randy was added on drums. - Steven

Do you feel God leading the band in a special direction? We have felt from the beginning our direction as a band has been to break down the barriers between the experiences of our lives and our faith. We do our best to avoid the "not a Christian band, but Christians in a band" response. As artists we cannot separate the experiences in our lives from our music. The amazing thing about a relationship with Christ is that it's holistic. We can't compartmentalize our sin from our glory. Whether our inspiration comes from a personal relationship with a friend, a romantic relationship, or the hope for an eternal glory and peace that will only be found in eternity, we have felt pressed to reflect that accurately - both the shame and redemption. Our hope is that there are others with the same questions we have, and that we can be a part of ushering them towards truth. - Steven

How does the band plan to further its ministry in the future? We've learned the hard way, that we can only do so much on our own. Anything we can do based on our own labor isn't really worth doing. We work hard, and we will, of course, keep doing that. But more importantly, we will strive to pursue God and others with a fierce integrity, and pray that He will bless us in our efforts. - Steven

Birthdays:
Jeremy: March 25
Steven: October 6
Jonathan: February 5
John: May 31
Randy: February 9

Favorite Bible Verses:
Jeremy: 2 Kings 6:15-17
Steven: Matthew 2:16-20
Jonathan: Romans 12:1-2
John: Exodus 33:2
Randy: 1 Corinthians 1:19
& 9:24-27

Fan Email Address:
fans@themyriad.net

Websites:
www.themyriad.net
www.purevolume.com/themyriad

Booking Agency:
(Festivals and Colleges)
Third Coast Artists Agency
615-297-2021
www.tcaa.biz

(General)
The Agency Group
212-581-3100
www.theagencygroup.com

Avalon

Godly Friends

Melissa Greene

I grew up in a Christian home, attended church from a young age, and was involved in the ministries our church had to offer from when I was a child to a teenager. Despite all of this, I did not have many Christian friends growing up. Thank God that when I went away to college, my circle of Christian friends grew to an abundance! And even now, as I am getting older, and have been exposed to a wide range of people through the ministry of Avalon, God continues to bless me and enlarge my circle of Christian friends. I can truly attest to what a difference having Christian friends makes!

My godly friends have picked me up and cried with me when I have failed, and have rejoiced with me in my victories. I believe these are the attributes of a true, unchanging, godly friend. **Being a godly friend means imitating Christ in our relationships** everyday.

How do we do that? We do that by being trustworthy, compassionate, carefully listening at all times, helping in any way we can, edifying each other and by being devoted, faithful, and loyal to one another as friends in Christ. Jesus said in John 15:13-14 (NIV), "Greater love has no one than this, that he lay down his life for his friends. You are my friends if you do what I command." We may not ever have to actually lay down our lives for our friends, but we can practice sacrificial love by doing those things listed above.

"Two are better than one; because they have a good return

for their work: If one falls down, his friend can help him up. But pity the man who falls and has no one to help him up! Also, if two lie down together, they will keep warm. But how can one keep warm alone? Though one may be overpowered, two can defend themselves. A cord of three strands is not quickly broken" (Ecclesiastes 4:9-12 NIV).

I have always loved these verses. Without God in our relationships, a circumstance may overcome us, and oftentimes our friendships will fall to the wayside and be lost. How many times have you stopped being friends with someone over something small and insignificant? God is the glue that binds us together and makes us stronger than we ever could have imagined, when we put Him in the center of our relationships with our friends! Let us pray and ask God today and everyday, moving forward, how we can become better, godly friends to those around us.

More Verses:
Proverbs 17:17
Colossians 3:13

Prayer

Lord, thank You so much for all You have done for us. I pray that starting today I can show Your love towards my friends, and be the friend You would have me to be to others. Help me to forgive those that have hurt me. And I pray that I would be forgiven by anyone I may have hurt in the past. Fill me with more of Your precious love and kindness today so that less and less of my own flesh shows through. I love You so much and thank You for all You will do. In Jesus' name I pray, Amen.

UNPLUGGED
a deeper look

How did Christ-centered relationships help you in the hard times in life? During my college years, I made many mistakes. I eventually found myself on solid ground again, but it was only God's grace, mercy, and my circle of strong, Christian friends that enabled me to get back on my feet again. These friends graciously told me when I was wrong and then prayed with me until I got back to where I needed to be. I thank God for them! More recently, my friends have been my solid foundation, when I found out my father-in-law had cancer. My husband and I asked all of our friends and loved ones to pray with us for healing. I believe in the power of prayer, and praise God, my father-in-law is in full remission today. Not only did my friends lift my father-in-law up in prayer, they helped pray myself and my husband through a difficult time in our lives. What a blessing friends are!

What are some tips on finding friends that have a Christlike character? The first sign of finding a godly friend is to look for a person in whom you can readily see the fruit of the Spirit. Can you see Christ in that person no matter where that person is? In church, school, at the movies, or at the mall? I believe we should choose our friends very carefully during all stages of life, and should pray that God is in our friendships at all times. I especially believe it is important for teenagers to seek out other godly teens! Being a teenager is not easy, and it is much easier to be pulled down than to be lifted up. So teenagers, pray for God to bring other godly teenagers into your life!

How have your friendships with Avalon and other Christian music artists helped you? I am so grateful for my friendships in Avalon. My husband and I are also thankful for the friendships we have made with other Christian artists. It is so wonderful to be able to be open and honest, and to feel

free to talk, cry, pray, or be overjoyed with the circumstances of life. There are so many ups and downs of being involved in the industry, and with our ministry in general, that it is a huge blessing to be able to share these with other artists who may be going through the same things.

BACKSTAGE PASS
getting to know

How did the group meet and form? Janna Potter Long and Jody McBrayer are both original members of Avalon. They met in a previous group, Truth, where they traveled, sang, and ministered in churches together. Janna auditioned for Avalon, and she recommended Jody. Over the years we have had members change due to God's leading and timing. In September of 2002, Melissa Greene joined the group. Newest member, Greg Long, filled in after Michael Passon's departure, and after much prayer, joined Avalon in fall of 2003. Greg also happens to be Janna's husband. The first Avalon baby was born in May, 2004 (Greg and Janna's)!

Do you feel God leading the group in a special direction? We have felt a reconfirming of the calling of this group and why it was started. We want to achieve God's highest standard of excellence in sharing the gospel, singing, worshipping, and speaking, and to serve the body of Christ to the best of our ability. We, as a group, have grown so much in Christ over the past nine years; so our hope is that you hear a maturity and a truth that only God can reveal, in both the triumphs and trials that He has brought us through.

How does the group plan to further its ministry in the future? We are so excited about the future of Avalon's ministry! We have truly become a family, and we are dedicated to each other, as well as to the ministry. No matter what the days ahead may bring us, Avalon, the ministry, is here to stay.

Birthdays:
Janna: February 5
Melissa: June 26
Jody: June 25
Greg: December 12

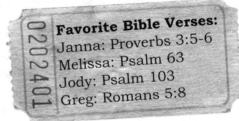

Favorite Bible Verses:
Janna: Proverbs 3:5-6
Melissa: Psalm 63
Jody: Psalm 103
Greg: Romans 5:8

Booking Agency:
Jeff Roberts & Associates
615-859-7040
www.jeffroberts.com

Fan Mail Address:
Avalon
P.O. Box 150867
Nashville, TN 37215

Website: www.avalonlive.com

MICHAEL TAIT

GODLY PARENTS

Growing up, my dad was a great example to me. My mom was also a great example, in the sense that she was what we called a "Proverbs 31 Woman." I remember that so fondly - my mom, never complaining, such a servant. My dad always lived out what he preached. He didn't just talk about it at home. You saw him do it in his cab, on the streets with people, loving us when we were kids, and trying to provide positive people and environments for us as kids growing up. I had a charmed life in that sense.

But I have a brother who is in jail for drug abuse and just a lot of dumb things. A good guy, ninth and tenth grade all-state at football ... he just kind of threw his life away. I never really saw my parents denounce him or say, "You're the worst," though. They loved him, and they embraced him, and they cared for him through all that time. I'd imagine that's hard, to see your child start straying away. But my mom and dad loved that boy, and they do to this day. My dad's in heaven now, but he died loving him and hoping the best for him. My brother's still in prison, but he knows the Lord. He's learned a hard lesson, but a dcTalk song says, *Some people gotta' learn the hard way.* Sometimes we have to learn that way. I have no question that my parents' love for him was a big part of him coming to the Lord. They were that example of unconditional love.

Times have changed, situations change, locations may change, but the same thing my parents went through in 1945, you kids are going through today. How you deal with it, and maybe some of the repercussions are different, but parents

Michael Tait Michael Tait Michael Tait Michael

do understand. Your job is to go where your parents are and think, "Okay, the parents have lived through it. They probably understand a little better than I do, and they try to work with me. Let me try to work with them." **You need to open up to your parents.**

Yes, my family had our downfalls and our problems, but just seeing the integrity there with my mom and dad, their friendship and their marriage, says a lot to me. We were a family that went to church together and stayed together.

More Verses:
Colossians 3:20-21

UNPLUGGED
a deeper look

God disciplines His children, as godly parents discipline theirs. How can teens accept discipline from their parents with a willing spirit? You have to listen and realize that a loving parent will only discipline you with the hopeful response that you try to walk the straight and narrow. True Christian parents do not enjoy chastising their kids. They do it out of necessity and out of obedience. It has to be done, and it saved my life ... my parents disciplining me. I could have been a "wild boy," growing up in Washington, D.C. You can gain a lot from your parents' discipline and need to appreciate it.

How can you grow in your walk if your parents are not Christians? Some of you aren't as fortunate as I was. If you have parents who aren't Christians, but you are a Christian, you can still grow in your walk. I think praying for your parents and fasting for your parents is a big deal. It's kind of tough, because you almost become the parent, spiritually speaking, but you have to be the example. You have to be the cross-bearer, loving them and living "right" in front of them, so they can see your example as their offspring. If you're not in

a "perfect" situation, there are other believers. The church is out there, youth groups are out there; good Christians, Bible study, counseling is out there - I think it's important to have some sort of outside support, once again, somebody helping you to bridge that gap. A mentor would be great - helping you understand that. Sometimes it's hard to get past the pain and realize there is a God out there that cares about you.

BACKSTAGE PASS
getting to know

Favorite Books: *Wild at Heart* by John Eldredge and *The Purpose Driven Life* by Rick Warren

Musical Influences: Nat King Cole, U2, Stevie Wonder ... I'll stop there; that could go on forever.

What is God teaching you now? I think I have this ongoing lesson coming from God, to focus. I'm like a kid in a candy store; I have a hard time focusing because I want to do everything. And God says, "Okay, if you don't focus, I can't really pour into you. I can't give you this awesome power." I'm learning patience, and I'm learning how to truly die to what I think I want. One of my records is called <u>Lose This Life</u>, for goodness sakes. It feels good to satisfy the flesh. That's the danger.

How has your family helped you in your walk with God? Just Mom and Dad living what they preached - saying it, and then walking out the door and living it.

How do you plan to expand your ministry in the future?
Music's obviously my major platform. I wouldn't mind getting into film; I wouldn't mind getting into Broadway, if that came my way. Music is the tool that God has given me as my gift to use, so wherever it takes me, I'll go. The main thing I'll keep doing is making records, whether it be with Tait or dcTalk, or I'm praying, outlets with secular artists. That's a big prayer request lately. That God will open more doors in the secular world for me to really influence people.

Birthday:
May 18

Favorite Bible Verse:
Proverbs 11:30

Website:
www.taitband.com

Booking Agency:
Creative Artists Agency
615-313-8787
www.caaccm.com

Fan Mail Address:
Tait
227 3rd Ave. N.
Franklin, TN 37064

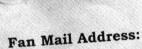

Fan Email Address: taitband@taitband.com

STARFIELD

GOD'S GRACE

Jon Neufeld

*A*lthough I was blessed to grow up in a Christian home surrounded by prayer and devotion through the example of my parents, it still took me a long time to even scratch the surface when it came to understanding grace, and living in the freedom that it permits me. It can be a difficult thing to not feel the weight of condemnation as a result of our sin. Paul says in Romans 8:1 (NIV), that " ... there is now no condemnation for those who are in Christ Jesus." We are meant to live in freedom from guilt and condemnation because of the sacrifice Jesus made for us. Paul also says in Romans, Chapter 6 (NIV), "What then? Shall we sin because we are not under law but under grace? By no means ... You have been set free from sin and have become slaves to righteousness." **Grace is not a license to sin**, but instead, it should inspire us to be people of integrity that serve and honor God with our lives.

It is a promise that we need to grab hold of. One of the main lines in a song of ours called "Revolution" says: *I am a war already won, I'm a revolution.* That's how we need to understand grace. The battle has been fought and won by Jesus; now all we need to do is depend on God, and ask for His help to be the hands and feet of Jesus in the world today. This doesn't mean we won't sin, but it does mean that when we do fall, Jesus doesn't see us as any less in that moment. His love and His grace are unconditional and unending.

In my life, I find that I consistently slip into undisciplined, selfish habits that pull me away from my relationship and intimacy with God. But then I always slowly find my way back to surrender, repentance, and forgiveness. This "coming back"

Starfield Starfield Starfield Starfield Starfield Starfield Starfield is one of the most freeing and beautiful things we can do as human beings. God doesn't count how many times we fall away; all He cares about is that we come back to Him again and again, and are slowly transformed more into His likeness. That's the mystery and the beauty of grace.

UNPLUGGED
a deeper look

How have you seen God's grace affect others' lives? Grace has the power to transform a person from joylessness to true fulfillment. I've seen friends of mine go from a place of being bogged down by condemnation and guilt for their sin, to a place where they are living in freedom. These people are so refreshing. They are the kind of people that are honest and real, and don't pretend to be something they're not. It's easy to really get to know a person who understands and receives God's grace.

How has God shown you a better understanding of His grace? I believe understanding grace is a lifelong lesson, but God has shown me more about grace specifically through my relationships with the other guys in the band. Being in such close quarters all the time means that we have to work hard to maintain humility and a mutual respect for each other. I have learned what it means to extend grace and to keep a short record of wrongs for others. This has helped me to understand how God sees us, and how His grace works.

Do you have any tips for teens on how they can accept God's grace in the fullest way? First of all, understand it for yourself. Read the Word, hear what Paul has to say, and what Jesus has to say about grace. The most important thing that a person needs to understand is Romans 8:1. This is essential to receiving grace. We do not live in condemnation for our sin. God doesn't see our sins, because He has already dealt with them on the cross. We need to let this freedom inspire us towards integrity and a closer walk with Jesus.

BACKSTAGE PASS
getting to know

How did the band meet and form? Tim (my older brother) and I both grew up playing and leading worship at church in youth group and church worship bands. At some point we decided to play some coffee shops together, where we butchered U2 and Jars of Clay cover songs. Several years ago, we got the chance to form a band around us, and be the "worship band" at a few local festivals in Canada. We started taking every opportunity we could get, writing and recording our own songs. Today we can look back and really see the hand of God on our band and on our lives individually, teaching us and showing us His will day by day, bringing us to where we are now, with Shaun and Gordy as members of the band.

Do you feel God leading the band in a special direction? We feel called to write songs for the church - to be a band that leads people in worship. As a touring band, we want to focus our energy on drawing near and worshipping God in a corporate setting. Our hope is that a Starfield concert feels like a church service, with a little more rock 'n' roll. We feel as if God wants us to write the soundtrack for a generation that is searching for a faith that is relevant. We want to communicate the truth of salvation in a way that isn't manipulative, but instead, in a way that is full of grace and love. Our prayer is that our songs can communicate in this way.

How does the band plan to further its ministry in the future? We just want to continue to be faithful in the small things - pursuing God as individuals and as a band, making time for the things that are really important in life: friends, family, reading the Word, and prayer. In the larger scope of things, we really want to stick to our original vision, which is to complement the "already in process" work of the local church all over North America. We want to be servants, encouraging and building up the body of Christ. We are always praying for fresh vision and purpose - that God would show us what needs to be said, and how Christians in this generation need to be challenged. On a practical level, this means we want to be on the road a lot, just getting out there - playing and leading worship wherever and whenever we can.

Birthdays:
Tim: April 7
Jon: July 31
Gordie: September 27
Shaun: January 14

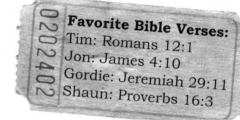

Favorite Bible Verses:
Tim: Romans 12:1
Jon: James 4:10
Gordie: Jeremiah 29:11
Shaun: Proverbs 16:3

Website:
www.starfieldonline.com

Booking Agency:
Creative Artists Agency
615-383-8787
www.caaccm.com

Fan Email Address:
starfield@starfieldonline.com

THE ELMS

GOD'S PROTECTIVE HAND

Owen Thomas

I woke up in a hospital bed, about 30 hours after we were in a terrible car wreck, and I'd never been as scared as I was in that moment. I'd never been in any kind of road mishap that would put me in the hospital. The roof of the van was totally smashed, like a pancake. We shouldn't have walked away from the ordeal. I had some severe head and neck trauma and Chris had to have some knee surgery, but there's no way that we could have survived something like that, unless God and His angels were in our company. We really believe that that's what happened - that God was there with us. You hear people talk about how faithful God is, but for me, it's extremely personal, simply because God was very faithful to us that night. It has a literal meaning for us. We've lived it.

Living life, though, we can lose our focus, and what it truly means to be a Christian. We get consumed with the details and the rigors of life: our van, our vision, the album coming out, the tours we were on, but a car accident like that - that has a way of bringing you back into focus. There's a line in our song, "You Saved Me," inspired by the accident, that says, *When all my ambition became my religion, still I knew You were around.* At the very core of the whole thing, it's just trying to advance God's Kingdom in a way that represents Him well.

We always ask for protection, and that's another very real way that He shows us His grace. I've known some extremely godly people, and I can think of one right now that had a huge impact on my life. A woman that I knew in Missouri, who was a wonderful woman of God, got killed by a drunk driver one night on her way home from taking her kids to their friend's house. None of us are worthy of God's sacrifice or worthy of grace. It was a gift that He gave to us, but if there was somebody who was worth it, it was this woman; she loved God and loved people so much. I'm sure her family asked, "God, I thought you were supposed to protect us. What's the deal? Why didn't you protect my mom, or my wife?" I know that God does protect His children, and even when it seems that maybe His provision has taken a different role than what we think it should, He's still on his throne.

I know that God doesn't want His children to hurt. I know He doesn't want His children to be in pain. I know that as much as God is our Protector, Satan is always at work. **Hope should be in just knowing that God is still on His throne.** I don't have to know all the answers - I don't know why she died. But I'm sure she's loving life now. I think that God's will and His provision go hand in hand, and I think just to know that He's still on His throne is extremely comforting, the greatest kind of provision.

UNPLUGGED
a deeper look

Genesis 15:1 says that God told Adam He would protect him. All through the Bible God protected His people. In what other ways have you felt God's protection in life today? Our band spends 200 days a year or more, on the road. We had that one mishap, and even in the extreme circumstance of it, God was able to protect us. Over the course of the last three or four years, I've probably spent 80% of my time driving around the country and only had *one* accident. That's an enormous testament of God's provision to me. Life is dangerous. We hope to make the most of everyday, and just leave the details in God's hands. Doing all of the traveling that we do, it's obvious that God protects His children.

When you accepted Christ, did God begin to protect you from worldly temptations? I've really petitioned God to keep me from temptation, help me to not even be placed in situations where I'm tempted, as opposed to giving me strength

once I'm faced with temptation. Those are two different things. I try not to put myself in positions where I would compromise myself with temptation that I know can be a vice to me. I don't know that any human has enough fortitude, aside of God's help, to ward off those temptations. We may want to believe we do. Even the person who feels the closest to God, in their humanity - in a situation where they're faced with their one greatest temptation, doesn't have that kind of strength. Our flesh wants to glorify itself.

Exodus 33:22 says that God will cover us with His hands. What does that mean to you? It means a lot to me. It's kind of a cool picture to think about in a literal sense - where you can actually see God shielding you. It feels very personal because of the nature of the name of our band. The Elms is the name of my uncle's home in London, a 16th century converted hotel completely surrounded by trees, to the point where if you're walking by on the street, you can't even see his house from the road, because the trees are so dense. I've always thought of that as a provisional theme: God's protection so thick around us, so prevalent, that our enemies can't even see us. His hands are on us - in times that we feel alone, that we just need to feel loved, that what we're doing is making a difference. He's our Comforter. God really does take care of His kids. I'm grateful to God that He's protected my vision and my calling so many times. How gracious God is that He would protect us, protect our vision, protect our hearts, protect our minds, protect our bodies, and our everything.

BACKSTAGE PASS
getting to know

How did the band meet and form? The Elms began with me and my brother, Chris, deciding that it was "high time" we started a rock 'n' roll band. When we decided to do that, the only guy that we could think of to play guitar was my best friend since fourth grade, Thom. We called him up, and Nathan joined us about a year and a half ago. Although we've known Nathan for six or seven years, it's great to finally have him in the band.

Do you feel God leading the band in a special direction?
Over the course of the last couple of years, we've come to
realize the enormous need that people have to be hopeful.
We've gotten the chance to do a lot of touring outside of just
exclusively Christian events, and we've seen a lot of people
in the world who need to know that there's hope available to
them. Our band really feels like it's incumbent upon us to tell
them about God's love.

**How does the band plan to further its ministry in the
future?** We just want to give people something to believe in
and hope for, to let them be a part of our band, a part of the
global vision of The Elms, as opposed to just being a fan of it.

Birthdays:
Owen: July 29
Thom: March 8
Nathan: September 22
Chris: November 6

**Favorite Bible Verses
and Books:**
Owen: Luke 12
Thom: Micah 6:8
Nathan: Matthew
Chris: Psalm 46

Website:

www.theelms.net

Booking Agency:
The Agency Group, Ltd.
212-581-3100
jordanburger@theagencygroup.com

Fan Mail Address:
The Elms
P.O. Box 1214
Seymour, IN 47274

Fan Email Address: Contact@theelms.net

ZOEgirl

Good Enough?

Chrissy Conway

"*For* it is by grace you have been saved, through faith - and this not from yourselves, it is the gift of God - not by works, so that no one can boast" (Ephesians 2:8-9 NIV).

Growing up, I was a pretty good kid. I did well in school. I was involved in my community. I listened to my parents (well, most of the time). If you asked me if I believed in God, I would have said to you, "Yes, of course." If you'd asked me if I thought I was going to heaven and why I thought so, I would have said, "I hope so, because I think I'm a good person." I spent the first eighteen years of my life just "hoping" that I was good enough to get into heaven. I had never read the Bible - I didn't know I really could read the Bible. It always seemed too overwhelming to read.

Right after my high school graduation a friend of mine, who I knew was a Christian, took me to a huge Christian crusade. That was the night that changed my life forever. For the first time, I heard the gospel being read. That night, I realized how incapable I was of getting into heaven on my own, and that all of my good deeds were worthless without Jesus. I realized that I would never be good enough on my own to stand before a mighty and perfect God. I found out who Jesus really was and what He did for me. I accepted Him into my heart that night. That is why I am here, seven years later, writing this to you.

The Bible says that **NONE of us are good. That is why we need a Savior.** It is not enough to go to church on Sundays, just to say you were there. It's not enough to go to youth group, hang out with Christian friends, listen to Christian music, read Christian books, or be a good person. When you really experience God, and when He becomes a reality in your heart, those things are done not because you feel like you have to, but out of love and excitement for God and His purpose for your life.

Most of you may have grown up in Christian homes. Maybe you've heard this same story a million times before. I want to challenge you to take a moment and really check the motives of your heart. Have you ever had a personal encounter with Jesus, or is this something your parents believe and you're just going along for the ride? At the end of the day, your family, your works, and your good grades combined will never get you into heaven. Jesus, Himself, said that He is the only way to God. The choice is up to you and the time is now to make it. No one is guaranteed to see tomorrow. One thing we have in common is that someday we will all stand before God and account for our lives. Knowing what I know now, I'm glad that I have Jesus on my side.

Prayer

Lord, I thank you for the gift of salvation. I thank you for Your grace. I pray that we would place all of our faith in you and not in our own capabilities. Help us to realize how much we need You. I pray that You would show us more and more everyday, how everything we have and everything we are, is because of You. I ask that You would reveal to each of us the things in our lives that we are trying to control on our own. I pray that right now we would surrender those things to You and discover the purpose You have for each of us. Amen.

UNPLUGGED
a deeper look

What are some ways that your life has changed since you accepted Christ and stopped just trying to earn your way into heaven? My life has changed dramatically in the past seven years, since I became a Christian. The biggest way it has changed is that I have gone from living my life for me and doing things my way, to putting God first in my plans and my decisions. I know for a fact that I wouldn't be in ZOEgirl if I hadn't surrendered my dreams and desires to God. I wouldn't have met my husband if I hadn't joined ZOEgirl. So, my life is completely changed forever since I accepted Christ and started following His plan for my life, instead of my own plan.

Are people saved if they don't know the exact day they received Jesus as their Savior or haven't had a dramatic conversion? Usually a person remembers the specific point in time when they gave their life over to Christ, but the Bible says that if you believe in your heart and confess with your mouth that Jesus is Lord, then you will be saved. If both of these things are true for you, then you are saved. However, if you've never "officially" spoken out about your faith - today is your day. Tell someone you know about what you believe, and make today your day of salvation.

How can teens who are wondering if they're really saved confirm their salvation? When you become a Christian, there is something about you that changes. It's not about having religion in your life. It's not about going to church, having Christian friends or listening to Christian music. When you have a relationship with Jesus, you KNOW it. You know it by looking at the condition of your heart … where it used to be and where it is now. Being saved isn't just a one-time experience. It's a constant, daily commitment of developing a relationship with your Savior. One way of confirming this is by looking back at the way you lived before committing your life to Jesus, and then looking at the differences afterwards. When you have a living, active relationship with God, you WANT to spend time with Him. Through praying and reading the Bible, God is constantly chipping away at the old you. He is molding you day by day. By allowing this to happen, you become more like Christ and closer to God everyday. People will see that you aren't the same person you used to be. By just being you, you will influence others around you, and inspire them to live that same kind of life.

BACKSTAGE PASS
getting to know

Favorite Book: *The Purpose Driven Life* by Rick Warren

Musical Influences: I am a big fan of CeCe Winans and Nichole Nordeman.

What is God teaching you now? God is teaching me to not just value, but treasure, my prayer time with Him. He's showing me more and more that life is much easier and more meaningful when my prayer time is consistent.

How has your family helped you in your walk with God? I have an amazing family in New Jersey. Now that I am married - I have twice the amazing family! I am so blessed to have the people in my life that I do. They are encouraging, supportive, and uplifting to me in every way imaginable. The family unit is so important, and without them, I wouldn't be doing what I'm doing today.

How do you plan to expand your ministry in the future?
I am open to whatever God wants my ministry to be - it's ZOEgirl right now; tomorrow it could be something completely different. I just want to be ready and available for whatever God has planned for me. I would like to continue using music as a ministry tool. I would also like to get further involved in children's ministry.

Birthday:
April 5

Favorite Bible Verse:
Proverbs 31:30

Booking Agency:
Jeff Roberts & Associates
615-859-7040
www.jeffroberts.com

Fan Mail Address:
ZOEgirl
c/o Proper Management
P.O. Box 150867
Nashville, TN 37215

Website: www.zoegirlonline.com

BETHANY DILLON

GOSSIP KILLS YOUR HEART

Until recently, the issue of gossip was far from my mind. I thought since I grew up in the church and was a good person, "venting" to my family and friends was not a big deal. Whenever the subject came up, my mind would automatically go to "that person" I knew, who really struggled with gossip. But within a couple of days, gossip was brought up in conversation after conversation. And, as always, God gently pointed out the bitter fruit it has produced in my heart.

What a convicting passage Ephesians 4:29-32 (NASB) is! It hits me right between the eyes when I read, "... do not grieve the Holy Spirit, ..." and "... forgive each other, just as God in Christ also has forgiven you." But it's so easy ... and fun. There is something about getting people on your side ... telling them something they wouldn't know otherwise. "She snubbed me! I really have tried to be nice to her. I don't know what her problem is." How many times have I said that? The truth is not always a comfortable thing: Gossip kills our hearts. Once we begin a relationship with Jesus, the new man has replaced the old. Our sinful nature has passed away and we begin to think, act, and even speak like Him. As believers, **we should be kind to one another, tender-hearted, and forgiving, because Christ is!** It makes me chuckle to think about how afraid I am of people talking about me ... yet, I find myself talking about others. I hope that people give me the benefit of the doubt, but how often do I jump right to conclusions? I want trustworthy friends that will build me up, but how often have I failed to control my words?

The wonderful thing about God's conviction is that He doesn't leave us feeling guilty. There is hope! One of my friends says, "Starve a habit to break it." I encourage you to be a blessing to the people around you by starving your appetite for gossip. Look for opportunities to build someone up in another person's company. Point out the things that you love about them. It is hard to bite your tongue when you would love to blurt something out ... remember, you reap what you sow. God will be honored when you seek to encourage and give grace to those around you.

Prayer:

Jesus, help me have eyes like Yours. I desire to see people as You see them ... I want to love people like You love them. I want to accept people with a tender heart and humble mind. Please give me a heart like Yours. I'm willing to give up my habit of gossiping, because I want to honor You in the way I live my life. Make me more aware of all the opportunities I have today to build up my brothers and sisters. Thank You for being patient with me! Amen.

UNPLUGGED
a deeper look

What can you do if you try to be kind to someone (even another Christian), and they still gossip about you? Still be kind to them. It's tough, but it is *so* important to put yourself in the other person's shoes. Grace is a much more powerful thing than we think. It takes true character to search for the good in anyone, especially someone who enjoys talking about you behind your back. Let the Lord uproot that in others - just do what you are called to do - love them. Be a picture of Jesus by choosing to talk about the good in people. Most people would rather see you live what you believe than just tell them.

Many Christian teenagers never intentionally gossip. Someone says something about someone else, and they absent-mindedly join in, or somebody has hurt or upset them, and they just believe they're "sharing their feelings." How can they realize "gossip is gossip" and they can't be exempt from that sin? I am so thankful for the few people in my life that I can truly vent to ... people that won't go out and tell everybody and their brother what I tell them in confidence. I'd encourage you to look for that person that really knows and loves you, and who will look at things objectively when you're hurt. Boundaries are very important, though. A good thing for me to be mindful of when I'm talking about someone else is to imagine them being in the room. Would I be sharing this story if he/she was standing right here? Pray that God would make your heart sensitive to that - that you would have a compassionate and selfless heart. When you love others as much as you love yourself, it'll be hard to talk about them behind their backs.

How should teens handle a situation where their friends are gossiping? When I'm in those situations, usually (a) I'm afraid of making a big deal about it, because I don't want to make my friends angry and (b) I don't want to come off like I'm self-righteous, because *I* know, and *they* know, I struggle with it myself. Pray for wisdom, because sometimes it's good to speak up and say something like, "Hey, I don't know if we should be talking about this. I know you don't mean any harm by it, but I just don't want to tear him/her down. Cool?" If you say it as nicely as possible, it's usually fine. There's nothing wrong with keeping each other accountable. However, other times it's wise to be thinking of ways to change the conversation, or interject something positive about that person.

BACKSTAGE PASS
getting to know

Bethany Dillon Bethany Dillon Bethany Dillon

Favorite Books: *The Bible* and *The Chronicles of Narnia* by C.S. Lewis

Musical Influences: Sara Groves, Jonatha Brooke, Jennifer Knapp, U2, Patty Griffin, Ben Harper, and Nichole Nordeman

What is God teaching you now? Because I'm gone so much with touring, at times I feel really homesick. I throw myself a pity party, thinking about all of the things I'm missing out on - youth group, hanging with my family and friends. I was so overwhelmed the other day, adding up all that following Jesus is costing me. Right then, God reminded me of all my faithful brothers and sisters around the world that risk their lives every day for Him and the sake of the Kingdom. They consider Him more than worth it! So I am learning how to live courageously, fixing my eyes on Jesus. The last thing I want to be is a coward.

How has your family helped you in your walk with God? Oh, my! How could I ever mention all the ways my family has helped me? The up-side of being gone is that I appreciate them so much more than I ever have. From my dad all the way down to my younger brother, Ben, I am inspired by all of them. God has blessed me with a family that loves Jesus. My dad has taught me how to be a compassionate person and what it looks like to have a servant's heart. My mom is the embodiment of sacrifice; she does so much for all of us that we're not even aware of. My sister, Kate, and I have so many good conversations. I learn so much from her, because she's constantly reading some book, or studying some deep, theological principle. I look up to my brother, Aaron, so much. He is one of the kindest, most genuine, humble people I know. He is such a source of encouragement in my life! My other brother, Matt, convicts me all of the time with the way he looks at life. He is so happy to be alive - he rejoices so easily. And, the youngest, Ben, is such an amazing kid. He has brought almost all of his teachers at school to tears because of his sweet heart - he's followed after Dad in being a servant. The more time goes by, the more I am encouraged and moved by each member of my family.

How do you plan to expand your ministry in the future? To be honest, I try to not have an agenda. I have a lot of dreams about things I would love to do in the future: be a mom, teach in the inner city, do missions work in Asia ... but, right now I'm just trying to be faithful in the big and little things that God has entrusted me with.

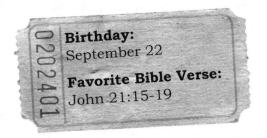

Birthday:
September 22

Favorite Bible Verse:
John 21:15-19

Booking Agency:
Third Coast Artists Agency
615-297-2021
www.tcaa.biz

Fan Mail Address:
Bethany Dillon
P.O. Box 150867
Nashville, TN 37215

Website: www.bethanydillon.com

HAWK NELSON

GROWING UP WITH GOD

Jason Dunn

rowing up in a Christian family, my parents always wanted the best for me, to put me in an area where I was always with Christian friends. I grew up in a Christian school. My school was held in a church basement. Every morning we'd start with a chapel service and pray for at least half an hour. Everywhere I went, I was surrounded by believers. Many people thought that was a bad thing. But it's good to have strong believers to encourage you and lift you up, and it's good to be accountable to your friends. Some of my friends thought I was "sheltered" or "uncool" because I went to church six days a week.

Growing up in a school where they make you memorize chapters of God's Word at a time is somewhat frustrating and annoying when you're 15 years old. But **I can absolutely look back on my years at school and see where He has led me, and how He's worked in my life**. I can call on the Scriptures I learned as a child when times get difficult now. I always hear the familiar Scriptures like, "I can do all things through Christ who strengthens me" (Philippians 4:13 NKJV), those verses I've grown up with and been fed my whole life. Now that I'm older, those always come to my mind, and I'm like, "Wow! I'm so glad I had to learn those as a kid." That's what gets me through the day, every day.

I didn't really grasp the importance of how significant it was to be in a Christian home. I said, "I don't want to be in a Christian school." I wanted to be more like my friends who didn't grow up there. I didn't rebel from it; I just didn't agree with it 100 percent. Now that I'm older, I realize that it was a great thing. You have to have a spiritual maturity to be really thankful for what you've been brought up in.

Being that immersed in the church environment absolutely had a strong impact on me. The thing is, you don't start to realize the effect it has on your life until you're on your own, maybe not attending church as much as you used to, or even would like to. Growing up, I just got used to that environment, and I took it for granted. Now that we're on the road pretty much all year-round, I don't get to go to church every Sunday, so it's a lot more difficult than it was as a kid. Then again, having a strong foundation in God, I just start using what I know. I use what I learned, and that helps a lot.

I thank God every single day that my parents sent me to a school that was based on the Word of God.

UNPLUGGED
a deeper look

Have you drawn on the foundation developed during your years of Christian schooling to help you through difficult times? Last year in North Carolina, we had just finished a show and gotten something to eat at the local Waffle House. Just as I finished paying, these guys with guns jumped over the counter, and I ended up having a gun to the side of my head. I honestly thought that it might be the end, but I didn't doubt where I was going to go, because I knew, being brought up as a believer. I wasn't afraid about where I would be if that trigger *was* to be pulled. Even though I escaped with only having my wallet stolen, the experience made me realize that you never know when your time is. You always need to stay grounded and plant your seeds in the good soil.

Hawk Nelson Hawk Nelson Hawk Nelson Hawk Nelson Hawk Nelson

The Bible says that we should "live in the world, but not be of the world." How can youth who are raised in a Christian home, and so immersed in church, step out of their comfort zone when they go out into the world and not be drawn into that? After high school, I didn't really live in the world, but when we toured, we played a lot of bar scenes. I started to realize, "Wow! I'm glad I didn't do this. It's not where I'd want to be," but I did have a taste of what it was like. It's been really cool because I can talk to kids who haven't necessarily been brought up in a Christian home. That's what I really feel that I want to do, go into the world where kids don't have a spiritual background, and I can tell them that there's a lot more to life than just going out getting drunk every Friday night, because it's not worth it in the long run. A lot of people wait until, "Once I'm old and on my death bed, I'll give everything over to God, because right now I'm having fun." But you can. I'm *having* lots of fun. Sure, we're different from other people, but that's what we want. We want to make that difference in kids' lives because if we're just the same as everybody else, no one's going to listen to us.

BACKSTAGE PASS
getting to know

How did the band meet and form? We met in Canada. We all played in different bands around the "Ontario Scene," as it was called. Eventually, we all came together after high school and formed Hawk Nelson.

Do you feel God leading the band in a special direction? Yes! We feel God has called us to go into places where there is not a whole lot of light. We feel we are able to be that light, whether it's a huge halogen lamp or just a flick of a lighter. A light is a light.

How does the band plan to further its ministry in the future? We plan to play for as many kids as possible. Right now we try to take it one day at a time, seeing where God would want us to be.

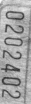

Birthdays:
Jason: December 26
Daniel: August 17
Jonathan: June 23
Skwid: June 15

0202402

0000405

Favorite Bible Verses:
Jason: Proverbs 4:5-6
Daniel: John 3:16
Jonathan: Galatians 2:20
Skwid: 1 Corinthians 13:4

Website:
www.hawknelson.com

Booking Agency:
Third Coast Artists Agency
615-297-2021
www.tcaa.biz

Fan Mail Address:
Hawk Nelson
P.O. Box 391
Franklin, TN 37068

Fan Email Address: mail@hawknelson.com

Hawk Nelson Hawk Nelson Hawk

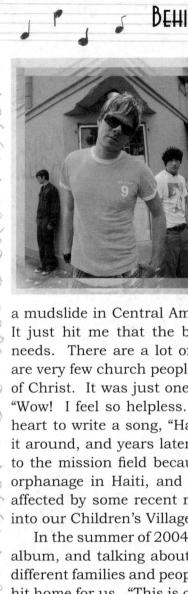

AUDIO ADRENALINE

HANDS AND FEET

Mark Stuart

I was watching TV one day, and I saw there had been a mudslide in Central America that had killed 10,000 people. It just hit me that the body of Christ has to meet people's needs. There are a lot of people "playing church," but there are very few church people really becoming the hands and feet of Christ. It was just one of those moments where I was like, "Wow! I feel so helpless. How can I help?" God laid on my heart to write a song, "Hands and Feet." Now God's brought it around, and years later, we've seen a lot of missionaries go to the mission field because of that song. We're building an orphanage in Haiti, and some of the orphan kids that were affected by some recent mudslides, will hopefully be brought into our Children's Village.

In the summer of 2004, we'd been touring for the <u>Worldwide</u> album, and talking about missions. We were commissioning different families and people to go on mission trips, and it really hit home for us. "This is our tenth record, and if we're going to leave a legacy, now is the time." It was something God put on our hearts.

It's a way to tie in music - our platforms as Christian artists, and give something back to some of the less fortunate people around the world. Religion that God finds pure and faultless is when we look after widows and orphans. Here in America, where most of our fans are, we have everything. We don't have a clue what the rest of the world lives like, and this is a good opportunity for us to stretch our fans, and to let God take them to a whole other level. It's a chance for us to go make our faith real and allow God to work in our lives. While we become the hands and feet of Jesus, things happen.

"And how can they preach unless they are sent? As it is written, 'How beautiful are the feet of those who bring good news!'" (Romans 10:15 NIV).

UNPLUGGED
a deeper look

How did the Hands and Feet Project form? We all came together at the same time with a vision, and my parents were retiring from full-time ministry in Kentucky. My dad said, "Hey, I'm thinking about going back to Haiti to do mission work," and we decided to work together. God put a simple idea in all of our hearts. He opened up several doors at the right time, and we just said, "Yeah, let's do it."

How would you like to see Hands and Feet grow? He can take Hands and Feet wherever He wants. I'd like to see different Children's Villages planted around the world. I'd really like to see Christian music - fans, bands, and artists, take on other orphanages - raising support, and championing Children's Villages in parts of the world that might need it.

BACKSTAGE PASS
getting to know

How did the band meet and form? We first started at a Bible college in Kentucky and had a really passionate desire to do music. I was also called to do mission work, and it was actually when I was in Haiti with my parents, way back, that God told me my mission field was to do Christian rock and to reach out to a generation of Americans.

Do you feel God leading the band in a special direction? God's definitely leading us in different ways, and pushing us, and we feel His hand on our ministry in a lot of different ways. We are working with the orphanage in Haiti, the Hands and Feet Project, and we're excited about that. God's really put it on our hearts to not just sing about missions, but to do missions, and to get involved with our fans. Record-wise, we've really felt like God has directed the album <u>Until My Heart Caves In</u> - just to sing about keeping your faith passionate, and making the melody of the gospel the forefront of your life ... not just talking about it, but singing it with your life, until you can't do it anymore, and your heart gives in.

How does the band plan to further its ministry in the future? Just be faithful. There's really nothing I can do, or plan on doing, that I can control. I can control my heart, and I can be disciplined with my intimacy with the Lord. As far as where ministry goes, that's just one day at a time, wherever God will take us. The biggest way to further our ministry is to let go of trying to figure out what we're doing in the future, and do it today with some real conviction, to seek God's face today. A great way to further our ministry is to get it going right now.

Birthdays:
Mark: April 14
Tyler: December 31
Will: February 25
Ben: August 14

Favorite Bible Verses:
Mark: James 1:27
Tyler: Proverbs 3:5-6
Will: Numbers 6:24-26
Ben: John 3:16

Booking Agency:
Third Coast Artists Agency
615-297-2021
www.tcaa.biz

Fan Email Address:
info@audioa.com

Website: www.audioa.com

RUSS LEE

HE WILL DIRECT YOUR PATH

"*T*rust in the LORD with all your heart and lean not on your own understanding; in all your ways acknowledge him, and he will make your paths straight" (Proverbs 3:5-6 NIV).

Everybody who has ever lived has had bad days. The secret to success in the Christian life is not avoiding struggles, but pushing through them with God's strength. The more that I talk honestly about where I have been and where God has me, the more I realize that situations may vary, but our feelings during difficulty really do not. All of us have doubts, fears, anxiety, and disappointments when things don't go our way. I think that most people want to keep a strong faith and the right attitude, no matter what they're facing. Here are some ways to do that:

• **Speak to God honestly about how you are feeling.**
Tough times are made for crying out to God. Get away to somewhere quiet and really tell God what's on your heart. He won't be offended or surprised.

• **Take time to let Him respond to your struggles.**
Once you've spoken to Him honestly, then it's time to listen to His response. He speaks through His Word, friends, spiritual leaders (i.e. pastors, authors, mentors, and parents). Once you've stated your case, it's time to have an open heart to God's response. He will speak in His perfect way and His perfect time (Luke 11:10). **God has great plans for you** (Jeremiah 29:11). We have to trust Him enough to hear and accept His response. His ways are higher than our ways. That demands for us to bow at His feet and say, "Speak, Lord, your servant is

listening ..." (1 Samuel 3:9 NIV) as well as, "... not my will but yours be done" (Luke 22:42 NIV). This is the proper attitude toward a holy God who speaks to us from a heart of love and truth.

• **Let your friends walk with you through the hard times.** Don't be dishonest about how you are doing. The Bible says, "... a brother is born for adversity" (Proverbs 17:17 NIV). Together in Christ, we can make it through the most difficult times. After all, we have His promise that He is with us, even to the very end (Matthew 28:20) ... and He never breaks a promise!

Prayer

Lord, help us to trust You completely, even when all that we can see doesn't make any sense or feel very comfortable. You have proven that we can trust You. We know that your plans are bigger and better than ours. We want to live like we believe in You and trust You with all our hearts. Help us to do just that. For Your glory always, Amen.

UNPLUGGED
a deeper look

Would you mind sharing some struggles you've had throughout your life? I grew up in a fairly large family (four kids). Being the oldest child, I felt a great responsibility to care for the others, as my parents struggled with divorce, alcoholism, and mental disease. We felt helpless and hopeless many times. We never knew what the day would bring. Our parents truly loved us, but they had many problems. I ran to drugs and friends who weren't Christians for support. They partied with me, but really couldn't help me. My struggles and insecurities are things that I have had to continue to overcome on a daily basis. God has really been there and been strong on my behalf in difficult circumstances.

How have you seen God help you and make you stronger through your trials? God has brought the right people alongside me over the years to strengthen my faith, to let me know that I am not alone, and that I am a new creation in Christ who can do all things in Him as He strengthens me. I am a better decision-maker because of struggles. I also know that God is faithful because He has been so faithful in my difficulties. I can rest in Him because I know that He is on the job and never lays down my problems. He keeps working. He never walks away, no matter how hard things can get. The secret is to make up your mind to trust Him and love Him, no matter what comes. His plans are perfect, and His ways are higher than our ways. He is in control. We have to decide to believe that enough to live it, as we trust Him. It's an exercise of faith to say, "I'm not holding onto this or trying to figure it out. I'm gonna' run to the Lord and lay this down at His feet, worship Him, and rest in the assurance that He can and will handle it." You always make it through and see miracles along the way when you take this approach.

How can teenagers overcome their trials? Stay in God's Word. Speak to Him honestly about everything from your heart. Go to a good church that loves you and teaches you the absolute truth of God's Word. We MUST learn about Him. This helps us understand that we can trust Him. Getting to know Him more gives us new glimpses of His big heart of love!

BACKSTAGE PASS
getting to know

Favorite Books: *The Bible*, *My Utmost for His Highest* by Oswald Chambers, *Mere Christianity* by C.S. Lewis, and *What The Bible Is All About* by Henrietta C. Mears

Musical Influences: Russ Taff, James Taylor, Al Jarreau, Al Green, and Aretha Franklin

What is God teaching you now? He is teaching me the importance of daily, honest conversations with Him and a strong work ethic.

How has your family helped you in your walk with God? We all try to support and encourage each other. We are all very involved as a family with church activities. They all keep up closely with my career and ministry so they can feel like they're in the middle of it with me. They pray for me and encourage me so much. I can't put a value on their part of my career and ministry.

How do you plan to expand your ministry in the future? I have been to Okinawa to minister to the Marines and sailors stationed in Japan. We are currently touring all 50 states and 6 major continents in celebration of 25 years of ministry. Too much going on to even talk about. Just pray for us. Our opportunities are great.

0202401

Birthday:
November 13

Favorite Bible Verse:
Proverbs 3:5-6

Website:
www.russlee.com

Booking Agency:
Russ Lee Music
booking@russlee.com

FM
2 0
1967

5¢ U.S.POSTAGE

Fan Mail Address:
Russ Lee
P.O. Box 11147
Murfreesboro, TN 37219

Fan Email Address: email@russlee.com

Russ Lee Russ Lee Russ Lee Russ Lee Russ Lee

DANIEL'S WINDOW

HEARTBREAK HILL

Bill Coleman

My brothers and I passed through the turnstiles and onto the "T" platform. The train doors slid open and we jumped aboard, our eyes scanning the inside of the car for some empty orange seats. We were making our way to the streets of Beantown to cheer on Dad as he ran the Boston Marathon.

The historic neighborhoods of Boston and its surrounding New England communities are quite charming, and they provide a great backdrop for such a famous athletic event.

It was an amazing sight to see such a crowd of runners pass by, as we observed from the steps of a building along the route. We hoped to catch a glimpse of Dad, and eventually did see him from a distance, his head bobbing in and out of sight amidst the mass of numbered runners. After capturing the moment on camera, we cut across town to watch again at a different point along the route.

There is a notorious section late in the 26-mile course, known to the runners as "Heartbreak Hill." It's a 5-mile section of winding uphill grade, which threatens to take the steam right out of what would have otherwise been a strong, steady pace. If the runners can stay focused and strong through this test of endurance, they can be assured that the worst is behind them, and they are only 5 miles from the finish line.

Anyone, from time to time, can feel like they're stuck on "Heartbreak Hill" - a draining stretch of what seems to be one struggle after another. Even though we know that our troubles will eventually be behind us, working through those moments can consume our energy and thought so intensely, that it becomes easy to lose perspective on how close we actually are to completing the race.

Sometimes heartbreak comes in the form of broken relationships. Maybe we've lost trust in someone that we once looked up to, who always seemed to be able to carry the weight of the world on their shoulders. Maybe we've even lost confidence in ourselves.

Might it be that **these let-downs are actually a launch pad from which we can jump into the arms of our loving God**?

"I don't mean to say that I have already achieved these things or that I have already reached perfection! But I keep working toward that day when I will finally be all that Christ Jesus saved me for and wants me to be. No, dear brothers and sisters, I am still not all I should be, but I am focusing all my energies on this one thing: Forgetting the past and looking forward to what lies ahead. I strain to reach the end of the race and receive the prize for which God, through Christ Jesus, is calling us up to heaven" (Philippians 3:12-14 NLT).

More Verses:
1 Peter 1:3-9

Prayer

Father, You bring strength to the weak. And when I feel strong, I know it's You who empowers me. You are the only one that will never let me down. Please help me to place my trust and reliance on You rather than in myself or another person. I pray that I will be a positive encouragement to those who need someone to cheer them on through difficult times. In Jesus' name, Amen.

Daniel's Window Daniel's Window Daniel's Window

UNPLUGGED
a deeper look

So many youth in this generation turn to drugs, sex, or alcohol before running to God in their struggles. How can they learn to jump into His arms first? God loves us above our fleshly desires and misdirected chasing of satisfaction. "I have seen all the things that are done under the sun; all of them are meaningless, a chasing after the wind" (Ecclesiastes 1:14 NIV). God's purpose is restoration and right relationship with us. He is not a police interceptor waiting to catch us on His radar. If we can remember that God is the ultimate Provider and Source of all that is truly good, it will help us to seek Him first in all aspects of life. In yielding the right of way, we can see the direction God is moving. There are many choices to be made in life, but let's not let the choices we make now affect the rest of our lives in a negative way.

If kids can't find the strength to run to God and just want their trials to end - through suicide or another form of violence - how can they see that they are close to the "finish line," and with God's help, they can make it? When hope is lost and we ask ourselves, "What's the point?" let's remember that Jesus was so focused on redeeming us, that He did not give up on His mission to save us during His darkest hours. If we're having our worst day ever, we can look to Jesus and know He had a worse day when the sins of the world were on His shoulders, and He was nailed to a cross. But the fantastic thing is that He died so that we might LIVE! (1 Thessalonians 5:10).

BACKSTAGE PASS
getting to know

How did the band meet and form? Our singer, Heather, met our guitarist, Alby, at a music related photo shoot. They shared a common vision to put a band together. Jesse, the drummer, is Alby's cousin, and they had a history of making

Daniel's Window Daniel's Window

music together in the past. I got a call from Heather to attend a basement rehearsal of a "new band" that needed a bass player. It turned out that I had already known Alby from one of my music classes. Caleb was attending the same church as Heather, and about six months in, he joined us as keyboard player. A year and a half later, Caleb asked for Heather's hand in marriage.

Do you feel God leading the band in a special direction? We've always seen a special blessing on worship. There's a creative and artistic side, too, and we are seeking God's wisdom on how to make those two elements coincide. We have an underlying goal of letting people know that God wants to meet them right where they are.

How does the band plan to further its ministry in the future? We tend to take things one year at a time. We have set our sights on a new recording project, and have resumed the creative process of writing songs. In recent past, we have been leading worship at many youth conferences nationwide. We hope to continue to have opportunities to do that, as well as improve as a band musically, professionally, and spiritually.

Favorite Bible Verses:
Heather: Proverbs 3:5-6
Caleb: Acts 20:24
Alby: John 3:16
Bill: 1 John 4:9
Jesse: Philippians 4:13

Birthdays:
Heather: June 4
Caleb: February 10
Alby: October 14
Bill: August 28
Jesse: February 10

Booking Agency:
OneDay Promotions / 219-879-0890

Website: www.danielswindow.com

Fan Email Address:
dw@danielswindow.com

DARLENE ZSCHECH

HIS PASSION -
OUR PASSION

*P*assion ... how we need it in our world. Imagine us all with no passion.

It seems to paint a solemn picture of life! Just think about all the mysteries we've discovered so far, and of all the good things helping to make a difference in people's lives today. Someone's passion is behind it. Man was created uniquely and full of passion. Adam loved to walk with God in the evening. He even named every plant and animal in the world. Passion is different from being driven by our selfish desires and greed, because it originates with our Creator.

God was so passionate to have fellowship that He made man and woman in His own image. He was passionate to create life for us filled with love, peace, laughter, and fulfillment ... all that is good. How He loved us! He was passionate about the smallest thing. He even made a smile.

How precious and perfectly wonderful life was, until we allowed sin to enter in. Our choice to break the one command God had given us separated us from Him, and put us on a path leading to death and destruction. Here the ultimate example of passion was shown. Proverbs 15:11 (KJV) says, "Hell and destruction are before the Lord, how much more then the hearts of the children of men." God, so loving us, gave His beloved Son to live and die, and His Son gave His life to save us.

His passion is us. He made a way for us to worship Him and walk with Him again. Just spending time worshipping in His beautiful presence fills us with desire to see people touch

Him. We see homeless people, abused people, abandoned children, the lost, both rich and poor, who don't know their Maker and the eternal depths of His love for them. We long to see them know Jesus as their first love, for loving Him is true passion. How we long to see them healed, made whole, and find true fulfillment in Him - for His passion has become our passion.

He said, "I will build my church and the gates of hell will not prevail against it" (Matthew 16:18 KJV). He gave us gifts individually and said, give yourselves wholly (passionately) to them (1 Timothy 4:15). He said to come to Me, "for my yoke is easy and my burden light" (Matthew 11:30 NIV). All we need to do is love Him and do what He puts in our hearts to do. The rest is up to Him. His burden, His passion.

Thank God He gave us His Holy Spirit and His Word to lead and guide us: from writing a letter to feeding a child, from being a missionary to being a light in our work place. Even the smallest things, like a smile, all come from Someone's passion and knowing that Someone.

Prayer

Lord Jesus, thank You for loving me; for Your passion to save me and have me live eternally with You. I live to love You and serve You. Teach me Your Word so that I can know You and be filled with Your passion for the world. I praise You and thank You that Your glory is going to fill the earth as the water covers the sea.

UNPLUGGED
a deeper look

Throughout what seems to be a growing darkness among the youth of today, do you see kids rising up to be the church and starting a revival, a new Great Awakening? I see revival starting with those who are not satisfied by living in a materialistic generation, but who become desperate for the outpouring of the Holy Spirit and to see God glorified in the earth. We're all called to love, serve, witness, and forgive. It's a matter of allowing the Holy Spirit to guide us through the Word and keeping focused on what He's called us, individually, to do.

How can teens invest their passion in worthwhile things and not get angry over something like a traffic jam? When our passion is ultimately to know and become like Christ, then something like a traffic jam is the perfect opportunity for all of us to practice!

While it's important for teens to have a passion for God, do you think it is also important for them to have a passion such as music or art, that they can pour their heart and soul into? God delights in us completely enjoying music, arts, and all the other gifts and desires He's given us, just as any loving, earthly father would. He is the most creative, most pure, full of life and funniest person in the universe. We just need to love and seek Him first, and keep ourselves and our gifts untainted from the world.

BACKSTAGE PASS
getting to know

Favorite Books: *The Bible*, *The Lady, Her Lover and Her Lord* by T.D. Jakes, and *The Heavenly Man* by Paul Hattaway. I love anything by Charles Spurgeon and Eugene Peterson.

Musical Influences: The muso's I love to listen to are Sting, U2, Delirious, Tim Hughes, and Lauren Hill.

What is God teaching you now? That above all, He is faithful.

How has your family helped you in your walk with God? If there is one place where I can be myself, it is with my family. They truly keep me focused in making sure I am living every moment with the future generations in mind.

How do you plan to expand your ministry in the future? I plan to continue to be faithful with all He has placed in my hand today, and trust Him with tomorrow.

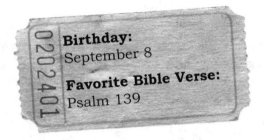

Birthday:
September 8

Favorite Bible Verse:
Psalm 139

Booking Agency:
darlenez@hillsong.com
+612 8853 5390

Fan Mail Address:
Darlene Zschech
Hillsong Church
P.O. Box 1195
Castle Hill, NSW 1765 Australia

Website: www.darlenezschech.com

SILERS BALD

HOW SHOULD WE THEN LIVE?

Warren Bazemore

$\mathcal{I}$f we have been redeemed by the grace and goodness of Jesus, and have been adopted into the family of God, then we are stuck in the middle of two ageless truths ... we are part of the culture of Christ, and we are part of the culture of the world we live in every day. We live in a culture that has turned its back on the claims of Scripture, and that same culture has become increasingly cynical towards those of us who bear the title, "Christian." While resting in the belief that only a sovereign God can warm cold hearts, how do we go about being the most effective ambassadors of this relevant, life changing gospel of grace?

The prophet Jeremiah lived a life that today's believer can relate to. He lived in the midst of a culture that had known the truth of God, and was in the midst of turning away from that truth. Jeremiah tells us how it came to happen to his people, and in reality, how it happens to all cultures that abandon God. In Lamentations 1:9 (NKJV) he says, "... She did not consider her destiny. Therefore her collapse was awesome; She had no comforter ..." The culture of Jeremiah's day erred when it stopped thinking of its destiny, or end. All around us we see ads that tell us how to look younger, feel younger, be prettier, grow more hair, lose more weight, or how to fit in with the right people. We are told to forget the one thing we are born sure of ... that we all have an ending. **The reality of eternity weighs heavier with each passing day**. We are not an end unto ourselves, and our hearts know that this is true. Encourage your friends to be a thinking people.

Look for the answers that your hearts yearn to find. Live an authentic, engaging, thinking faith. Use the tools of culture like movies, music, and television to engage in dialogue that probe the things of eternal weight. Pray that God allows you to seize the moments, and direct the culture you live in towards the God of all answers, and the comfort that never fails.

UNPLUGGED
a deeper look

Our society is so image based. Do you think it's important for teens to have an idea of godly self-image and self-esteem? A "godly self-image" should simply be man's way of saying, kill your pride and see yourself from God's point of view - washed in the blood of the righteousness of Christ. The problem is SIN! Our culture is fragmented because of it, and it has left relationally unstable, incredibly busy, lonely, pleasure-abusing, stressed-out children in its wake. You must get to know who you are in all your flaws and desires, and recognize where you are weak and most likely to fall. For example, if you've lived with parents and a father, in particular, who have not shown you that you are a delight, and are beautiful, and to be treasured, then you most likely have not accepted that the God of the universe has "... fearfully and wonderfully ..." (Psalm 139:14 NIV) made you, and even as He was crafting you in your mother's womb, He was setting you apart to be His "sons and daughters" (2 Corinthians 6:18 NIV). You must ask God to rip from your hearts those things contrary to what He says about who you are and why you matter, and with the Father's grace see YOU from HIS point of view! - Shane

Some teens might be fearful of "having an ending." How do you advise them to prepare for eternity without fear? When we first begin to look at our final chapter in this life, we ought to come to the topic with trembling. It is only a fool who looks at death flippantly, or pushes it out of his mind, because it is too sober a thought. It is for that very reason that we must approach it, and the sooner, the better. Here are some very quick things to consider:

• Jesus wept when His friend Lazarus died (John 11:35). He loved His friend and was sad when he died. He wept for the sadness of sin that brought death to this world, and so should we. Losing the people we love is sad, and our sadness is a reminder of the consequence of sin.

• The great hope and truth of the gospel is the swallowing up of death, itself. The Gospels resound with the resurrection of Christ Jesus, and throughout the letters of Paul we read of the work Jesus did, in order that we might, alongside Him, be conquerors of even death (1 Corinthians 15).

• We, as Christians, believe that this life is not the final or most important chapter. Eternity is real, not some dusty fable concocted in centuries past. Death is the scale that measures what matters and forces us to reckon with our own eternity. Death is the great equalizer, and it forces all of us to consider the claims of Christ, who is indeed the resurrection and the life (John 3:16, Romans 6:23, 1 Timothy 6:12, Titus 1:1-3).

The precious promise of eternity is the bedrock of Christianity. It is a watermark of believers. We are all fading away, but eternity remains. Heaven and hell are real places, and for those who have been bought by the grace of God, know that you can face eternity and death alongside the Author of eternity, and the Great Defeater of death. - Warren

BACKSTAGE PASS
getting to know

How did the band meet and form? Growing up, Shane was active in choirs and singing, and I was active in theatre and drama, so we knew each other that way. Jason, our drummer, went to high school with me, and wound up being one of Shane's roommates in college. Marcus, our violin and dulcimer player, had grown up in church with Shane since they were 4. In 1994, we started playing music together for Fellowship of Christian Athletes in college. That's how we all met and reconnected. It wasn't anything where we said, "Ten years from now, I'd like to have a record deal and play 200 shows a year." It was like, "Let's start playing music together." I think that's part of why God's allowed us to do it for so long - because it was so obviously His design, because we didn't plan it. - Warren

Do you feel God leading the band in a special direction?
Life is changing; we're all married. We love playing music
together still, playing in front of the people that God allows us
to, but we're trying to balance that with being home and being
with family - making it not a high priority, but the *absolute*
priority for our lives. We're just trusting God that He'll lead us
in the places that we need to go; we're watching, and listening,
and waiting for God to lead us in that way. - Warren

**How does the band plan to further its ministry in the
future?** We try to be advocates of honesty and authenticity in
both the art that we engage in and our daily lives - that there's
nothing trite about it, that we're real people, trying to honor
God. The way we trust God to further what we do is that the
people we've impacted will be led to do the same in their own
lives, whether they're a musician, or a banker, or a baker, or a
candlestick maker, that they do it in an honest and authentic
way, that allows people to see that whatever they do with their
professional and private life, they honor God with it. - Warren

0000405

**Favorite Bible Verses
& Books:**
Warren: Romans
Shane: Philippians 3:12-14
Jason: Ephesians 5:8
Marcus: Galatians 2:19-21

0202401

Birthdays:
Warren: May 12
Shane: January 29
Jason: May 29
Marcus: October 3

Booking Agency:
GOA, Inc.
615-790-5540
www.goa-inc.com

Website:
www.silersbald.com
www.archmusicgroup.com

Fan Mail Address:
Arch Music Group, LLC
2021 21st Avenue South
Suite 120
Nashville, TN 37212

Fan Email Address:
Go to www.silersbald.com

BUILDING 429

HUMILITY

Jason Roy

*H*ow many of us are truly humble? As I sat at my house and started to think about writing a devotion on this topic, I couldn't help but question my motives as the frontman of a Christian rock band. My mind kept rolling over moments in my life when I was the opposite of humble - remembering times when a completely imperfect guy acted like he had all the answers to hand out. Then I started thinking about kids today and how hard society has made it to be humble. Everyone is singing their own praises, and hey, let's face it, they get noticed because of it. Football stars swagger into the room and proclaim themselves the greatest ever, and the TV rolls on, adding to their legendary status. Rock bands keep answering questions like, "What makes your band unique?", with self-praise sessions. For crying out loud, the most popular guy in school is the most arrogant person you've ever met and he's ... well, the most popular guy in school.

Read Philippians 2:5-11.

So here is the question: Do you want a legacy that points to you, or a legacy that points straight to God? **Humility is about the willingness to be a servant.** It's boasting about those around you, when no one would blame you for boasting about yourself. It's about winning an award and lifting up the person who you triumphed over. For those of us with meaningful relationships with the Lord, humility is just the by-product of a life spent chasing Him. I'm not able to do anything without God preparing the way and leading my every step, and neither are you. Our accomplishments are not our own; they are His, and humility is the only reasonable response to accomplishment, if we are truly seeking to be imitators of God!

More Verses:
Matthew 18:1-4
1 Corinthians 4:7
James 4:10

Prayer

Father, I am not the humble person I should be. You know me inside and out, and You know how I've failed in this part of my life. Lord, please begin to change my heart so that by my life I may begin to draw people to You. Allow me to choose humility even when I am tempted to brag, and keep my heart and mind steadfast in pursuit of You. In Jesus' holy name, Amen.

UNPLUGGED
a deeper look

John the Baptist gladly proclaimed the name of Jesus above his own, and the Bible says to humble ourselves under the mighty power of God. Does this mean our own self-confidence must suffer? Absolutely not, it just means that we have to keep things in perspective. We must remember that our confidence should only be in the Lord. When we place our trust and hope in the Lord, we begin to understand that the gifts we have been given are special, and given for a specific reason. Knowing that, we are able to draw from His strength, and in His strength we are capable of anything. We must remember that we are deserving of nothing ... and capable of nothing in our own strength. With every new challenge comes a new opportunity for the Lord to show Himself faithful and strong. Every ball game, every test, every accomplishment is a moment that God has brought to fruition in order that His name might be glorified through you. John the Baptist understood this fully, even as he was given the honor of baptizing Jesus.

What can teens do daily to leave behind a godly legacy of humility and service? The first big thing is to pray that the Lord would give us the ability to be humble in every circumstance of the day. Without a constant connection to the Lord it's impossible to be godly, because as we all know, we are self-centered people born into sin. The second is to constantly read the Word of God and fill our hearts with words spoken in humility and love. Finally, in the moments of truth that come, we must shrug off our natural instinct of self-preservation and self-glorification and remember to be a servant of the Lord, and handle ourselves with humility. An easy way to do these things is to pray without ceasing ... even carrying on conversations with the Lord throughout the day. Whether it be in your head or out loud, discuss every situation with the Lord as if in a conversation, and the Spirit will be much easier to discern.

How can teens comprehend reaching their full potential in Christ and understanding the fact that they are fearfully and wonderfully made, without becoming arrogant? A big part of not becoming arrogant is a part that we tend to leave out at the end of each accomplishment. That part is simple ... praising the Lord. I don't expect you guys to break out into Sunday morning worship services if you hit the game-winning shot, but when the moment comes, remember to worship the Lord and thank Him that the opportunity was yours, and that He allowed the strengths that He has given to shine through you. "... Blessed is the man who trusts in the LORD, whose confidence is in him. He will be like a tree planted by the water that sends out its roots by the stream. It does not fear when heat comes; its leaves are always green. It has no worries in a year of drought and never fails to bear fruit" (Jeremiah 17:7-8 NIV).

BACKSTAGE PASS
getting to know

Building 429 Building 429 Building 429 Building

How did the band meet and form? This is a question that can only be answered by the word, "God." We didn't grow up in school together; we weren't best friends in college; we were barely even acquaintances, but in 2000, Scotty and I got together and wrote our first song. We both knew that God had given us gifts, and we wanted to give them back to Him. At first, we played for fun and to worship God, but soon we recognized that something special was going on around our performances, and that it felt as though the music we were playing was having profound effects on those who heard it. Michael was a good friend who had just left the ranks of another band. Jesse was added to play guitar and keys. That brings us to the place we are today.

Do you feel God leading the band in a special direction? We are a band that is still growing, still learning new things about ourselves. We are heading in the same direction we've always tried to follow, and that is the path that follows after God. We don't know what the future will hold, but we know that if we stay on course, it's gonna' be a completely life-changing ride. Hopefully, the music will get better, and the ministry more potent through the years, because that is the goal. The Lord has begun to allow us to use our platform lately to further such causes as World Vision and Redeem The Vote. One step at a time, and one life at a time; that's our motto.

How does the band plan to further its ministry in the future? To date, our focus has been on the mission of our name (Ephesians 4:29) and the effort of building the youth of America up again. Esteem is a word seldom used by youth these days, and this is a generation of people who are faced with more temptation, sin, and consequence than any generation before. The effects of that leave us with young adults who wonder who God is, where He is, and why they haven't met Him in a real and meaningful way. While there are lots of reasons for kids to stray outside the church doors, there are a lot of reasons to remain inside the doors, as well. We feel like God has called us to challenge the youth of America to stop trying to know all of the *information* about God, and to begin to strive to KNOW Him. There is another challenge that goes with that to the churches of America: We've got to begin to connect our young people with God, not with programs, not with church services, but with evidence of God in our own lives. That is the challenge to the body, and the challenge that lies before us in the future.

Favorite Bible Verses:
Michael: 2 Corinthians 4:5
Jesse: Joshua 1:9
Scotty: Jeremiah 33:3
Jason: Zephaniah 3:17

Birthdays:
Michael: December 6
Jesse: December 18
Scotty: March 5
Jason: August 9

Website: www.Building429.com

Booking Agency:
Creative Artists Agency
615-383-8787
www.caaccm.com

FOREVER CHANGED

"I CAN HEAR YOU, BUT I'M NOT LISTENING"

Dan Cole

*I*n high school, all of my friends were convinced they each had Attention Deficit Disorder (ADD), and most of the time I felt the same way. I remember years ago, sitting in my Spanish class, blankly staring at the chalkboard, not being able to read or pronounce nearly any of the words. Because of this, I would either become frustrated with my teacher for not doing her job right, or fall back on blaming my lack of understanding on this extreme case of ADD that I had allegedly been battling with for years. At the end of the class session, my ears would say, "Well, I *heard* everything the teacher said! What's the problem?"

My favorite Scripture for some seven years has been James 1:19 (NIV). It reads, "My dear brothers, take note of this: Everyone should be quick to listen, slow to speak and slow to become angry ..."

Although it may have appeared that I was listening in my classes, I really wasn't - I was only hearing. In all honesty, I was a goof-off the majority of the time, and I wasn't really concerned about the material my instructor was teaching about. Right there was the problem. That type of attitude, of not really caring about what people have to say - a selfish attitude, inevitably leading to frustration and anger.

The problem of "not listening" transcended into other areas of my life, as well. I used to battle daily with interrupting people. Most of the time, I didn't really want to listen to what people had to say, and thought what I had to say was much more important. I was often quick to SPEAK, and slow to LISTEN, being the complete opposite of how James instructs us to be.

Forever Changed Forever Changed Forever Changed

It took me a long time to even realize I had a "listening" problem; in fact, a close friend of mine had to point it out to me. You would think as a musician and lover of music, I would be better at using my ears. But **as James points out, the problem isn't my ears; it's my attitude**. If we love people as Christ does, we should want to listen to what others have to say. Besides, if we can't even listen to other people - how are we to listen to our heavenly Father?

Prayer

Lord, You are the only true God. Thank You, Lord, for always listening to my prayers, and never turning a deaf ear to me. Father, I pray that I can do the same to others. Lord, help me become a better listener. Help me become quick to listen, and slow to speak. Father, strengthen me to do this, and ultimately better Your kingdom because of it. In Your Son's name I pray, Amen.

UNPLUGGED
a deeper look

Will our personalities affect whether we are quick to listen, slow to speak, and slow to become angry? If so, how can we overcome that to become who Christ wants us to be in Him? Our personalities do affect how well we listen, and how much or little we talk. With a daily effort to listen as Christ does, one can overcome his natural instincts. - Dan

If teens struggle with listening to others or to God, how can they change their weakness into a strength used to advance God's Kingdom? I'm sure many teens struggle with listening to others, as myself and many friends did when we were that age. A monumental lesson that teens can learn is to strive to be humble. Remember that what others have to say is important. In fact, you could learn much from what others have to say. - Dan

Will our listening skills and actions mentioned in James change immediately after our attitude does, or will it take time and work on our part? This type of change will certainly take time, and much work. Changing our attitudes takes hard work and preparation, and our actions will need much developing and planning. Prayer and meditation are extremely important when striving to listen as Christ did. - Dan

BACKSTAGE PASS
getting to know

How did the band meet and form? The band was started in Tallahassee, Florida where Dan, Ben, and Nathan met in high school. By 2003, the whole band was living in Orlando, and in December, a long time friend, Tom Gustafson, took over as bassist. Tom actually became a Christian after going to a few shows and getting to know the other guys in the band. Forever Changed spreads its time between Tallahassee and Orlando when we aren't out on the road. - Nick

Do you feel God leading the band in a special direction? I've definitely seen a huge progression in the band in the past year alone - through songwriting, and more importantly, how we approach being in a band. It's not something we look at as a luxury or as something just for fun. God has shown us how powerful our gifts are, and how we need to be using them. There's no way we could do this on our own, and even though there's nothing wrong with being in a strictly secular band, we all feel like our specific direction is to be a ministry. Hopefully, we can be accepted in the medium of being a ministry band in the general market. - Nathan

How does the band plan to further its ministry in the future? I think with a backing label like Floodgate, we'll be able to really progress in getting out there and playing more shows to more people. That in itself will help the ministry aspect of the band, as well as gaining popularity. - Nathan

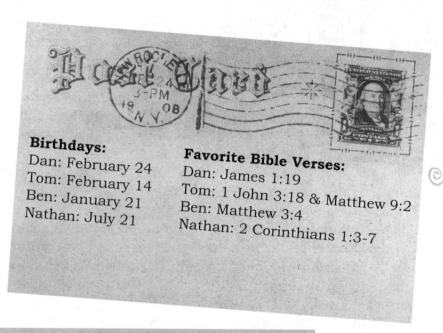

Birthdays:
Dan: February 24
Tom: February 14
Ben: January 21
Nathan: July 21

Favorite Bible Verses:
Dan: James 1:19
Tom: 1 John 3:18 & Matthew 9:2
Ben: Matthew 3:4
Nathan: 2 Corinthians 1:3-7

0000405

Booking Agency:
The Kenmore Agency
978-745-4287
www.thekenmoreagency.com

0202401

Website:
www.foreverchanged.net

CARRIED AWAY

I WILL LIVE FOR YOU

*B*eing three young girls with very different dreams, it was a miracle when God brought us together to start Carried Away. We each had to make different sacrifices in order for God's plan to prevail in our lives. When we focused in on God's will, it became clear that He had ordained a future for us in ministry together.

Pam: Ever since I was a kid, I wanted to teach. Even as I got older, I planned on going to University to get my teaching degree, and then go on to take a position as an elementary teacher. This plan was not something that God had in mind for this part of my life. I realized that I had to make a very important decision that would change everything. Was I going to go ahead with the plan that I had for myself, or choose to live for Him and trust that He had a vital plan for Carried Away? I chose to set aside my teaching dream and obey the calling that God had on my life to be a part of Carried Away.

Christine: My family is really important to me, so being away from them when traveling is really hard. I miss out on a lot of things at home, from my brother's soccer games, to my sister's graduation. Being away from home a lot is something that I had to give to God. Even though I do miss out on a lot of things, it makes me appreciate being with them even more. To get through this everyday challenge, I think of the twelve disciples that followed Jesus. They left their family, friends, and all their possessions to live a life following Christ. I am now starting to discover that the blessings far outweigh the sacrifice.

Colleen: While Jesus Christ was whipped and beaten, we were being healed, and when He died, we became alive.

I grew up in a Christian home, surrounded by Christian friends who encouraged me immensely. However, there came a time when I struggled with relationships during my late teen years. I was trying to fill a void inside of me. I wanted to feel love, and I found it when I began going steady with a guy for quite some time. This relationship came to a halt three years ago, when I realized that God had a love for me that I couldn't find in a relationship. I knew I had to desert my old ways of living, in order to surrender to God's love that is bigger and better. This was a sacrifice for me, but God had promised in His Word a good and perfect plan for my life. I decided to be totally committed to what He wanted for me. This was when God's will for my life became clear through Carried Away.

Have you noticed a pattern in each story?

In order for God to use each of us, we need to sacrifice everything in our lives first. It's only then that God can complete His will through us. We need to offer ourselves daily and allow God to work in our lives. We want to challenge you to live to the fullest and LIVE FOR GOD!

More Verses:
Romans 12:1-2

Prayer

Dear God, thank You for the sacrifice You made on the cross. Help me to make my life a living sacrifice, holy and pleasing to You, and reveal to me Your perfect will. Give me the courage and wisdom to live only for You. In Your Name, Amen.

UNPLUGGED
a deeper look

Will following God's plan for our lives always involve sacrifice? In our humanness, certain aspects of our life might seem to be a sacrifice, but when we commit our ways to the Lord and trust in Him, He gives us a desire in our hearts to do what He has always planned for us. Psalm 37:4-5 (NIV) says, "Delight yourself in the LORD and he will give you the desires of your heart. Commit your way to the LORD; trust in him and he will do this ..."

Will our blessings be fewer if we don't give up the things God calls us to sacrifice so we can follow His will? 1 Samuel 15:22 (NIV) says, "But Samuel replied: 'Does the LORD delight in burnt offerings and sacrifices as much as in obeying the voice of the LORD? To obey is better than sacrifice, and to heed is better than the fat of rams'."

"Through Jesus, therefore, let us continually offer to God a sacrifice of praise - the fruit of lips that confess his name" (Hebrews 13:15 NIV).

God sees deep inside us. He sees our commitment level, and our attitude. If we're totally connected with God, and He's calling us to do something, we want to offer that as a sacrifice of praise to please God, as it says in Hebrews. Did He not sacrifice everything for us? We could never pay Him back, but we can be obedient to His calling. God blesses our obedience to Him.

BACKSTAGE PASS
getting to know

How did the group meet and form? Colleen and I are sisters and Christine is our cousin, so there was always a natural connection. Growing up, Colleen and I saw Christine at family gatherings and other functions, but we did not really know a lot about her. It was not until about five years ago when she started coming over every weekend, that we developed a lasting friendship. All three of us loved singing, and grew up in musical families; so when Christine came to Colleen and I with a Point of Grace song for a Musicfest competition, it was an easy decision to join her. We ended up winning first place. The following year we entered Musicfest again, and won first place in two categories. Churches in the area started calling, wanting us to sing. It was then we started wondering if this was something God wanted us to do. We began singing in many different churches in our hometown, and from there God started to open doors that we didn't think possible. That's how our ministry for Carried Away began, and we continue to look forward to the plans that God has for us in the future. - Pam

Do you feel God leading the group in a special direction? We believe that God is leading Carried Away to minister to youth. Being youth ourselves, we know how hard it is to be a Christian in school and to live a godly lifestyle. Youth of today are being pressured into premarital sex and drugs more than ever before. We want to tell people that God has a purpose for each of our lives, and it's bigger than what anyone can ever imagine. We also want to encourage this generation to live a lifestyle of worship, holy and pleasing to God. - Christine

How does the group plan to further its ministry in the future? For us, Carried Away has been one aspect of our lives that we haven't had to fully plan. Ever since the beginning of this ministry, we've allowed God to totally take it and make it into what He wants. We have so many ideas for Carried Away's future, but our ultimate goal is to further the gospel of salvation throughout the world. We believe in doing everything with excellence, so as we move on in Carried Away, we want to strive to do our best - whether it be performing onstage, or sharing with people offstage, we are simply trying to be the best we can be for God. - Colleen

Birthdays:
Pam: September 22
Colleen: May 17
Christine: May 13

Favorite Bible Verses:
Pam: Philippians 4:4
Colleen: Jeremiah 29:11
Christine: Romans 12:1-2

0000405

Booking Agency:
booking@carriedaway.ca

Fan Email Address:
info@carriedaway.ca

Website: www.carriedaway.ca

SKILLET

INTIMATE FELLOWSHIP AND PRAYER

Jesus had the most intimate relationship with the Father that we have ever seen. One thing Jesus did to maintain this intimacy was to wake up early in the morning and sneak away to spend time with Him. We should learn from His example and develop this discipline - intimacy with God, learning to hear His voice more clearly, learning to pray effectively, and learning how to love Him better. It is good to simply spend time in His presence, with no other agenda but to be with Him. Too many times we can be quick to tell Him what we want and then go away, never waiting for Him to speak to us. What if you only asked your friend for things you wanted and talked about yourself? You would never let him speak; you would never fellowship. What kind of a relationship would that be? That doesn't sound too attractive, does it? We can be this way in our relationship with God. We are always talking and asking, instead of fellowshipping and sharing life together.

Many people wonder what to do to have a relationship with God. We recommend reading the Psalms, then begin to write your own. Within this book, we see the author pouring out his heart to God. Sometimes they begin and end with praise, sometimes they are questioning, sometimes his focus begins with himself and his own circumstances, but they always end with hope. You will find as you begin to walk in closer fellowship with God, that even in the direst of circumstances, **there is always hope, because God, Himself, is hope**. Learn to pour your heart out to the Lord, with your focus always on Him. You will always find hope, no matter what comes your way.

Skillet Skillet Skillet Skillet Skillet Skillet Skillet

The most famous prayer in the Bible is Jesus' "the Lord's prayer." This prayer started off with, "Our Father who art in heaven, hallowed be thy name" (Matthew 6:9 RSV). This persuades us to begin our prayers by praising God. One is never in a better relationship with God than when he is worshipping Him. This can be a cure for not knowing what to say to God. It also is a cure for constantly asking God for things, instead of enjoying His Presence.

Here are some easy examples of how to speak praises to God:

•   "God, You are awesome! You are wonderful in every way, and I love You."

•   "I worship You with all of my heart, and You are my one true passion."

•   "Thank You, God, for saving me from hell and from my sin. I worship and exalt You."

•   "There is no one righteous but You, and there is no one good but You. You are perfect and Your mercy lasts forever!"

For the last year, Skillet has enforced the "Mandatory 20." This is time specifically set aside to simply fellowship with God - not Bible study, but just time to be with the Lord. We do this every morning before we see each other, regardless if we are leaving at 3:00 A.M. or 12:00 P.M. We have found this discipline to be very fruitful and invite you to join us. There are many other disciplines that we can develop to help us become more like Jesus, and to help us renew our minds. The ultimate goal is to know God better and to be more like Him. He is the desired end and reward.

Another Verse:
Ephesians 6:18

Prayer

God, I want more than anything to know You. I pray that You equip me with the powerful presence of the Holy Spirit, that I may dwell in righteousness and live in victory. I long to see Your name glorified over all the earth. Be glorified in my life, as I learn to walk in the Spirit.

UNPLUGGED
a deeper look

When we write psalms to God, can He reveal flaws in our own Christian walk? When we write psalms to God, it is us expressing our worship to Him. As we become more intimate with God, He shows us our weaknesses. There's no better way to be intimate with God than by speaking our praises to Him. By doing it outwardly, it becomes more real to us. In the Bible it says, from the fruit of your lips, you'll praise Him. The more we begin to speak those praises to God, the more we believe it - the more it challenges our spirit. The real issue with worship with young people is they don't know how. They're like, "I really wanna' worship God, but what does it mean to sing praises to God? I don't know what it means to sing." If you are not feeling like God is showing you things in your life that need to change, then there should be a real concern about your relationship with Him. It is great that God shows us these things. So, when we begin to profess our love to God (which is what I really mean by writing psalms to God), we will become more intimate with Him. - John

Once we set aside time to spend in His presence, many times we let our minds wander. What should we do during this time to focus on Him? All of us know how hard it is to make ourselves have time with God. My battle has been a wandering mind. It's still as hard as it was when I was 15. I find it very difficult to read or pray because of this. If we can concentrate for five minutes, it's okay to take a break. Some people think that if they can't pray for an hour straight, then why pray at all? Well, every conversation that we have with a friend does not last for 30 minutes or an hour. Sometimes we want to call someone just to say, "Hi," or maybe just to hear a friendly voice. God wants to be our friend, and we need to learn to talk to Him in that way. We don't have to pray for an hour and a half; just create communication. We have to will ourselves to do it; it's just like working out - we set aside that time to work out everyday, and we'll notice our body changing. We'll notice that we feel different. It's just like that with the Lord. We set aside that time and pursue Him on a consistent basis, just speak to Him, and we'll notice change. - John

Skillet Skillet Skillet Skillet Skillet Skillet

BACKSTAGE PASS
getting to know

How did the band meet and form? The band met in Memphis, Tennessee, and started at our church, so we could play at some evangelical outreaches. We were not planning on being a professional band, but God had other plans! We were all from different bands when we started, which is why we called the group Skillet. It was like cooking - taking all of these different ingredients and throwing them together. - John

Do you feel God leading the band in a special direction? God is leading us to be relevant in a world where it is becoming increasingly more acceptable to talk about Jesus. Jesus is becoming a fad, and we want to be a voice of true Christianity to a generation of passionless people. We're trying to do more shows with mainstream bands and get more mainstream radio play. We're really working to get the message out and do our little part of showing the world what radical Christians are supposed to live like. - John

How does the band plan to further its ministry in the future? Our focus is to build an audience in the mainstream market. We have been touring the Christian market for about ten years now, and we love it. We don't want to quit doing it, but we plan to keep growing our fan base. My heart has always been for the lost. We toured in 2004 with a mainstream band called Saliva. It was a thing we really had to pray about, and we felt God calling us to do it. Afterward, I knew more than ever that God has called me to do that. - John

0000405

Booking Agency:
Jeff Roberts & Associates
615-859-7040
www.jeffroberts.com

Website:
www.skillet.com

020240

Birthdays:
John: April 7
Korey: July 21
Lori: October 29
Ben: April 15

Favorite Bible Verses:
John: Romans 8:38
Korey: Psalm 37:4
Lori: 1 Thessalonians 5:23-24
Ben: Psalm 63

0000404

TAMMY TRENT

IT IS WELL WITH MY SOUL

It may not be well with your circumstances, but it can be well with your soul - what a statement that runs deep inside my heart. Standing on the edge of the water at Jamaica's Blue Lagoon in September 2001, I couldn't breathe, I couldn't see through my tears, I couldn't move. It was certainly not well with my circumstances at that very moment.

I was on a much needed trip (part vacation, part mission) to Jamaica with my high school sweetheart and later husband, Trent Lenderink. Trent and I had met at the tender age of 15, in our youth group, so seven of our eighteen years were dating before marriage. We had just spent seven days together, playing in the sun and laying on a tramp in the ocean. I remember thinking to myself, "It can't get any better than this." I wasn't prepared for what would happen next.

On our way to begin the mission trip, we stopped off at the legendary Blue Lagoon, so Trent could go free diving. There was nothing unusual about that, since Trent had been diving since the age of 12, and would dive on every vacation we ever took. What *was* unusual was when Trent sank beneath the surface that afternoon and never returned.

The search began and continued through the night and into the next morning. The morning of September 11, 2001. I will never forget standing in front of the TV, watching the second plane plow into the twin towers in New York City. Moments later, the phone rang with the news of Trent's recovery. The world was falling apart, and my personal world was falling apart. Trent had not survived. "Oh, Jesus, what happened? What went wrong?" My whole life changed at that moment,

Tammy Trent Tammy Trent Tammy

and I knew it would never be the same again.

Honestly, I will never be able to answer all the questions that I've had this side of heaven, so I stopped asking long ago. I am a girl who still feels broken, yet very complete. I am a girl who has experienced healing, yet I think I'll be healing the rest of my life. But because I have Jesus, I have hope, and because of that hope, Trent is now a part of my future, not my past. I'm constantly amazed at the Lord's commitment to us in the worst moments of our lives. It is one thing to call Him "Shepherd," it is another to be carried by Him when you can no longer stand. **It might not be well with your circumstances today, but it can be well with your soul.** Trust. Believe. Have Faith. Stand Strong. Have Courage. You are never alone. Every fallen tear is always understood. Life is hard, but God is good!

Another Verse:
Psalm 34:18

Prayer

Jesus, I give You my life today. All the good - all the bad - and ask that You make something beautiful with it. Only You can complete and fix a broken heart. A shattered world. I might not like my circumstances today, but please help me to see that it can still be well with my soul through You. In Jesus' name, Amen!

UNPLUGGED
a deeper look

We've heard you talk about a maid you believe God brought into your life when you couldn't reach anyone on that terrible day. Could you share that story? That is an amazing story, and it would honestly take some time to tell you the miracle that God brought into my life one very painful morning, while all alone in a hotel room in Jamaica. I was able to tell of that breath-taking moment in my book, *Learning to Breathe Again*, so I hope you're able to pick that up and read it in full ... truly amazing. But I can tell you that in that very critical moment in my life, in the middle of all my questions, even as a believer, I knew that God had sent me an angel, and I knew that He was very, very real, even through my tears.

When we reach heaven, do you think we will receive answers to the questions of life, or will we just be satisfied without answers once we're with our Father for eternity? I think we'll be in complete relationship with Jesus, and part of relationship is spending time together, talking, dreaming, loving, adventuring together, life - so I believe we'll have lots to talk about and laugh about. I'm sure seeing Him face to face will make everything clear to me, but I will be amazed at how it all came together (especially my husband's life and death), so I'm quite sure we'll sit under a beautiful tree and reminisce about life itself.

BACKSTAGE PASS
getting to know

Favorite Books: Whatever I'm reading at the moment. Right now it's *I Married Adventure - Looking at Life Through the Lens of Possibility*, by my good friend, Luci Swindoll.

Musical Influences: It will always be Amy Grant for me. She was my first concert at the age of 9, and her music was such a part of my growing years. Now, I have her cell phone number. Oh, my goodness. I'm still freaking out!

What is God teaching you now? Patience. Slow to anger.
Rest and be still.

How has your family helped you in your walk with God?
Just watching their lives is the biggest example I've had. Their
faith has never changed, no matter what their circumstances.
My family means so much to me and has always surrounded
me with love and support. Knowing they're all believers is a
great comfort. We'll all be together forever.

How do you plan to expand your ministry in the future?
Interesting question. I don't know what God has in store for
me, honestly. I just completed my first studio album in six
years entitled <u>I See Beautiful</u>. It is truly the journey of my life
put to music. My plan is to take it one adventure at a time and
give God all of the attention along the way.

0202402

Birthday:
April 11

Favorite Bible Verse:
Jeremiah 29:11-13

Website:
www.tammytrent.com

Booking Agency:
Tammy Trent Ministries
615-837-3880
anita@tammytrent.com

Fan Mail Address:
Friends With Tammy
P.O. Box 1701
Brentwood, TN 37024

Fan Email Address: tammy@tammytrent.com

Tammy Trent Tammy Trent Tammy Trent Tammy

JEFF DEYO

LEARNING HOW TO BLESS THE LORD

Revelation 5:11-12 (NLT) paints us an incredible picture of thousands and millions of angels gathered around the throne of God, along with the living beings and the elders all singing this song together: "The Lamb is worthy - the Lamb who was killed. He is worthy to receive power and riches and wisdom and strength and honor and glory and blessing." WOW! I can't wait to join with the angels one day to sing that very song to the King of all Kings - the Son of the one true God of all the Universe!

David adds his cry for blessing to the King in these famous words from Psalm 103:1 (KJV), "Bless the Lord, O my soul: and all that is within me, bless his holy name."

I have come to realize how absolutely essential it is for us to **give all glory, honor, riches, strength, power, and blessing to God!** It is vital that we join our hearts and voices daily in the song the angels sing to Him! In fact, to be a Christian and to *not* bless God is almost impossible! It is unthinkable and disastrous.

Knowing God is about a two-way relationship. We haven't joined a "Bless Me Club." When we treat Him like heaven's Santa, we advocate that blessing should be a one-way street. And that closes up the windows of heaven faster than just about anything! Of course we don't bless God *so that* we will receive His blessing. God cannot be tricked. We bless Him out of the abundance of love for Him in our hearts. Then, because He absolutely LOVES to bless His people, He gladly heaps His supernatural blessings upon us!

An equally important reason for blessing God is simply

because He created within all of us a desperate need to do so! Sometimes we just need to tell ourselves, "Self, look around. Look at all that God has done for you. Look at who He is. Has He not given you life and breath? Has He not forgiven you when you deserved death instead? Has He not provided every single thing you need? Has He not wiped away your tears and given you joy and peace everlasting? Has He not allowed your heart to continue to beat over and over again? Has He not been slow to anger and quick to pour out His mercy? Come on, self ... BLESS THE LORD! BLESS HIS HOLY NAME!!"

God does not ask us to bless or praise Him because He is in *need* of our blessing. He has no needs that we know of, or that we can meet for Him. He is the embodiment of blessing! He is love. He doesn't need love. He is light. He doesn't need light. He is hope. He doesn't need hope. Even though He truly enjoys it when we bless Him, He simply has no need of our "tiny," "measly" blessings. He commands us to bless Him because of the great need we have in our lives of putting Him first! There is no question that God deserves all blessing, and honor, and glory, and strength, and riches, and power! And He is greatly pleased in seeing His creation honor and bless Him in the way He designed!

More Verses:
Galatians 6:7, Matthew 6:33, Luke 9:24, Psalm 134, Philippians 2:5, and 1 Corinthians 9:21

Prayer

Lord, thank You for being such an incredible God! Please teach me the power of blessing and honoring You with my lips and with my life. I love Your blessings, and I long to love blessing You and others as much as I enjoy receiving blessings from You! I know this is what Your Kingdom is all about, so please guide me as I seek to make my life a blessing to all! I love and trust You. In Jesus' name I pray, Amen.

UNPLUGGED
a deeper look

Why is it important for teenagers to bless God in their younger years? It is so important for teens to recognize that they are not *just* the future of the church. Teenagers are truly the center of the body of Christ RIGHT NOW! It is amazing how many young people were used by God in the Bible. David was a teenager when he was anointed king and when he killed Goliath. Mary was a teen when she gave birth to the King of Kings. Students need to realize that living for God starts *now.* Our teen years are not just years of waste, where we can do whatever we want, while waiting for our "serious" adult years. These are the years that mold us into the people we are going to be when we are adults. Now is the time to get serious about God, to begin praying for godly wisdom to be able to make right choices. Just think of all the people you can touch and bring to Christ when you realize that you were born to serve Christ with every breath - not just as an adult, but from an early age. Imagine the influence for God you can have on your peers when you finally begin to grasp that everyone is called to "full-time ministry" - not just pastors and musicians. Whether at school or at work, the reason you exist is to make disciples. Christ has commissioned you to do so. There is no other purpose for your life.

Why is our attitude toward God so important to our everyday life? Our attitude toward God shows who we are. We can say all day that we love and trust God, but when trials come, we find out exactly where we stand. If we truly honor God as Lord, we live it out even when troubled times come. If we really trust God, we won't sin by worrying about the future. Jesus was the ultimate example to us of what we should be. We must understand that we cannot compare ourselves to others. We should never say, "Well, at least my attitude is better than most people's." God never looks at it that way. He always compares our attitude to His Son's. Jesus set the standard, and no other standard counts. The final reason to keep a godly attitude in every day life is to be an example to others. Everyone is watching you. Each person who calls himself a Christian is on the "stage" every day, just like I am. We are all being watched. People want to know if it is different being a Christian.

We are expected to do whatever we can within the confines of Scripture to win people to Christ, so use every opportunity that your "stage" allows you to be an example of a true believer.

BACKSTAGE PASS
getting to know

Favorite Books: My favorite author is John Bevere. He is teaching things that many of us have *never* heard before, yet that are *huge* in the Bible! When you read his books, you almost think to yourself, "How have I missed that truth all my life?" The books of his that I would recommend for students are *The Fear of the Lord*, *Under Cover*, and *Drawing Near*.

Musical Influences: I loved artists like Phil Collins and Chicago and Christian bands like Petra and Michael W. Smith. I finally got a cassette player in my junior high years. I would sit for hours playing and rewinding songs, trying to pick out the chords on the piano so I could play along. Later on, it was dcTalk and still, MWS that whet my musical appetite. Don't tell anyone, but I even had a life-size poster of Michael from his Big Picture days.

What is God teaching you now? God has been teaching me a lot about serving and loving him in balance. Some people think of God only as their King. They focus mostly on His holiness and bigness. Others concentrate on God's grace. They realize God says we can approach His throne with boldness, and they think of Him more like a friend. The problem is that when we only think of God as King, or only as friend, we miss out on the real God. God desires us to approach Him as *both* King and friend. He wants us to come boldly, with humility. He wants us to draw close - but still act in reverence. He wants us to sit in His lap and bow at His feet. Psalm 2:11 (NLT) sums it up, "Serve the Lord with reverent fear, and rejoice with trembling." God desires us to approach Him with rejoicing and trembling at the same time! We can only do this by faith; faith comes by hearing and hearing by the Word of God. We are able to approach God correctly only when we truly know who He is and that happens mostly through the Word.

How has your family helped you in your walk with God?
I grew up in an awesome family! My parents loved God and always kept us involved in church and activities that involved God. My father has worked for Youth for Christ for over 40 years! I also married an incredible woman of God. Martha's heart has been tender toward the Lord since I've known her. And it's cool, because the thing that has kept our relationship strong is our like-passion for loving God! Having family members who love God has continued to keep me accountable my whole life. What a blessing to have a godly heritage.

How do you plan to expand your ministry in the future?
My top two desires for my ministry are to help people learn to love God and to love people. I will always be a lead worshipper, because that is what God called me to do. The way I use my gifting may vary over the years, but it will always involve helping people do those two things. I will continue writing worship songs with the hope that people will be able to use them to worship God in their churches, conferences, and around campfires. As long as God allows me to, I will travel, leading people to worship the King. I will continue to make resources available on our website, as well, because I love to write encouraging articles and provide chord charts for worship leaders and musicians.

Website:
www.jeffdeyo.com

Fan Email Address:
jeff@jeffdeyo.com

Birthday:
November 5

Favorite Bible Verse:
Zephaniah 3:17

Fan Mail Address:
Jeff Deyo
WorshipCityMinistries
P.O. Box 24675
Nashville, TN 37202

Booking Agency:
Jeff Roberts & Associates
615-859-7040
www.jeffroberts.com

DAY OF FIRE

LET THE LORD BE YOUR GUIDE

My name is Josh Brown. I was born in Jackson, Tennessee. I grew up in a divorced home, and at age 15, I began using drugs and alcohol to escape feelings of insecurity and depression. I also started playing guitar and writing music. I had big dreams of one day becoming a rock star. I started singing in bands and was immediately drawn into the rock and roll nightlife. My popularity grew and so did my addictions. Eventually, my band scored a recording contract. After recording our first album, we hit the road to tour the United States. By this time, I was highly addicted to narcotics. I was even shooting up. I found myself completely controlled by fear and depression. My band was now touring with many bands that I watched on MTV. I thought that this level of success would somehow bring fulfillment and purpose into my broken life, but I was wrong. Loneliness consumed me as I searched for comfort inside another drug binge. That binge ended with a near-fatal overdose of heroin. I went to rehab to get cleaned up for awhile. I started to realize that I had a hole inside of me that could not be filled by the things of this world. The more that I tried to fill this hole with money, sex, or fame, the emptier I became. I needed something more in my life. I felt less than human. I began to cry out to God for some sort of relief. I began reading the Bible in search of hope. One night while watching a Christian TV station, the good news of Jesus Christ was explained to me. All people are born sinners. Our sins keep us separated from God. The fear and emptiness in our lives comes from our separation from

God. God loves us so much that He sent His only Son, Jesus Christ, to die on a cross to take the punishment for our sins. God then raised Jesus from the dead so that we could have a new life with Him. Everyone that accepts Jesus Christ as Lord and Savior will have eternal life. Through Jesus Christ, we no longer have to live as slaves to fear and depression. That night I gave my life to God. I asked Jesus to forgive me of my sins and to be Lord of my life. I began looking deeper in the Bible to learn about God and what He wanted for me. I learned that God wanted to be number one in my life, and that if I truly wanted to have peace, I would have to do things His way.

Soon after that, my girlfriend, Adrianné, and I decided to get married. We started attending a local church and depending more and more upon the Lord. God took away my desire for drugs completely, and freed me from my addictions by the power of the Holy Spirit. He gave me a new mind and filled my life with an undying hope. I found my purpose and peace inside of Him. **God became my Provider, my Healer, my Shelter, and my Strength.** He completely washed away the sins of my past, and He wants to do the same for you. Jesus says in John 3:16 (NKJV), "For God so loved the world, that he gave his only begotten Son, that whoever believes in Him should not perish, but have everlasting life." For God did not send His Son into the world to condemn the world but to save the world through Him. Jesus says in Matthew 11:28 (NIV), "Come to me, all you who are weary and burdened, and I will give you rest. Take my yoke upon you and learn from me, for I am gentle and humble in heart, and you will find rest for your souls. For my yoke is easy and my burden is light." If you are tired of the life that you have been living and would like to begin your life with God, please say this prayer with me:

"God, I know that I am a sinner. I believe Jesus is Your Son and that He died on the cross for my sins. I believe that You raised Him from the dead so that I could have a new life with You. Please forgive me of my sins and fill me with Your Holy Spirit. Be the Lord of my life, free me from my depression, and teach me how to live."

Romans 10:9 says, that if you confess with your mouth Jesus as Lord and believe in your heart that God raised Jesus from the dead, you will be saved. If you said that prayer with me and meant it in your heart, you have just been born again into the Kingdom of God. God has become your Father, and you have eternal life with God on earth and in heaven. This is the beginning of your life with God. To build your relationship with Him, you must devote time to Him everyday with prayer and studying the Bible (the book of John in the New Testament is a great place to start). Also, learning to hear and obey the voice of the Holy Spirit will guarantee your success in this new life. It is vital that you find a group of believers to worship with and attend a Bible-believing church with a pastor that teaches the Word of God. Let the Lord be your guide.

UNPLUGGED
a deeper look

You said your life was basically a mess before you found Christ, between drugs, depression, loneliness, and the stressful life of touring. How do you advise teens who are in the same types of situations to: 1) Recognize the danger they're in and sins they're committing, and to 2) Turn their life around? Most people that are doing drugs know it's dangerous and fundamentally wrong, but at some point, they cross a line and get to a point where they don't care. Instead of trying to talk to them about drugs, I talk to them about the symptoms that cause them to use drugs, which are the depression, and the emptiness, and the feelings of purposelessness. Once you figure out what you're created for, and once you realize that you have a purpose on this earth, life is much better. It has more meaning. Inside Jesus you can find that purpose, and you can find that fulfillment. God has a life for you that is exciting and dangerous. God desires us to be walking in faith and on the edge. Church is great, but church is more than going to a building for a certain number of hours a week. Being a Christian is more than going to church on Wednesday and Sunday, not cussing, and not smoking. Following God is actually going to bring excitement, meaning, and purpose to your life.

How important do you think it is for kids to find God early in their lives, before they're tempted by drugs, fame, and sex, and an ungodly lifestyle takes control? No doubt. I didn't have that experience, and I made a lot of bad decisions. It cost me a lot. It's detrimental not to know God. I do not wish that anyone would have to travel the roads I've been down. It took me 25 years to figure out that I couldn't do it on my own, and when I look at my daughters, my prayer is that they would know and love God even more than I know and love God - so they can have greater success earlier in life. I see kids growing up in churches now; their parents have been obedient and sought God. They have been a good example to their children, and their children are amazing. They are doing things that the elders in the church aren't even doing yet, and it's very encouraging to me. I know that there's hope for this generation. When a person encounters God for the first time, they find out that God is real - He's more than an idea. He's more than something your parents talked about. He's actually a living being. He created the universe. When you come into contact with Him, it changes you. The only way a teenager's going to be changed is by getting in the actual presence of God. God hates sin, but He loves sinners.

BACKSTAGE PASS
getting to know

Favorite Books: *Under Cover* by John Bevere and *Wild at Heart* by John Eldredge

Musical Influences: The Cars, Pink Floyd, just bands like that.

What is God teaching you now? God is teaching me about community, about how to be the church on the road, instead of depending on being able to get to a building to worship God. I'm learning to seek God with my band and my family - how to be godly inside the structure of the band.

How has your family helped you in your walk with God?
God shows His love for me through my family constantly. I have a solid foundation in my family - my wife, my children, my brother and his wife, my mom. God has put these people in place, and no matter what I'm going through, no matter where I've been, they are there for me. They always have love.

How do you plan to expand your ministry in the future?
I see branching out to the world, and people that do not know God coming into contact with God through our music. I see us continuing to travel the world, not just spreading the gospel through talking about it, but by walking it out in front of people, by the grace of God. He is allowing us to love people in bars, to love people in churches. It's through Jesus and Day of Fire.

0202402

Birthday:
November 15

Favorite Bible Verse:
Matthew 11:28

Fan Email Address:
info@whizbang-inc.com

Booking Agency:
Creative Artists Agency
615-383-8787
www.caaccm.com

FM
2 D
1967

5c
U.S.POSTAGE

Fan Mail Address:
Day of Fire
P.O. Box 100993
Nashville, TN 37224

Websites:
www.essentialrecords.com
www.dayoffire.com

EVERYDAY SUNDAY

LETTING GO

*O*ne rainy day, my fiancée and I popped in the movie "Crouching Tiger, Hidden Dragon." Two Chinese people were talking, and we're reading along, and Chow Yun Fat's character says, "Nothing can be taken from a man that he does not cling to." She suddenly sits up and rewinds the tape (yeah, it's a video tape), so we can read it again. It truly *is* a profound statement, and it's actually a thought that we've talked about before. It's probably been said before by other philosophers and theologians, but the idea is simple and staggering. What we do not hold onto cannot be stripped away. This can apply to all of life - material possessions, time, relationships, the past, fears … It takes me to Jeremiah 10:23 (NIV), when Jeremiah confesses to God, "I know, O LORD, that a man's life is not his own. It is not for man to direct his steps." The more I think about it, the more real and practical it sounds.

Need of nothing is the greatest of freedoms - freedom for God to use us in amazing and powerful ways that we might not have been available for before. The hard part is letting go, which really boils down to trust. Am I willing to fly blind? Do I really believe that God knows best for me and will show me what He wants with my life? Easy to say and easy to agree to, but harder to apply in the real world. Let's go back to Jeremiah. I can imagine Jeremiah, a man who actually heard the voice of the Lord every day, who stood alone as a righteous man, preaching repentance to the nation of Israel. I can see him after a long day of preaching and his fuse is short. He comes to God, and recognizes that he is still holding something back. So he sighs, raises his arms, and says, "I know, O LORD, that my life is not my own …"

Everyday Sunday Everyday Sunday Everyday

Try reminding yourself of that today, and you'll be amazed how much more of yourself you find to give to others, and how free you feel when you realize that your life is not your own.

UNPLUGGED
a deeper look

When teens are bombarded daily with advertisements telling them they "need" more and more stuff to fit in, what are some ways they can begin to loosen their grip on material possessions? I think getting confidence in who you are as a person, and as a child of God, is the most important thing to realizing your importance is not in material things or possessions. A lot of it has to do with the way you're raised and taught to handle things as they come along in life. The more you realize that nothing in this life is yours, and it all belongs to God, the easier it is to let go of being selfish.

The best thing to do is to know the difference between our wants and our needs. God will provide everything for our needs as long as we are faithful. We need to be careful with what we want and how much we want. Teens need to stay away from debt to get things, and save towards them. Teens need to learn the value of a dollar before they can see the difference between what they need and what they want. You don't need new clothes every month, but if you are spiritually and financially responsible in tithing, rent, or the things you need, it will be much more rewarding to get something you want.

Sometimes it's very hard for teens to let go of their dreams and trust that God has something even bigger. How do you advise teens to get to that point? I think dreams are an awesome thing to have. I think God puts passions on our heart for a reason, but the most important thing is finding where God wants you. I believe He will show you that by opening and closing the right doors in your life, when you're in His will and working hard. I believe that's the best way to be in a place where He can show you what adventures and great things He has in store for you.

What we cling to can be taken from us. What things should teens hold on to, and what should they let go of? First of all, they need to hold on to God, and who they are in God. That is where all true wisdom, confidence, love, and comfort come from.   Then when the other things come and go, you'll be able to have the right attitude about it. Someone once told me that if you put God in the center, everything else will work itself out. I have found that to be true in my whole life, and I am confident in the things to come. It does not mean you won't face hard times, because hard times come. It's more about what kind of foundation you have built when those times come. Read Job 1:20-21.

BACKSTAGE PASS
getting to know

How did the band meet and form? Trey started the band when he was 16. We all met through our youth group, and most of the band has been together since June, 2000.

Do you feel God leading the band in a special direction? I feel the band being led in a special direction, whether it be to make a new record or if God has a different direction for us.

How does the band plan to further its ministry in the future? We are always striving to further our ministry by trying to better ourselves. We can't reach people with problems that we haven't tried to better in ourselves.

Birthdays:
Jesse: April 12
Trey: September 10
Chris: December 20
Dan: September 8

Favorite Bible Verses and Books:
Jesse: Psalm 37:4
Trey: Romans 12
Chris: Proverbs
Dan: James

Booking Agency:
Jeff Roberts & Associates
615-859-7040
www.jeffroberts.com

Website: www.everydaysunday.com

JOHN DAVID WEBSTER

LIFE'S LESSONS

God's taught me a lot of things lately, including the importance of family. A lot of times in life, we look at all of the important things we have to do for God, but we overlook the people that are closest to us. I think that's what God's been showing me - look around at all of these people that are in your life, the people you're surrounded with, the people that love and minister to you. They are miracles. When I sing my song "Miracle," I can feel a connection with what's really important in life, coming down to the basic part of life, which is relationships.

God's also really been teaching me about His grace. A lot of times, I think people look at Christian artists, and they think, "Wow! He has it all together. What's it like to go out and represent God?" But I minister as much by my failures - realizing that I'm just like everyone else. I think it frees them up to say, "I'm not perfect, but I know Someone who is."

The other day I was telling my son, Zion, that we need to tell people that God loves them. That's something even my kids can understand. He asked me, "Doesn't everyone know that God loves them?" I said, "No, not everyone knows," and he responded, "Well, why don't we tell everyone?"

At times, each one of us fights with what God really wants us to do. When God asks us to do something, or go somewhere, or talk to someone, we find that inward battle. One of the things that's been changing my life is a simple prayer - "Lord, have your way in me." Inside there's a battle raging, but **there's a freedom of release when you just let it go and give it to God** - no matter if you've been walking with the Lord for a long time, or have just come to know the Lord - to

John David Webster John David

recognize the beauty of surrender, and to say, "Lord, have your way in my life."

I've felt called to music ministry my whole life. I remember seeing Christian artists that would come and play in town; there was just something different about them, and there was something that drew me. Their music was really good, but I knew there was something underneath it. I just knew that was what I was going to be doing, ever since I was a kid. I know it's something that God's called me to do. I've followed that calling. He's shown me that He will give me the grace I need to be a spokesman for the faith.

"So then, just as you received Christ Jesus as Lord, continue to live in him, rooted and built up in him, strengthened in the faith as you were taught, and overflowing with thankfulness" (Colossians 2:6-7 NIV).

UNPLUGGED
a deeper look

How can teens overcome the frightening feeling of being vulnerable when they tell God to have His way with them? It's terrifying to say, "Okay, Lord, have your way in me, and take this." I'm a control freak at times, and giving it to God, saying, "Have your way in my life, with my kids, my marriage, my finances, being on the road and away from my family ..." feels so good and so right. I don't know why I fight it so much, but that's what I feel like my message is - to share about my struggle with asking God to have His way in my life. People respond to that, and they want to open up, as well.

What rewards have you seen by letting God take control of your life? The greatest reward is just knowing that I'm seen for something way bigger than me. When I'm singing for the Lord, I'm singing things that I really believe in. There's something humbling about it - just knowing Him. When we get to heaven, we're going to take all of the rewards that we've gotten and throw them down, because they're not going to mean anything compared to Him. He's the one that made all of the rewards. The blessing of singing and playing music is so awesome. How many people would love to play music for a living? And God's given me a chance to do that. It's an awesome thing.

BACKSTAGE PASS
getting to know

Favorite Book: *The Ragamuffin Gospel* by Brennan Manning

Musical Influences: Peter Gabriel, Sting, Bono, Rich Mullins, Keith Green, and the list goes on and on and on.

What is God teaching you now? He's teaching me to not take things so seriously sometimes, and to let go of things and just enjoy the people around me. Life is short.

How has your family helped you in your walk with God? It's amazing; it's a sense of home for me to come back to. My wife, and my kids, and I all feel called to do what we're doing. In a nutshell, my family's a blessing.

How do you plan to expand your ministry in the future? Right now, to play as much as I can, and everywhere I play, whether it's for 5 people or 5,000 people, to play my heart out.

Website: www.johndavidwebster.com

Booking Agency:
The Breen Agency
615-777-2227
www.thebreenagency.com

Birthday:
February 15

Favorite Bible Verse:
Matthew 5:14

Fan Mail Address:
John David Webster
Blanton, Harrell, Cooke and Corzine
5300 Virginia Way, Suite 100
Brentwood, TN 37027

Fan Email Address: jdw@johndavidwebster.com

ERIN O'DONNELL

LISTENING TO GOD

I have a friend whom I admire for lots of reasons - her humor, energy, wit and fearlessness, just to name a few. But I noticed something about her recently that I believe God used as a lesson for me. You see, I believe **God can** and does do that ... **use everyday people in everyday situations to help shape us into the person He longs for us to be**.

In the midst of giving each other updates over lunch, on what had been happening in our lives, this friend used every opportunity to encourage and support me. I didn't realize it until well after the last bite had been eaten, and I had gone on with my day, but I felt better about everything. My load seemed lighter, and I knew I wasn't alone.

It wasn't that I went into that meeting feeling particularly needy or lonely - and it wasn't that anything that was said was particularly awe-inspiring or profound. It was that I came out feeling that someone saw me - truly saw me. Not only that, they were happy to meet all of me - the good, bad, and the ugly. She was merely there, happy to listen, and quick to offer encouragement and praise with things I had been working on. She gave reminders that God was at work in my areas of struggle, and laughter at how life continues to catch us by surprise.

I didn't know I needed it, but God used my friend to keep me going and remind me that I am loved by Him. And He continues to do so. All around me. When I really listen, I can hear Him.

Erin O'Donnell Erin O'Donnell Erin O'Donnell Erin

Prayer

Heavenly Father, thank You for teaching me about encouragement through my friend. Help me to continue to learn, and grow, and to cheer my friends on in this life. Give me ears to hear what others need. Help me to be an encourager and remind me how powerful words can be, and how the wrong ones can trample a tender heart. Help me to freely give of my time. Let me be one You can use to make another's burden feel lighter. And above all, allow me to be a reminder to others of how much You love them. Amen.

UNPLUGGED
a deeper look

What should teenagers expect when they're trying to hear from God? I think God speaks to us quite clearly, like when you have a check in your gut about a particular situation, or a real sense of calm and peace about an upcoming event. The world would say, "Follow your conscience," but I believe that is our heavenly Father guiding our steps and speaking to our hearts.

The Bible says Christians should learn to quiet their hearts and minds - is that the best time to really hear God? God can speak through any noise or situation, but having a heart that is quiet and a mind that is not thinking about a million other things, can only help foster a better relationship with Him.

BACKSTAGE PASS
getting to know

Favorite Books: *The Ragamuffin Gospel* by Brennan Manning and *Breathing Lessons* by Anne Tyler

Musical Influences: I love everything from jazz to Christian pop. I studied music in college and have a great respect for those who can create it, no matter the genre.

What is God teaching you now? To continue to listen ... to have patience ... to remember what is important.

How has your family helped you in your walk with God? My family teaches me about real love everyday ... how selfish I can be ... how unkind. They also teach me about forgiveness and grace. I am blessed to have such wonderful people in my life.

How do you plan to expand your ministry in the future? Haven't really thought about it. I love playing music and will always do that on some level.

Website:
www.erinodonnell.com

Birthday:
March 11

Favorite Bible Verse:
Romans 8:38

0202402

Booking Agency:
GOA, Inc.
615-790-5540
www.goa-inc.com

5¢ U.S. POSTAGE

Fan Mail Address:
Erin O'Donnell
c/o O'Donnell Productions
604 Countryside Ct.
Franklin, TN 37069

Fan Email Address: mailerin@comcast.net

ZOEGIRL

"LOVE ME FOR ME"

Kristin Swinford

Do you long for someone to understand and accept you for who you are? Have you ever found yourself pretending to be something you're not in order to measure up or meet someone's expectations? The real question is probably, "Who hasn't?" It seems so difficult in this day and age to be satisfied with ourselves and the person God has made us to be. Once we finally start to become content, doesn't that twinge of self-doubt start to come in? That lovely little voice inside says, "They won't like you unless you" ... or "If only you looked like ..." This very subject is what the song "Love Me for Me" talks about. It explores how, in the search for acceptance from others, a person can become something foreign to who and what they really are, while trying to please everyone else. In the verses, we used the metaphor of a circus act to portray a girl caught in her own identity crisis. She feels like she's on display up on the trapeze, and everyone is not only watching, but they can see that she's not being true to herself. She's frustrated and tired of pretending. A counter voice enters after each chorus and in the bridge saying, *"There is someone who loves you for you, and God loves you for you."*

I know in my life, other peoples' opinions have always mattered far too much to me, and I've often found myself longing for someone to truly understand and accept me without reservation. Although I have been blessed with great friends, a wonderful loving family, and an amazing husband, I still have those moments where I feel like the person I am inside and out isn't good enough. I feel that I'm destined to fall or let them down, or that somehow they'll be disappointed with me. This has perplexed and hindered me for so long, and honestly still creeps back in my life here and there. My only resolution to this is trusting that God does love and accept me. Where's my proof? It says in the Bible that Jesus Christ died for me, for all those imperfections and sins that have marked and tainted me. Romans 3:23-24 (NIV) says, "For all have sinned and fall short of the glory of God, and are justified freely by his grace through the redemption that came by Christ Jesus." Because of that redemption, meaning I have been freed from the consequence of sin, I am reassured that when God sees me, He doesn't see what I see or what anyone else sees. **He sees His child that was cleansed and made perfect through Jesus' sacrifice.** Therefore, He loves us for who we are and have become in Christ. We are His redeemed children, His beloved; He doesn't play the games we play in human relationships, nor does He string us along with lies or enforce unattainable expectations on us. No matter how insecure, imperfect, unfit, or seemingly undesirable we are, the fact that God still desires the most personal and intimate relationship with us is the greatest form of love, and the truest example of acceptance we could ever experience.

UNPLUGGED
a deeper look

How do you recommend that teens stay true to their values with so many magazines and other media sources pressuring them to fit a particular look? In order to stay true to godly values, we have to focus on Him, not fashion. We need to draw closer to Him, not temporary fixes. Much of the content in magazines encourages us to be completely self-absorbed, and focuses on outward beauty. God made us for His glory, to fall in love and be absorbed with Him, not ourselves and our outward appearance. The images we see in magazines have gone through many transformations to make things appear flawless, which can be very intimidating when you measure yourself up to what you see. We have to remember that those are people's standards, and God's standards are different. He doesn't measure us according to how trendy we look. He sees us as His valued and treasured creation that He paid the greatest price for.

How can teenagers determine what God thinks about their image and fashion sense? Asking God to show us what He thinks is very important. If you have a certain "image," think about your motives for having that image. Do you spend more time on your image and fashion sense than your relationship with God?

What are some practical ways teens can form godly friendships with both guys and girls? Choosing friends that share your faith and help and encourage you in your walk with God is really important. Always be yourself. If you have to be something or someone else in order to gets someone's attention, or for others to like you, then something is wrong. One true friend is better than ten friends that pressure you to change and compromise what you know is right. God loves you for who you are, and a true friend will, too.

BACKSTAGE PASS
getting to know

Favorite Books: *The Chronicles of Narnia* by C.S. Lewis and *Don't Waste Your Life* by John Piper

Musical Influences: Cindy Morgan and Sting

What is God teaching you now? I feel like God is teaching me about wisdom right now. Wisdom in the choices that I make, in how I respond and deal with others, and I think He's showing me more and more every day how to be a strong and solid woman of God.

How has your family helped you in your walk with God? I was baptized with my dad when I was 6, which was a very important and impacting moment in my life. My parents were very supportive and helpful to me when I realized that my calling was in music ministry. They have always stood by me in faith that God had a special purpose for my life. I will always be so thankful for the strength they gave me and the strong belief they had in me.

How do you plan to expand your ministry in the future?
I have been so blessed to be involved with the ministry that God has given ZOEgirl. It has always been our prayer that He would guide us every step of the way, and as we've focused on His will for our ministry, many doors have opened up for other opportunities in missions. We are continuing to seek God for any ways that we can be more effective and serve Him and others better. We'll see what He has in store!

Birthday:
December 15

Favorite Bible Verse:
Ephesians 4:2-6

Booking Agency:
Jeff Roberts & Associates
615-859-7040
www.jeffroberts.com

Fan Mail Address:
ZOEgirl
c/o Proper Management
P.O. Box 150867
Nashville, TN 37215

Website: www.zoegirlonline.com

FFH

MARKED BY GOD'S GLORY

Jeromy Deibler

What **is** worship?

In a world where the term "Worship" has become so associated with a musical style, most of us have lost objective touch with what worship really is. No doubt, worship is experienced in a powerful way when we sing of our love for the Father. But it is so much more than that! It's a refuge of the heart in the things that are true and holy. It's a spirit towards God that ushers in His glory and puts us in the middle of that glory. It's a pursuit of the face-whitening presence of God that changes us from the inside (spirit) out. Moses experienced worship on the wilderness mountaintop. He encountered God in such a way that it left him forever marked by God's glory. That's what our worship, our time with God, is supposed to do ... mark us with the glory that comes from the Father alone. The disciples had the anointing of that glory on them when they hit the streets after Pentecost. Their time with Jesus left in and on them an unmistakable manifestation of His power and presence. That's what worship should do to us.

Two extremely important things happen when we pursue the presence, face, and glory of God in worship ...

First, we are changed into the glory that we are in the midst of. **We become glory, the aroma of Christ to God.** We take on the characteristics of Jesus and our hearts are changed to be more like His. Second, we are prepared by glory for what's to come. We are commissioned and anointed to live life. We are marked by God's glory in such a way that, whatever comes next, we can undertake it with the unmistakable presence of God. Moses came down from the mountain, full of face-bleaching glory, to be God's voice to His people and tell them what He (God) expected of them for generations to come. The disciples left the experience of Pentecost where tongues of fire settled on them, to go and preach the gospel with unprecedented power and authority - even in languages that they themselves didn't know.

This isn't just Old Testament "Bible stuff." This is real, it's for today. God wants to put His glory on you, as well. He wants to mark you with an unmistakable brand that draws people to Him through you. But it doesn't come without pursuit. Jesus knew this, that's why He sent His disciples off and went away to quiet places to pray. He had to purposefully get alone with God to experience His glory. In Matthew, before His historic walk on water and calming of the storm, Jesus was away on the mountaintop, spending time with the Father. What followed was unprecedented and unquestionable. And what was the response of the disciples? "Truly You are the Son of God" (Matthew 14:33 NIV). Jesus was marked by God's glory for unmistakable ministry.

Prayer

Father, I want to be Your glory here on earth. So first of all, give me a hunger and thirst for mountaintop time with You. Then change me, make me more like You. Mark me with Your glory, so people around me know that You are real and working still today. Remind me that it is Your glory, not mine. Let me not steal any of it from You.

UNPLUGGED
a deeper look

How can teens pursue God to become marked by His glory?
Spend time with God, that's the most effective way. Jesus got
alone with the Father; He's our example. - Jeromy

**What can teens do to radically change their personal time
with God?** There are lots of things you can do to enhance
your time with God. Remember, it's a real relationship, much
like any other relationship. Time spent hanging out with
my family at dinner is a lot different than alone time with my
son, just he and I. It's the same way with God. If we spend
quality time with Him, we will get to know Him on a different
level, than if we just meet with Him in passing every once in
awhile. - Jeromy

**Will we automatically become like Jesus when we worship,
or does it take time, prayer, discipline, and a change inside
of us?** Both. I believe that we do automatically become more
like the Father when we spend time with Him. Again, it's a
relationship. Chances are, you act like the folks that you are
around the most, but like any other relationship, it takes time
and work to go deeper. That's where prayer and the other
spiritual disciplines come in. - Jeromy

**Do you believe times of worship bring us nearer to the
heart of God?** Definitely, without a doubt. There is constant
worship in heaven. When we worship we join in that spirit.
That brings us closer to God's heart. - Jeromy

BACKSTAGE PASS
getting to know

How did the group meet and form? FFH began in 1991 at a
small camp in Pennsylvania. Jeromy and I have known each
other since we were born; our parents were actually friends.
We joined two other guys at this family camp and sang for
a youth night service. Along the way, Jeromy met Jennifer

in Nashville at the GMA Convention; a year later they were married, and she began traveling with us. Shortly after that, one of our original guys left and we asked Jennifer to take his place. In 1997, we met Michael at a camp in Roach, Missouri where we were doing a show. He was recruiting kids for his Bible College and leading Praise & Worship. In 1998, we found out our guitar player was leaving, so we asked Michael to join. - Brian

Do you feel God leading the group in a special direction?
Over the past two years, we've realized there is more to life than just FFH, especially with us having kids. However, I think now we are feeling that God is calling us to be out there more than ever, and because of that, we are enjoying the road, shows, and being with each other, more than we ever have. God is calling us to reach people for Jesus; the only way we can do that is to be out on the road. - Brian

How does the group plan to further its ministry in the future? I think now, more than ever, our goal is to tell people about Jesus. To do that, we feel like God is pulling us outside the walls of the church - not outside of the people, but the actual walls. We love playing in mainstream areas such as theatres, ball fields, fairs, and so on. We know some folks will come to those venues, but will never set foot in a church. The ministry potential is huge. Our goal is to continue that, and continue to be out there on the road telling people about Jesus. - Brian

Birthdays:
Jeromy: August 19
Jennifer: June 14
Brian: July 27
Michael: November 8

Favorite Bible Verses:
Jeromy: Romans 10:8
Jennifer: Jeremiah 29:11
Brian: Colossians 3:17
Michael: 1 Thessalonians 4:11-12

Booking Agency:
William Morris Agency
615-963-3000
www.wmaccm.com

Fan Mail Address:
FFH
P.O. Box 1328
Franklin, TN 37064
Website: www.ffh.net

RACHAEL LAMPA

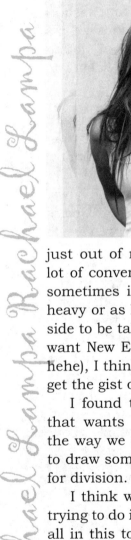

MATH COMPETITION

Weird title for a devotion, huh? Well, I hope that by the end of this, it will make a little more sense to you. Being a girl just out of my teens, I would say that I have engaged in a lot of conversation. Sometimes it's about hair and makeup, sometimes it's about sports, sometimes it's about God. As heavy or as light as the conversation was, there was always a side to be taken. I didn't like my friend's hair or I did, I didn't want New England to win the Superbowl or I did (I didn't ... hehe), I think God is like this or I think God is like that. You get the gist of it.

I found that, for some reason, there is something in us that wants everyone else to see things and believe things the way we do. I am totally guilty of it. And in our attempt to draw someone onto our side of things, we only make room for division.

I think we get so caught up in adding up our points and trying to do it faster than each other, that we forget that we are all in this together. Sharing God is not a math competition. We are so engulfed in the desire to be more right than the person next to us, that we forget that God loves them just as much as us.

I think that theology and accurate interpretation of Scripture is extremely important, for it is the foundation of what we believe, but also high on the priority list should be LOVE. That is where it all started, right? **God loved us enough to send Jesus to us, who loved us enough**

to die for us. As we receive that love, we need to allow it to fill us to the point of overflowing, and then give it away. Only by doing this can we even begin to get our point across.

Love first and see how things change.

Another Verse:
1 Corinthians 16:14

Prayer

Lord, I pray that You will give me the instinct to love before I even begin to formulate my opinions. Let everything I think and say come from a place of genuine love. I know that before I can even be capable of doing this, I need to first receive Your love. So give me the humility to fall on my face and allow You to refresh me in Your true love. I thank You so much that we are not all the same and that You make us original and unique. Help me to embrace and love that about myself and others. Thank You that I can talk to You about anything and everything anytime. I love You so much! Amen.

UNPLUGGED
a deeper look

As we take sides, how can we determine if we're "taking the side" God is on? It is important that if we claim to be on God's side, that we walk with Him and seek Him on a daily basis. Some of us are the strongest advocates for God when

we are on the defense. The more we know about Him, the closer we will walk with Him. When we are coming from a place of peace and acting in love, we are on God's side.

Can God remove our selfish desire for being right, and fill us with His desire for oneness? Absolutely. Again, as we seek Him, we learn about Him and His nature. We already know how much He loves us through His actions. It is up to us to receive that love and consequently, reciprocate it. In the process of falling in love with God, we find that it is no longer about being right or winning the game. It's about being in love with Him and becoming one. It flips our world around, along with our priorities and motives.

BACKSTAGE PASS
getting to know

Favorite Books: *Blue Like Jazz* by Donald Miller and *Hinds' Feet on High Places* by Hannah Hurnard

Musical Influences: Stevie Wonder, Aretha Franklin, Coldplay, Keane, and Sixpence None the Richer

What is God teaching you now? That it's okay to sit back and soak Him in. I've always been someone to go 90 miles per hour through every task in life. He's showing me the beauty in slowing down and how much I miss out on when I run too fast.

How has your family helped you in your walk with God? They stay real with me. They are the best at telling me what I need to hear, whether I want to hear it or not. They help me to look at my life from the outside, and help me to keep myself in check. Most importantly, they talk to God about me, and that's the most special thing in the world.

How do you plan to expand your ministry in the future? I hope to jump out of my comfort zone and spend time with people that don't think or live the way that I do - make them wonder about the joy and love that's inside of me, and where it comes from. Whether that's through music, or church, or some community program, I feel like God is gearing me up for something like that.

Birthday:
January 8

Favorite Bible Verse:
Proverbs 3:5-6

Website:
www.rachaellampa.com

Booking Agency:
Creative Artists Agency
615-383-8787
www.caaccm.com

Fan Mail Address:
Rachael Lampa Fan Mail
P.O. Box 331366
Nashville, TN 37203

Fan Email Address: rachael@rachaellampa.com

BRAD MILES

MATTHEW 10

This passage is one of the hardest and most exciting passages in Scripture. In this chapter, Jesus is sending out the twelve disciples. This is the first major thing that they have been asked to do, and I'm sure they were really excited. Listen to the instruction Jesus gives them, though.

First, He tells them not to take any money or anything they could use to provide for themselves. He is commanding them to leave themselves completely at the mercy of the places they will be going. Immediately after telling them this, He tells them that He is sending them out like sheep among wolves. He goes to great lengths to describe how they will be persecuted, how they will be alone, how even those closest to them will betray them. Honestly, everything Jesus describes happening to them actually happened to Him. When I read this passage I can feel my stomach drop. Jesus says, "Leave behind anything you could take that might help you on your journey and go out into the world like sheep among wolves." He might as well have said, "Tie pieces of raw meat to your legs and walk through the lion's den." He calls them to do something and then immediately tells them, "This is going to hurt."

I can tell you that, over the last year, I have felt much like those disciples must have felt. It's easy to become discouraged or confused when you do exactly what you feel like the Lord is calling you to do, and that calling leads you into incredible hardship or even hurtful situations. I have spent time crying out to Him and questioning Him. I have wondered what He could possibly be doing, and I have questioned the truth of the promises found in Romans 8:28 and Jeremiah 3:11.

There is more to this passage, though. Listen to Jesus tell the disciples that He will provide for them. Hear Him say that He will rise up against those who treat them badly. He lets them know that things are going to be hard, but He doesn't leave them there. He says, "God knows when two sparrows, who are sold for a dollar, fall to the ground. He has numbered every hair on your head, so don't be afraid. You are much more valuable than sparrows."

This Christian life is not easy. It often leads us into hardship. It polarizes even the people we love, and we have to lose our life to really find it in Him. The promise is that **the wonder of knowing God somehow begins to happen when we have to trust Him completely**. The promise also is that He only acts in our best interest. It doesn't always feel that way. Sometimes we just have to blindly trust that it is true. In that trusting, though, the glorious mystery of a relationship with God is revealed.

Prayer

Lord, please help me to not allow my circumstances to dictate what I believe to be true about You. Help me to learn to trust You completely and to follow You fearlessly. Give me the strength and the wisdom to place my life in Your hands even when I am most afraid to do that. Remind me that I will never regret a decision to trust You.

UNPLUGGED
a deeper look

Does God understand when we question His commands and our calling? The wonderful thing about God is that He is big enough for our questions. Jeremiah 29:13 says, we will seek

Brad Miles Brad Miles Brad Miles Brad Miles Brad Miles

Him and we will find Him when we seek Him with all of our heart. He is faithful to come to us, and ultimately, the answer we seek is His love. God, Himself, is our answer. We find peace in the knowledge that God is good and at work doing good in our lives. Questions, followed by faithful obedience and trust, cause us to grow immeasurably in our relationship with God, and allow us to see His goodness and blessing at work in our lives.

As humans, we often want to take control - but isn't that when we need God the most? What can we control? We don't have and never will have control. Even when we feel like we are taking the reins, God's sovereignty trumps all of our efforts. When we feel like acting outside of our relationship with God, apart from His counsel, we are playing into the hands of the Enemy, who seeks to devour us. As we abide in Christ, we act in accordance with the leadership of His Holy Spirit. This is the path of victory. Striking out on our own, making decisions not based on an intimate relationship with the Father, leaves us exposed. Satan would like nothing more than to convince us that God is not an active part of our daily lives, that we don't need to "pray without ceasing" (1 Thessalonians 5:17 NKJV), as Paul exhorts us to do. If we marginalize God in our lives, we allow the Enemy access. Christ in us is our hope of glory.

If we say no to God's leading, can we fulfill the purpose He has for our life? This is a tough question. I don't think we can live the abundant life He desires from us if we resist His will. God's purposes and sovereignty are so far above my limited understanding that I have difficulty getting my mind around them. I'm not sure that God is ever surprised by my disobedience. I do think, however, that I miss His blessing for me when I choose to ignore His calling.

BACKSTAGE PASS
getting to know

Favorite Books: *The Jesus I Never Knew* by Philip Yancey, *A Tale of Two Cities* by Charles Dickens, and *Revolution in World Missions* by K.P. Yohannan

Musical Influences: U2, Coldplay, Creedence Clearwater Revival, Counting Crows, Delirious, and David Crowder

What is God teaching you now?   That knowing Him and seeking His face are all that matter. The stuff that I do for Him is just stuff without a consistent relationship with Him. He is teaching me to passionately pursue knowing Him.

How has your family helped you in your walk with God? My wife and daughter are pictures of God's grace to me. If I ever doubt God's faithfulness or His desire to bless me, all I have to do is look at my family to see that He has, and He is.

How do you plan to expand your ministry in the future? I just want to be used by God to pour out His Holy Spirit in me and on others. I want to experience the powerful movement of His Spirit through my life and music and watch that transform lives. Over the past year, God has been drawing me to a place where that is all I care about.

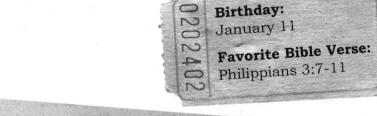

Birthday:
January 11

Favorite Bible Verse:
Philippians 3:7-11

Booking:
Amy Miles
918-289-8557
amiles8595@yahoo.com

Fan Mail Address:
Brad Miles
c/o First United Methodist Church
1115 S. Boulder
Tulsa, OK 74119

Website: www.myspace.com/bradmilesmusic

CRYSTAL LEWIS

MEMORIZING SCRIPTURE

As a kid, I remember being rewarded for memorizing Scripture verses. We got "Bible Bucks." We got points toward a camp scholarship. We got applause when we recited them in front of the congregation on Sunday night. Yes, you could easily consider this bribery. What we, the kids, didn't realize was that we were being doubly rewarded. We received our bucks, points, and applause, yes, but we also received valuable knowledge and the beginnings of wisdom with each memorized verse. The act of committing a verse or passage of the Bible to memory means becoming so well acquainted with a thought, a value, a concept, an idea, a command, that it becomes cemented in your mind. So much so, that when the time comes for that idea or command to be put into action, it's immediately accessible. Okay, I'm totally dating myself here, but in the movie "The Karate Kid," Daniel is taught a number of karate skills without his knowing it, through the teaching of washing and waxing the cars, sanding the floor, and painting the fence. He is so irritated by the fact that he's been doing chores instead of actually training in karate, that he loses his temper and explodes with frustration at Mr. Miyagi, his wise and knowledgeable teacher. Mr. Miyagi responds with a series of punches and blocks that Daniel is able to defend, and is pleasantly surprised at his ability to do so. Turns out, he's been training all along. Memorizing Scripture can have this effect, as well. We learn them, memorize them, and when the time comes (i.e. when we are faced with temptation, weakness, sadness, fear), we are able to combat those things with the Word of God as our strength.

The Bible says in Psalm 119:11 (NIV), "I have hidden your word in my heart that I might not sin against you." Does that mean that if the writer of that psalm had not hidden God's Word in his heart that he would've sinned? Maybe. Probably. God speaks to us through His Word. If we don't know His Word, how can we know what to do and what not to do? The Bible is a source of strength and power. In Hebrews 4:12 (NIV) it says, "... the Word of God is living and active. Sharper than any double-edged sword ..." In Ephesians 6 (NIV), the Word of God is referred to as "the sword of the spirit," part of an armor that must be put on. I think these references to weapons and armor signify the fact that we are in a battle! We are pursued by an Enemy that wants nothing less than our destruction. John 10:10 (NIV) says, "The thief comes only to steal, and kill and destroy ..." We must fight!! And **the way we fight is by the Spirit, with the Word**.

The first step is to get out your Bible and begin to read it. As you come across verses that speak to you, inspire you, motivate you, or convict you, write them down. I like to write things more than once, in different places. For instance, I might write the verses down in my journal, and then transfer them one by one onto small cards that I can tuck into my pocket or purse. One idea is to choose one verse to learn and memorize each week. Just keep reading it until you can recite it by memory. Repeat it to yourself as often as you think of it. Before long you'll have a collection of verses, both written on paper and on your heart, that you can draw from whenever you need them.

Be encouraged that God knows exactly what you need to hear and when you need to hear it. He will faithfully speak to you through His Word as you faithfully seek Him.

More Verses:
Psalm 119:9-11
Deuteronomy 6:6-9
James 1:22
Colossians 3:16

Crystal Lewis Crystal Lewis Crystal Lewis Crystal

Prayer

Jesus, I pray that You will teach me Your ways through Your Word. I ask for Your strength to keep me on the right path. I want to hide Your word in my heart, that I might not sin against You. My desire is to know You more and serve you better. Thank You Jesus, for the life You give. Amen.

UNPLUGGED
a deeper look

How has memorizing Scripture helped you personally? It has helped me realize my need to do so! I have been in situations where I needed help, mentally/spiritually, and I couldn't recall a verse. It's like almost drowning. Now I know how badly I need it. The Word of God is my protection, my weapon. I live by it.

How can teenagers learn not to become bored with Bible verses just because they hear them a lot? You've got to change your perspective. I grew up hearing the same Bible verses over and over, too. When I finally wised up and decided to be willing to look at things differently, I began to see the truth and life-giving power of the Word. It takes humility. It takes willingness. It takes surrender. It doesn't take physical eyes to see, it takes spiritual ones.

What are some tips for teenagers on memorizing Scripture? Songs work great! Putting a simple melody to a verse will cement it in your mind. I also like to write verses down on business-card size cards. Technology being what it is today, this is something that can be done in very creative ways. Use your imagination. Then put them all together in a box or basket and take one randomly every Monday morning on your way out the door. Keep it in your pocket or your purse and read it every once in awhile during the day. When you're reading your Bible, each time you come across a verse that you want to remember, write it down and add it to your collection. Jesus speaks to us in many ways, always through His Word. When we meditate on a verse or passage of Scripture, God will speak, comfort, heal, and strengthen.

BACKSTAGE PASS
getting to know

Favorite Books: *Hinds' Feet on High Places* by Hannah Hurnard, *East of Eden* by John Steinbeck, *The Screwtape Letters* by C.S. Lewis, *Waking the Dead* by John Eldredge, *Wisdom of Tenderness* by Brennan Manning, and *A Wrinkle in Time* by Madeleine L'Engle

Musical Influences: My musical influences are quite varied. I like, appreciate, and am inspired by a lot of different kinds of music. My earliest influences were Keith Green, the Winans family, and Aretha Franklin.

What is God teaching you now? God continues to teach me the importance and necessity of cultivating the fruit of the Spirit in my life - and the importance of surrender and trust.

Crystal Lewis Crystal Lewis Crystal Lewis Crystal Lewis Crystal

How has your family helped you in your walk with God?
Being married and having kids sheds a whole new light on being the bride of Christ and on the relationship between God and I as father/daughter.

How do you plan to expand your ministry in the future?
I don't. If God has a plan that includes me, great!

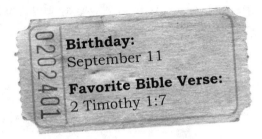

Birthday:
September 11

Favorite Bible Verse:
2 Timothy 1:7

Website:
www.crystallewis.com

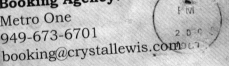

Booking Agency:
Metro One
949-673-6701
booking@crystallewis.com

Fan Mail Address:
Crystal Lewis
c/o Metro One
425 30th Street, Suite 10
Newport Beach, CA 92663

Fan Email Address: questions@metro1music.com

NewSong

More Than A Feeling

Michael O'Brien

$\mathcal{M}$ost people believe that if you see someone walking around with a smile on their face, life must be treating them pretty well - or maybe they are just having a good day. True? Maybe. Most likely not. I have found in this day and age, that there is much more going on in someone's heart than the look they may be displaying to those around them. While the world is singing, "Don't worry, be happy," I can't help but think, is life really about happiness? After doing some personal research, I've come to believe that it isn't. As a matter of fact, the Bible states that we will suffer. Make you want to be a Christian? Maybe not. But don't stop there; the best is yet to come.

When you become a Christian, a common problem may arise. A simple smile can become a mask. Or better yet, a lie. I've met people who generally don't want to be a burden, so they don't deal with the real issues that they may be facing in life. They keep it to themselves. They may even become their own counselor. They may say things like, "You have nothing to complain about. You aren't starving. You have a roof over your head and a good job. Get it together. You are fine." I used to be just like that until it finally caught up with me and my foolish heart. A funny thing happens **when you are open to the Holy Spirit working in your life - He actually will**. But I confess, it wasn't happy time. I heard someone quote a Scripture that says, "Joy comes in the morning ..." (Psalm 30:5 NKJV), but guilt and shame were there for me. The still, small voices came, also - things like, "You're not a Christian? You'll never be what God wants you to be. You might as well give up." The feelings that came from hearing something like that were overwhelming. But I knew there was more to the story. Good news. Jesus had overcome the world. I had to cling to the promise. I knew God would never allow me to go through anything that He knew I couldn't handle. That gave me hope beyond my human perspective.

I love James 1:2-3. I know that he is not talking about denying the pain that you might be going through. It's not implying that if something tragic happens in your life, to put on a smile and say, "Great!! This is awesome!! More pain, please!!" I think the joy he's talking about is more than a human feeling. It's believing by faith that God will never leave us or forsake us. Knowing that, we have a shoulder to cry on. He is right there hurting with us. I think joy also comes from knowing that God is there to teach us something about ourselves, if we are open to it. Don't get me wrong; feelings are good, but I don't think our goal in life is to be happy. I think our goal in life is to be more like Christ. That may bring many more feelings than one may think. I have also learned that pain is part of the healing process. So don't miss out on this thing called joy. It's something worth looking into.

Prayer

Lord, help me to face the trials that come my way with a joy that only comes from knowing You - knowing that You are there to help me through it.

UNPLUGGED
a deeper look

What are tips you would give teens on how not to lose the initial joy they have after just accepting Christ into their lives? Believe in what the Bible says about being saved. If you believe in your heart that He died for you, and you have confessed with your mouth that He is Lord, you are saved and no feeling can take that away. Cling to the promise. - Michael

Do you think our joy grows as we mature as Christians and in the assurance of heaven that we have? I think it becomes harder because you love more people. More people, more problems. It's in the valley where we find hope. Heaven is an awesome place, but we have a life to live down here, and with it comes trials. Excitement comes in knowing that this is not the end of the story ... - Michael

MY PURE JOY

Billy Goodwin

On Christmas Eve in 1980, I watched in amazement as my baby daughter was born into this world. We had already chosen her name, but the next morning when I came into the hospital room to visit my wife and newborn daughter, our name for her was confirmed. I saw her little head sticking out of a Christmas stocking that she was stuffed in. She was our little "Joy," and we were excited about the joy she would bring to our lives in the years to come.

I became a Christian more than 40 years ago, and my journey with Jesus has been filled with joy and peace that passes understanding. Even though joy is usually associated with an outward expression of emotion, I think real joy goes much deeper. My wife and I have been married for more than

Newsong Newsong Newsong Newsong

32 years, and over those years, our love for each other has grown much deeper because of the time we have spent working through struggles, as well as sharing victories together. She gives me great joy in my life, not just because of what she does, but for who she is and for her unconditional love for me. It is the same in my relationship with my heavenly Father. **The more time I spend with Him** and learn about His nature and character, **the deeper my love for Him grows** and the more joy He brings to my life.

When I reflect on God's forgiveness in my life, it brings me joy (Romans 4:7-8). Even when troubles come in my life, I can view them as opportunities for joy (James 1:2). Because I have received such love from God, it makes me want to bring joy to Him in the way I live and serve Him. Joy is a fruit of the Spirit (Galatians 5:22), and it will always be present in the life of someone who is living in a right relationship with God.

UNPLUGGED
a deeper look

Oftentimes teens get caught up in overcoming a trial. As James 1:2 tells us, how can we view these troubles as opportunities for joy? We need to view trials in life the same as we view any other challenge. As we step up to the challenge and overcome the problem, it makes us stronger and builds character in us. We grow stronger physically by exerting beyond the demand placed on us. We grow stronger mentally by applying the things we have already learned to solve a problem, and we grow stronger spiritually by exercising the faith we have and trusting God to always work things for our good. There is little joy in focusing on the trial we are facing, but if we focus on God's desire to grow us through the trial, this results in what is said in James 1:3-4 (NLT), "For when your faith is tested, your endurance has a chance to grow. So let it grow, for when your endurance is fully developed, you will be strong in character and ready for anything." - Billy

How can kids who lack joy examine their relationship with God, and find themselves excited about their faith again? When a trial comes that begins to take my joy away, I try to reflect back on the many times God has brought me through other trials. I always go to my favorite verse in Lamentations 3:22-23 and claim the promise that God's mercies are new every morning, and because of that, we are not consumed by the trials of life. When I reflect on God's unchanging nature in the midst of the confusion and turmoil of circumstances in my life, I can always have joy in His faithfulness. - Billy

BACKSTAGE PASS
getting to know

How did the band meet and form? The original four members attended the same church. We felt God calling us to take the leap into public ministry for Him; so we leapt.

Do you feel God leading the band in a special direction? Our unity of purpose has always been a call to ministry, so we strive to keep following in that direction.

How does the band plan to further its ministry in the future? Just to continue to trust God to guide us, to direct our ministry path, and to give us length of service.

NewSong NewSong NewSong NewSong

Birthdays:
Eddie: January 17
Matt: October 18
Billy: September 29
Michael: August 23

Favorite Bible Verses:
Eddie: Philippians 3:10
Matt: Psalm 119:11
Billy: Lamentations 3:22-23
Michael: Philippians 4:13

Website:
www.newsongonline.com

Booking Agency:
GOA, Inc.
615-790-5540
www.goa-inc.com

Fan Mail Address:
VanLiere-Wilcox
Attn: NewSong
P.O. Box 646
Franklin, TN 37065

Fan Email Address: hello@vanlierewilcox.com

Everlife

One More Mistake

"The greatest mistake you can make in life is to be continually fearing you will make one." - Elbert Hubbard

"For I am the LORD, your God, who takes hold of your right hand and says to you, 'Do not fear; I will help you'" (Isaiah 41:13 NIV).

As I spoke with a friend the other day, she told me that she was always fearful of doing the wrong thing, so she very often did nothing. She was so afraid of making the "wrong" decision that she took the "no risk" road, and just walked away. Unfortunately, she has reiterated that *that* road was filled with regret, dismay, and wondering, "What could have been?" and "What if?"

I began to mentally picture all of the accomplishments of people in history that "risked" all to complete their actions. George Washington, Martin Luther King, Alexander Graham Bell, the apostle Paul, and even Col. Sanders of the famous Kentucky Fried Chicken. He actually began over and over again so many times, that he was 65 years of age before his product was recognized - a true "faith walk." We would definitely be living in a different world if these individuals had never taken that "first step." What if these people had just given up before they even started, due to the fear of making a mistake?

Mistakes help us to learn both good and bad. Mistakes help us to listen and to reevaluate what we need to do right the next time. Is making a mistake enjoyable? Of course not, but I believe that it humbles us. We even forget about that other sin - the one of "not doing"- of omission.

"Anyone, then, who knows the good he ought to do and

doesn't do it, sins" (James 4:17 NIV).

Hmmm, that's a tough one, but God, as usual, has a way around it. No worries here. As leaders for Christ, we need to get rid of that fear of failure and replace it with a sound mind. Will doing that secure the fact that you will no longer make mistakes? Oh, no, there are more to come. But the biggest mistake that you can make is to not allow yourself to "make a mistake." If there has been something that the Lord has been leading you to do lately, and your fear has been one of making a mistake, then today is the day to take the leap, and learn from the outcome. **No worries; He will help you**!

Prayer

Dear Lord, You have given us a spirit of peace, not fear. Help us each time that "fear" knocks at the door, to answer it with "confidence" and the "blessed assurance" that You are right by our side. Give us the wisdom and discernment to "go" when we are supposed to and to "not go" when You want us to wait! We are listening, Lord.

UNPLUGGED
a deeper look

Could our fear of making a mistake prevent us from doing something that could make a difference in the Kingdom? Yes, I believe that fear in any sense makes us freeze up, run the other way, or shrink from opportunities we would otherwise have loved to take hold of. God has not given us a spirit of fear, but the complete opposite, that of love and a sound mind. Knowing that can help us when we seem afraid of showing compassion to others or sharing the gospel - our courage comes from the Lord.

He promises to always be with us, but the way will not always be easy. **Is there such a thing as a "no-risk road" when God has called us to a purpose?** We know that it says in Jeremiah 29:11 (NIV) that God has "… plans to prosper you and not to harm you, plans to give you hope and a future." We all have a purpose in life that God has called us to, but without bumpy roads, how will we appreciate the smooth ones? A "no-risk road" would mean a life lived without faith, and I don't believe that when God is in control of your life, He will ever let your circumstances bring you to where you aren't living and walking in faith.

Does the Bible say we should continue to pursue a goal, even though we are fearful? I do believe that we should continue to pursue the goal, even when fear and worry come along. The Bible says that perfect love casts out fear (1 John 4:18 NKJV), and God is the perfect love. Therefore, when we are called by God and become a little uneasy, just turn back to God and He will replace that fear with comfort and a reassurance of what you are supposed to do.

BACKSTAGE PASS
getting to know

How did the group meet and form? Wow, the three of us have been singing and doing dramas together since I can remember. We would always make up skits and perform them for our parents or neighbors. The group was "officially" formed in 1997, and it was actually Julia's idea. She was 8 at the time and came to me saying she wanted to start a band. I was all for it; it took a little convincing with Amber, but she finally gave in. We started, just wanting to have a positive effect on people's lives and have them go away from our concerts feeling more alive and free. We've been going ever since, and plan on doing this as long as we can. :) - Sarah

Do you feel God leading the group in a special direction? The three of us are blown away by the opportunities that God is allowing us to have. We feel so blessed to be doing what we love to do, with the ones that we love the most. We really want to be completely in God's will, always listening to His voice and knowing which step He wants us to take next. The direction of Everlife has always been changing lives in any way possible, whether that be playing concerts, doing radio interviews, or talking one on one after the shows. Whatever it may be, we are Everlife, to share the talents God has given to us and to show God to other people. - Sarah

How does the group plan to further its ministry in the future? Something all three of us have always wanted to do is to find a young group that is just getting started and help them along the way - to share with them what we have learned about the music business, and about being on the road - to help them further their own ministry. So many people have been mentors to us, and without their support and guidance, we wouldn't be where we are today. We want to keep doing what we're doing, playing as much as we possibly can, and being in God's will. - Amber, Sarah, & Julia

Birthdays:
Amber: May 31
Sarah: March 24
Julia: June 13

Favorite Bible Verses:
Amber: Jeremiah 29:11-13
Sarah: Philippians 4:13
Julia: Psalm 91

Website:
www.everlifeonline.com

Booking Agency:
Craig Bruck
International Creative Management Talent
212-556-5684
www.icmtalent.com

Fan Mail Address:
Everlife
P.O. Box 680175
Franklin, TN 37068-0175

Fan Email Addresses:
amber@everlifeonline.com
sarah@everlifeonline.com
julia@everlifeonline.com

OVERFLOW

PATIENCE AND GOD'S TIMING

Josh Cromer

*T*hink back with me over the span of your life. I don't know about you, but I can think of so many times when I had my mind made up that I knew exactly *what* I needed for my life and *when* I needed it. I can think of hundreds of plans I had for my life in my nearly 24 years on earth, and I just knew they were the right thing. I was so certain that I would follow through with those plans and dreams, finally realizing that they weren't the best idea. I would feel so sure that something was right, then everything would seemingly fall apart right in front of me. This would leave me questioning why it didn't work out like I had planned, and at times I would find myself angry with God, not knowing why He would let this happen.

God tells us in Jeremiah 29:11 (NIV), "For I know the plans I have for you, plans to prosper you and not to harm you, plans to give you hope and a future." As humans, the idea of not having absolute control of our "destiny" can be a concept that is hard to grasp, especially living in a society that tells us we must be "number one" or we're "no one." After being constantly bombarded with the idea that there is no room for second place, we don't want to put our dreams and desires in the hands of someone else, for fear that they may alter the outcome and cost us everything. This is in no way saying that having dreams and goals is wrong; in fact, it's encouraged, and the desire to succeed is admirable, but the problem comes when we let ourselves undertake the task of planning our lives apart from God. We should do as David did in Psalm 143:10

and **pray, asking God to guide us in seeking His will for our lives**, because we know His plan and timing for our lives is perfect, and His will is to prosper us and give us hope.

More Verses:
Psalm 37:5-7

Prayer

Father, thank You for being a God who loves me so much that You would send Your Son to die for me, so that I may experience real life. And Lord, I pray that as I live my life I would seek to do Your will and glorify You in all that I do. Grant me patience and a willingness to live every day of my life fully for You. I love You and I pray this in Your Son's name, Amen.

UNPLUGGED
a deeper look

Especially during the teen years, it's hard to wait for an answer for something we want. Is there anything teenagers can do to handle waiting and trusting in God's time? In the world we live in, we are not used to having to wait for things. We have "pay-at-the-pump" gas stations, fast food, and phones that go with us everywhere. The idea of not getting something done immediately has become a foreign thing to us. As a teenager, I think the easiest way to remain patient is to realize that the best outcome will result when we wait on God. If we take time to realize that God promises that He knows what is best for us, and that it will occur when He is ready, then it makes it easier for us to take comfort in waiting. When we pray and ask God to instill within us things such as patience, we must also ask Him for the strength to endure the tests that come along with it. With something such as patience, it seems as if the minute we ask God for it, a trying time happens. Why is that? It's because to develop something like patience, we must first put it into practice. These times are not always fun, and if we try to endure them on our own, we will usually fall flat on our face. We will rush to make decisions, or we will do something that we're questioning, just because the wait is driving us crazy. So, when you pray for patience, pray for strength and understanding of God's timing and His perfect will. - Josh

"Patience is a virtue." Easier said than done. How can teens understand what patience is in a godly perspective? Patience is so hard to put into practice. We want success now, we want a new relationship now. We want it all now. A quick fix isn't going to make us happy. We need to be patient with God to supply us with what we truly need. Let Him who sees and knows all decide when the time is right. We also need to be patient with one another, in spite of each other's faults. - Tom

Do you believe that God answers our prayers - even though it may take years to fulfill it? Yes. We have to remember that God doesn't always answer our prayers with a "Yes." The answer can very well be a "No." God opens doors, and He also closes them, but all are to our benefit. Remember that God sees the big picture, and we only see a tiny part of it. Even if we make a bad decision, God uses that to mold us into the people He wants us to be. Right now, things may not be exactly the way we like them, but as God's plan for us unfolds, we can look back and see that what God did was the right move. - Mark

BACKSTAGE PASS
getting to know

How did the band meet and form? We've been together for as long as I can remember ... Mark, Matt, Will, and I all grew up in the same small town in South Carolina. It wasn't until around the ninth grade that we decided it was time to start a band, so we devised a plan. For Christmas that year, we each asked our parents for our respective instrument, and that's when it all started. Josh is the group's most recent addition. God has blessed us so much. It constantly blows my mind that our job is to hang out with our best friends and play music together. And the coolest thing is, it's not just music, it is music that is effective for Him. - Tom

Do you feel God leading the band in a special direction?
We feel called to the church, whether it is the actual church establishment or places like youth camps. We know all bands have different callings in ministry, but for the five of us, being brought up in the church and knowing how important that was to our development, we want to offer encouragement and stay focused on the church. However, we will never limit God, so as we continue in our ministry, we are constantly praying about God's direction for us and seeking His will alone for this band. - Josh

How does the band plan to further its ministry in the future?
As a band, it has always been our desire to seek God's will for every aspect of what we do - from the style of music we play, to the lyrics we write, to the venues we perform in. From the get-go we have felt God calling us to be geared more towards the church (as in the body of Christ, not specifically the church building), and that is why we primarily do Christian events. As we continue to grow and put out records, we are constantly seeking God for guidance on who He wants our songs to speak to, what He wants us to say through our words and music, as well as where He wants us to go and play. His will and timing are perfect, and those are the things we seek to follow as we look to the future of Overflow. - Josh

Favorite Bible Verses:
Tom: Philippians 4:13
Mark: 1 Corinthians 9:19
Matt: Philippians 4:12
Will: Psalm 23:5
Josh: John 3:30

Birthdays:
Tom: March 25
Mark: April 12
Matt: April 11
Will: November 30
Josh: October 17

Booking Agency:
Jeff Roberts & Associates
615-859-7040
www.jeffroberts.com

Website:
www.OverflowRocks.com

Fan Email Address:
FlowFans@OverflowRocks.com

SARAH KELLY

PAUL AND SILAS APPROACH TO LIFE

$\mathcal{P}$aul and Silas were beaten that day. Probably bruised and bleeding, they chose to worship God in the middle of a jail cell at midnight (Acts 16). In a time that it might have looked to them like God was nowhere, and maybe even had forgotten them, they chose to take their thoughts captive and worship. This is what I believe "worshipping in spirit and truth" means ... releasing our faith in the middle of our circumstances - not pretending to not have doubts and hard times ... but worshipping through them. The day that I realized this, my life was changed forever. I don't know what you've been through lately, but what I do know is that no matter how far or how quiet God seems, He is waiting patiently for your blind trust. He wants to show you that **He knows what you want so much better than you ever will.** Paul and Silas probably weren't thinking, "Maybe if we worship, our chains might fall off and these prison walls might fall." No, they were probably thinking something more like ... "God, we can't see You or feel You right now, but we trust that You will bring us through this, and even though we can't see a way out, we trust that You will take care of us. Your will, not ours."

Later, it says that not only their own chains fell off, but everyone in the prison was also freed. I believe that the worth of our worship is not measured by the words in our song, but rather by the faith that we release into our lives through our song. It says in the Bible that if we have faith the size of a mustard seed, we can move a mountain (Matthew 17:20). If a couple of us will worship with all our hearts and all our faith, "living hallelujah"... instead of just singing it ... I believe those around us, even if they are not asking for it, will be changed and freed, just as those in the prison were freed.

"MATTER OF TIME"

(This is a song that I wrote out of the perspective of Paul and Silas. I tried to guess what their song might have sounded like.)

I choose to trust You even through the fire
Even when my eyes can't see, I know You're right beside me
I will always praise You, Lord, no matter what may come
Because You have been so faithful to me

So I will dream and I'll believe that what
You've promised soon I will see

It's just a matter of time till I'll see Your face ...
Till I'll dance in Your presence and sing out Your praise
It's just a matter of time till I'll hear You say,
"Well done."

Another Verse:
Acts 16:25

UNPLUGGED
a deeper look

Your devotion talks about "living hallelujah." How do you advise teens who may be going through tough situations to do this daily? Worship is more than a song, more than a lifestyle ... IT IS OUR LIFE. Where do our thoughts, talk, and time go? This is a good way to gauge what our life is worshipping.

We must praise God in thankfulness even when our hearts are heavy. Can doing this help to revive our spirits? It can do more than revive our spirits. I believe that our faith within our worship, during tough times, has the power to free us - and those around us, too.

Do you think Paul and Silas's worshipful attitudes affected the outcome of their situation - that they were freed from prison? Can we follow in the footsteps of Paul and Silas? I personally believe that it was the faith within their worship that freed them. If we believe that the faith of a mustard seed can move a mountain, like the Bible says, then how much can faith-filled worship in the middle of hard times accomplish? Worship was just a vehicle for their faith; I have experienced this in my own life, and they are my continual role models.

BACKSTAGE PASS
getting to know

Favorite Books: *Don't Sweat the Small Stuff - and it's all small stuff* by Richard Carlson and *The Money Book for the Young, Fabulous & Broke* by Suze Orman, and I love *Proverbs* and *Ecclesiastes*.

Musical Influences: Keith Green - from when I was a small child. I wrote my first song when I was 5 or so, on top of some of his chords. I guess you could say he taught me to write music.

What is God teaching you now? That He knows what we want so much better than we ever will. We can't dream big enough ... Take Me Away was an indie album to sell out of my trunk, so I could lead worship at my church for free ... and eight record deal offers and a Grammy® nomination later ... I am wondering whose life this is?

How has your family helped you in your new music adventure? My mom and dad have encouraged me since I was young. They always were telling me to sing loud, and boy did I listen! I have the best family a girl could ask for - not perfect, but no one ever has to wonder if they are loved.

How do you plan to expand your ministry in the future?
I am extremely excited about some of the doors that are opening for my band and me - looking forward to continuing going to public and private schools and colleges, and teaching songwriting. I believe everyone writes music, and I don't want to imagine my life without this outlet, so I am passionate about passing it on.

Birthday:
September 13

Favorite Bible Verse:
Acts 16:25

Website:
www.sarahkelly.com

Booking Agency:
Creative Artists Agency
615-383-8787
www.caaccm.com

Fan Mail Address:
Sarah Kelly
P.O. Box 159310
Nashville, TN 37215

Fan Email Address: sarahkellymusic@hotmail.com

WHISPER LOUD

PERSEVERANCE AND PERSISTENCE

Lauren Kaser

"Jeremiah did not resolve to stick it out for twenty-three years, no matter what; he got up every morning with the sun. The day was God's day, not the people's. He didn't get up to face rejection; he got up to meet with God. He didn't rise to put up with another round of mockery; he rose to be with his Lord. That is the secret of his persevering pilgrimage." - Eugene H. Peterson

When the road was rough and the path was long, Jeremiah chose endurance, because he knew the destination was worth it. When God places us in difficult situations and declines to eliminate the pressure, it is comforting to remember that **His grace enables us to keep going**. We have many opportunities for growth in our endurance, and we need to embrace all of them.

More Verses:
Romans 5:3-5

Prayer

Dear Lord, help me to seize the moment when I am facing trials, and do battle with Satan using perseverance and persistence. Help me to set my sights on pleasing God in every difficult situation that I face.

Whisper Loud Whisper Loud Whisper Loud Whisper

PRAY AND OBEY

Keri Blumer

*T*he most important thing in regard to your service in God's Kingdom is your ability to hear HIS voice. I know some of you are thinking …"Hear His voice … Does God REALLY talk?" … The truth is, **God does talk**, however, **the ears of our heart have to be focused and ready to hear God when He speaks**. Most importantly, they must be trained to hear God's voice … that's right, *trained* to hear His voice. We train by listening and obeying our parents, our teachers, our boss, people that are put in authority over us. Our life will never become anything if we can't train our flesh to listen and not just do or say *what* we want to, *when* we want to. I remember a time in my life when I was 18, still living at home. I was really praying for God to give me direction with my life. I was praying to hear His voice when my mom asked me to go get the keys to the car, and she was standing right by them. Being the good little teenager I was, I was thinking, "Go get them, yourself … what are you, lazy?" I remember plain as day, that little voice inside saying, "And you want Me to tell you what to do, when you can't even listen to your mother?"

Some of you reading this devotion right now might be having a really hard time getting along with your parents. (Trust me; it was only a couple of years ago when I was going through the same thing.) Sometimes your parents are going to ask or make you do something that you don't want to do, that just makes you mad (i.e. making you change clothes before you leave the house because they don't like your outfit, or not letting you stay out late to hang out with friends, or be alone with your boyfriend/girlfriend). And right now it doesn't make sense. You might be thinking, "I am old enough to make my own decisions." "They don't understand or trust me," or "It's MY life; who are they to tell me what to do!" It's not much different than when you were two years old, and you screamed for hours because your parents said, "NO!" when you were trying to stick a fork in the light socket and hurt or kill yourself. Now you are 14 years old and they are telling you not to smoke, or 16, telling you not to speed, or 18, telling you not to be alone with your boyfriend/girlfriend. These are all things that you have to listen and obey your parents about, 'cause they know what they are talking about. Listening and obeying isn't always fun, but it is for your own good.

PRESSING ON

Alana Warfel

"*F*orgetting what is behind and straining toward what is ahead, I press on toward the goal to win the prize for which God has called me heavenward in Christ Jesus" (Philippians 3:13-14 NIV).

Forgetting what is behind ... for me, I think that is the hard part. Paul is saying here that in order to persevere and press on, we must forget the past that holds so many mistakes and regrets, and look toward our goal - our prize. I've seen Satan dangle our sins and our mess ups, that God has already forgiven us for, right in front of our faces so many times. We have to just look past them and realize they are covered by the blood of Jesus! What has helped me the most in persevering through the hard times and being persistent in God's plan is this: I try to picture my life eternally, taking myself out of my present situations and focusing on the big picture - eternal life in heaven. I try to see my life through God's eyes. Also, it always helps to take my focus off of myself. I have to remind myself that it is NOT about ME! It is about serving God, and that means introducing people to Jesus Christ, my best friend. So I want to challenge *you* to **forget the past, press on toward heaven, look at your life eternally, and remember, it's not about you!** Most importantly of all ... PRAY! You want to persevere ... PRAY! You want to be persistent in God's plan ... PRAY!!

More Verses:
Romans 12:12
Proverbs 3:5-6

Whisper Loud Whisper Loud Whisper

Prayer

Lord, thank You so much for giving me the strength to endure anything that comes my way. Thank You for not giving me more than I can handle. Thank You for loving me so much that You sent Your Son to save me, that I can be in heaven with You someday! Lord, please give me patience to persevere through the hard times. And Lord, thanks for giving me what it takes to get through it all ... hope! I love You! In Jesus' name, Amen.

UNPLUGGED
a deeper look

How have you seen God work to help those who are pressing on in His service? I have seen my friends and myself be in need of specific things and amounts of money by a specific date, in order to go on missions trips that God has called us to go on, and God has always pulled through in providing *everything* that was needed! - Alana

God is constant! He is *always* working to help those who are pressing on for His service. - Keri

I know several people that put themselves in positions where they had to totally rely on God. The most amazing stories seem to come from those who had the ability and the opportunity to be very successful in the world's eyes, but they abandoned their opportunities to work in His service. I am convinced that those who are really seeking Him have nothing to fear, because God will direct their paths and take care of their needs. - Lauren

What tools can teenagers use to learn God's plan for them?
Nothing is better than the peace that comes inside of God's will.
This is truth - get into the Word of God to learn His plan. Those
are His own words! Next, ask Him. If you don't get an answer,
ask Him again. Don't forget to listen after you ask. Keep your
eyes, ears, and heart open. Ask the Holy Spirit to show you
things in the Word before you even open your Bible. - Alana

Honestly, there isn't a five-minute lesson plan that will give you
the exact details of what God's plan is for your life. Finding
God's plan for your life comes from living a daily life of worship
and praise to God. Then with every step of the day, God shows
you which way to go and what choices to make. I survive off of
every word that God says - that is how I pursue His will for my
life. And that is how I know His blessings are overflowing. - Keri

If we are focusing on having an intimate relationship with God,
and we are loving others as Christ loves us, we will stay in
God's will for our lives. I think God prompts each of us to a
decisive moment in which we surrender to His purposes. He
knows the desires of our hearts and He knows what is best for
us. The right doors will open and close because He wants to
make His children happy! - Lauren

BACKSTAGE PASS
getting to know

How did the group meet and form? Keri and I met through
an organization called American Kids when we were 12. I was
taking performance lessons from her mom, Rita (our manager
now). I joined a group Keri was already in called Kidz 4 Christ.
We have been singing together since then. Lauren joined us
in February, 2004. She was in American Kids, too. She also
went with us one year to GMA's Seminar in the Rockies, in
Estes Park, Colorado. We knew she was talented and in love
with God. She has done a tremendous job becoming a true
Whisper Chic! - Alana

Do you feel God leading the group in a special direction?
Yes. I feel that God is leading us to do what we call "Girl Fun
Days." We teach classes on being godly women, have fashion

shows, teach them some of our songs, and then end with a concert. We have been having a blast with the girls! - Alana

How does the group plan to further its ministry in the future? We hope to keep doing our "Girl Fun Days" and ministering in concert, God willing. We have a heart for girls and a vision to acknowledge the questions and problems that young women are facing today. We are currently putting on Girls' Conferences. We are hearing from so many of the girls and their moms ... just sharing that God moved in their lives at the girls' conference. It is so encouraging to our ministry when we hear from girls who have decided to restore their relationship with their mother or make a commitment to purity! Praise God for giving us the opportunity to be a part of that decision! - Lauren, Keri & Alana

Birthdays:
Keri: January 11
Alana: August 6
Lauren: April 17

Favorite Bible Verses:
Keri: Joshua 1:9
Alana: Psalm 25:4-5
Lauren: Proverbs 3:5 and
James 1:2-5

Website:
www.whisperloud.com

Booking Agency:
The Breen Agency
(615) 777-2227
www.thebreenagency.com

Fan Mail Address:
Whisper Loud
P.O. Box 856
Seiling, OK 73663

Fan Email Address: ritablumer@pldi.net

PHILMORE

QUIT FREAKING OUT

Justin Greiman

It seems lately like everyone I talk to is freaking out about the future. There is this mad rush to figure out what "God's Will For My Life Is," and then get immediately busy doing it. I'm not so sure that this is the way God intended it.

Take a look at 1 Thessalonians 5:16-18 (NKJV): "Rejoice always, pray without ceasing, in everything give thanks; for this is the will of God in Christ Jesus for you."

This passage doesn't mention where you choose to live, what career you pick, or even what kind of ministry you may be involved in. It reminds us that God's will is for us to be grateful and excited about what He is doing in our lives and to absolutely trust Him, both in the good times, and the not-so-good times. The rest is just details.

A few verses down in that same chapter is verse 24, "He who calls you is faithful, who also will do it."

Don't worry about how long things may seem to take in your life. We humans get so impatient and frustrated about time; God is interested in timing. He wants to connect us with others and bring things into our lives, but sometimes the timing isn't quite right yet. **He wants to make your life the most incredible life imaginable**, so let Him orchestrate the details of your life. And remember, Jesus didn't start His ministry until He was 30 years old.

So, enjoy your life with all the twists and turns that come along. Be faithful. Serve. Volunteer. Give. Come early and stay late. Trust God in every situation.

Just don't freak out.

More Verses:
Philippians 4:6-7

Prayer

God, I thank You that Your hand is on my life. I thank You that You have good plans for me. Help me to be patient, help me to trust You in every situation that comes along, help me to be faithful. My life is Yours, God. Use me the way You want to. Make me a blessing to everyone that I meet. And show people Your love through me. In Jesus' name, Amen.

UNPLUGGED
a deeper look

Do you think other people's "opinions" of what we're doing with our lives mean too much to us? Sometimes. Does the person *really* know you - your innermost dreams, goals, and desires? Or do they just give out advice to everybody? It is important to have at least one person in your life that you absolutely trust, that you are in "covenant" with, that can speak into your life. This person ought to know the Word of God intimately and be able to use it when discussing your plans for your life. They need to always bring you back to, "What does the Word say about ...?" A person with that kind of influence in your life can be huge in helping shape your destiny.

It is sometimes very hard to wait when we feel God's leading. Often we don't understand His timing. How can we learn to "wait upon the Lord?" Spend time with Him. Spend time in His Word. When you get to know Him and start to really understand His nature, you'll realize that He'll continually surpass your expectations. Things will always work out much better if you let Him bring things to pass, instead of making it happen on your own. He is able to carry out His purpose and do superabundantly, far over and above all that we dare ask or think, infinitely beyond our highest prayers, desires, thoughts, hopes, or dreams (Ephesians 3:20 AMP).

BACKSTAGE PASS
getting to know

How did the band meet and form? Kayle and I are brothers, so we met at a very early age.

Do you feel God leading the band in a special direction? Definitely. We commit a lot of prayer to all the details of writing and playing shows and everything else that we do. We feel strongly that God wants us to be out in the world, around people that don't know Jesus, and be a little light in a dark place. - Justin

How does the band plan to further its ministry in the future? For us, the band really isn't a ministry. It's a job, it's a creative outlet, it's something we're passionate about. Our lives are the ministry. God has called every believer to the ministry of reconciliation (2 Corinthians 5:17-18). Whether I'm a carpenter, or a salesman, or a guitar player, I'm going to love on people and show them what God is doing in my life, and how incredible He wants to make their life. I'm going to show them Jesus. - Justin

Birthdays:
Justin: October 13
Kayle: December 24

Favorite Bible Verses:
Justin: Colossians 3:1-3
Kayle: Romans 10:9

Website:
www.planetphilmore.com

SHAWN McDONALD

REAL OR FAKE?

"Oh come, let us worship and bow down: let us kneel before the Lord, our Maker" (Psalm 95:6 NKJV).

"I appeal to you therefore, brothers and sisters, by the mercies of God, to present your bodies as a living sacrifice, holy and acceptable to God, which is your spiritual worship" (Romans 12:1 NRSV).

As you read this, you are probably getting the sense that my writings are going to be about worship, and you are right. I am going to try to give a take you might never have thought of.

Our "Christian sub-culture" is all about worship. In fact, it has become quite the fad. "The latest and great Christian worship song." Now don't get me wrong, 'cause worship is the greatest thing we could ever give our God - to bow to Him and Him alone, how great is that? Music is so very close to my heart, and I believe it to be very powerful and healing, and a true form of worship. But worship could be, just being kind to a person that is in need of some kindness, or going into your room and hanging with God. I think you get the picture. Is the fad we're following truly worshipping God? My challenge today is more of a challenge of true and real worship. What I mean by this is that **worship is a lifestyle** - not a style of music, nor a song we sing, and definitely not something we do just Sunday mornings, but more **the attitudes of our hearts**. Doesn't God look at the heart of man? Or does He only look at our deeds? Was it not the Pharisees that would stand in the streets and sing and lift their hands to be seen - making people believe they were holy? Jesus said these men were just empty white-washed tombs (Matthew 15:8-9). How often do we go to church and sing the songs, yet never really think about God? We go home and say, "Worship was great this morning." What was so great about it? Was God really worshipped? It seems this is kind of how it has become. I know these are thoughts and words I have said before. I know that I am guilty of these things, but I hope for better days. I don't want to judge, so I can't say the motivation of one's heart, but I hope to reveal the truth and then encourage us to walk in it. I hope to live in our God and not just speak about Him. Let worship become the air we breathe and the day we live. Let worship become our lifestyle.

UNPLUGGED
a deeper look

Do you believe that how we receive the worship experience lies within our attitude? I do believe that our attitudes play a huge part of how we worship. I firmly believe that God is after our hearts, and our attitude plays a huge part of our hearts. I really think that you can worship God with anything outside of sin. If our heart is after God, then most likely our attitude will be, as well. It is the truth that sets us free, and our worship should be a freeing experience. If we are truly worshipping God, I think that people will be drawn in because of it.

How can Christian teens who desire to worship God with all of their beings change worship into something real, instead of the "popular thing to do?" I believe the only way we can truly worship God is with a wanting heart. You have to want it, making the popular thing disappear. Worship becomes real when it is truly something that you want to do. If the desire of your heart is to worship, then it really doesn't matter how or what it looks like. The Bible says do all things as if doing them before the Lord.

(left margin, vertical) Shawn McDonald Shawn McDonald

BACKSTAGE PASS
getting to know

Favorite Books: *The Ragamuffin Gospel* by Brennan Manning, *Blue Like Jazz* by Donald Miller, and *Waking the Dead* by John Eldredge

Musical Influences: Jenny Knapp, Shane & Shane, Ben Harper, and Dave Matthews

What is God teaching you now? To be Humble!

How do you plan to expand your ministry in the future? I plan to look to the Lord and let Him expand for me.

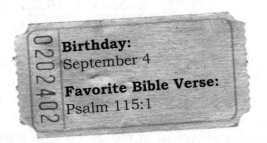

Birthday:
September 4

Favorite Bible Verse:
Psalm 115:1

Booking Agency:
Third Coast Artists Agency
615-297-2021
www.tcaa.biz

Fan Mail Address:
Shawn McDonald
P.O. Box 682546
Franklin, TN 37068

Website: www.shawnmcdonaldmusic.com

Joel Engle

Reverence For God

"But I, by your great mercy, will come into your house; in reverence will I bow down toward your holy temple ..." (Psalm 5:7 NIV).

Not too long ago, I had an interesting experience. I was in a hotel room in Nashville, recuperating from working on my latest recording project, when I inadvertently looked out my large bay window towards I-40 by the airport. Suddenly, I saw police motorcycles pass by, one ... two ... three ... eight ... ten ... and then police cars and black SUV's with antennas on top. Something big was going on in this town. At the end of the motorcade were ambulances and fire trucks. Then I remembered that the President of the United States of America was in town. Could this be the Presidential motorcade driving by my hotel? It certainly was. There had to be over 40 different vehicles pass by in its entirety.

I remember feeling a sense of awe and wonder. I thought about all the power and technology that was represented in that mile-long motorcade. The power to make life and history-altering decisions, and the power to protect the President from any would-be attackers. Several minutes later, I saw Air Force One prepare for take off. It was an absolutely huge and regal looking airplane. Needless to say, I was in awe. There was a moment of patriotic reverence that overtook me.

How much more reverent and in awe should we be when thinking about God? He is the King of Kings and Lord of Lords. He is the sovereign and all-powerful God of the universe, who is surrounded by the hosts of heaven who sing praise to His holy name night and day. **This is the God who spoke the universe into existence with the power of His Word.** This is the God who will judge the nations someday in His righteousness and wisdom. This is the God who sent His one and only, beloved Son to die on the cross for our sins. Should we not be in awe of Him every day of our lives? Should we not stand in allegiance with His Word and His way in all that we do? How often do we come into His sanctuary, utterly unamazed at Him? I know that I have been guilty of that many times in my life. We should never forget that this God is our Father and our Friend in Christ, and that we have access to Him through His Word and His Holy Spirit. We should never come to Him in a disrespectful manner, forgetting just how high and exalted He is - and how needy and dependent we are for Him. When is the last time that you and I stood in awe of God? The more I study Scripture for myself, the more I begin to realize just how huge, holy, and powerful God is and how much honor, reverence, and worship He deserves from me.

UNPLUGGED
a deeper look

What are some acts of reverence that you consider important to our spiritual discipline and walk with God? I think the first act of reverence would be to develop an intense love for God's Word. When we revere God's Word as the very breath of God (2 Timothy 3:16), we will develop what I like to call a "holy mentality." Obviously, the Bible teaches that as believers we don't have to live in the constant fear of God pouring out His wrath on us because of Christ's sacrifice, but it does teach that should respect and honor God in all we do or say (Colossians 3:17). I think that as we develop our heavenly mind-set (Colossians 3:1), that will turn almost everything we do into an act of reverence to God. The greatest act of worship is for us to surrender our hearts, and our minds, and our lives to Christ on a moment by moment basis.

Where should teens draw the line between having fun with their faith and being respectful and reverent toward God? There is absolutely nothing wrong with having a blast. If you hung out with me for awhile you might think I am crazy. I love sports and video games (although I am horrible at video games!) God created fun, but the way a Christian should have fun is very different than how the world has fun. I think the Bible gives us some awesome guidelines for our fun. Philippians 4:8 (NIV) says, "... whatever is true, whatever is noble, whatever is right, whatever is pure, whatever is lovely, whatever is admirable - if anything is excellent or praiseworthy - think about such things." God is not a killjoy. He is the most joyful and exciting person in all of the universe. He created life; He created us, and nobody understands fun like Him. The world has distorted what God has created. We find out what is acceptable through God's Word.

BACKSTAGE PASS
getting to know

Favorite Books: *Lifetime Guarantee* by Dr. Bill Gillham and *Commentary on Galatians* by Martin Luther

Musical Influences: Keith Green, Coldplay, Michael W. Smith, Sarah McLachlan, Matchbox Twenty, and Nichole Nordeman

What is God teaching you now? That I have to love God and people regardless of how I feel.

How has your family helped you in your walk with God? My wife is the kindest, most grace-giving person I know. She truly loves all people, regardless of who they are. She accepts people and truly cares for them. Her godly example in that area has really taught me a lot. My sweet little daughter, Elizabeth, has shown me how God must view us as children. I absolutely adore this child and constantly want to shower her with love and protection. I know that the Lord must feel that way about me, too. That's pretty cool.

How do you plan to expand your ministry in the future? I want to continue to write songs that impact people and authentically express my love and amazement at God. I would like to continue to build my conference ministry. I would also like to expand my influence on young people.

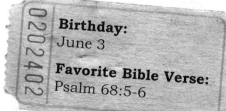

Birthday:
June 3

Favorite Bible Verse:
Psalm 68:5-6

Booking:
404-626-1728

Website:
www.joelengle.com
www.spin360.com

KENT BOTTENFIELD

SECOND CHANCES

There were way too many times in my career as a major league pitcher that my team would score a few runs and give us a lead, only for me to go back out to the mound next inning and give the lead right back to the opposing team. There were also numerous times when I did that, and my team would come back in and take the lead once again. I can't begin to explain the feeling of relief every time that happened. I felt like I had another chance to prove to my teammates that I was grateful for what they'd done, and I was up to the task of protecting the lead this time around.

Something similar recently happened to me in the game of life. At age 36 and only 3 years retired from the game, I drove myself to the emergency room with tightness in my chest. Once in the exam room, the doctors found my blood pressure was a little high, but all of my tests came back pretty normal.

When the cardiologist came in to see me, he said that even though my tests didn't show anything serious, he wanted to forego the standard procedure of a stress test for my heart and immediately do a cardio-catheter. This is where they go into your body through your leg and up into your heart to get a look at your arteries.

While I was lying conscious on the table and fully aware of what was going on around me, the surgeons' words hit me with a dose of reality I had never experienced in my life. I was informed that I had a 99% blockage of my main artery. It was later explained to me that had I not gone to the hospital, there was a good chance I would have been dead within hours.

Why did God allow me a second chance at life? Is it because He's good? Yes, God is good, not because He spared me, but because He's God!

Have you ever been given a second chance to make something right? Doesn't it feel great when you do?

Read Luke 13:6-8, and think about God as the owner of the field, Jesus as the man tending to it, and you as the fig tree. Have you become like the fig tree? I believe we all have at times in our lives, but **then comes the Son of second chances** who says, "Leave it alone for one more year, and I'll dig around it and fertilize it." Isn't it just like Jesus to stand up and take our failure to heart?

Maybe this short devotion is a part of your second chance. Are you ready to listen? Are you ready to honor God with your whole life?

Prayer

Oh, God, have mercy on me, a sinner. I realize that I am trying to keep parts of my life hidden from You. Thank You for being a God of second chances. I want You to take those ugly parts and make them beautiful again. I am grateful for what You've done for me, and through Your strength I will be up to the task of making the most out of this second chance for You. Amen.

UNPLUGGED
a deeper look

Can we make our own second chances as we study Scripture and are convicted of our sin? I believe that when we are studying Scripture, God reveals Himself through His Word. I don't believe we are making our own second chance; I believe it is one of the ways God reaches and teaches us, and provides us with that second chance.

Do you think the world confuses coincidences with God's second chances? Are we as Christians also guilty of not recognizing God's hand in these events? I believe a lot of times we are no different than the world in this area, because human nature lends itself to wanting control of a situation. We like to feel we have a say in a given matter and its outcome, so it can be more comforting to some to chalk it up to coincidence. I think the difference comes in the fact that a lot of people who don't have a personal relationship with Jesus Christ are scared of the idea that there is something bigger than themselves that they might have to submit to.

If kids are ready to listen to God but don't know what to do, what should be their next step? The best possible way is silence in prayer so God can be heard. Psalm 46:10 (NIV) says, "Be still and know that I am God." Psalm 62:1 (NASB) says, "My soul waits in silence for God only; from Him is my salvation."

BACKSTAGE PASS
getting to know

Favorite Books: Anything Max Lucado.

Musical Influences: Michael Card, Michael W. Smith, and Steven Curtis Chapman

What is God teaching you now? Understanding that He is in total control, and my worries and concerns are a sign of me not giving up that control to Him.

How has your family helped you in your walk with God? My wife is my rock on this earth. She can walk through anything with an incredible faith. God uses my children to show me how He loves me unconditionally. I never truly understood that or lived that before I had children of my own.

How do you plan to expand your ministry in the future? I would like to bring two more artists onto my label - two people with a combination of great talent and a true heart for ministry, not money and fame.

Birthday: November 14

Favorite Bible Verse: Romans 14:8

Website: www.kbott.com

Booking: 317-345-2871

JACI VELASQUEZ

SEEKING PEACE

"*P*eace ... it does not mean to be in a place where there is no noise, trouble or hard work ... it means to be in the midst of those things and still be calm in your heart ..."
(Unknown)

My brother gave me a card with this on the front and at the time I did not understand what it meant. I live in a very big city; it is the kind of place where you can go unnoticed very easily, and if you're not careful, you will never just be still and listen for the voice of God.

With all the work we get caught up in daily, the challenge is to *be* at peace. In Isaiah 26:12 (NCV) it says, "Lord, all our success is because of what you have done, so give us peace." I cry out for this everyday; I never even knew that I was in need of it, until one day I couldn't hear Him anymore. I was so caught up in the "hard work," I never just felt peace with the Lord and myself. My mother said something really cute the other day; she said it was "the art of doing nothing." I don't know about that, but I do know that probably has something to do with it.

Maybe we are afraid to slow down and find peace because of what we will find within ourselves. The truth is, only you and God know ... it says in Psalm 4:8 (NCV), "I go to bed and sleep in peace, because, LORD, only you keep me safe."

I will live by that one forever. We are always looking, moving, and seeking out the next big thing for our lives. **Let's just be still and calm in our own hearts, to hear His voice.**

"I leave you peace; my peace I give you. I do not give it to you as the world does. So don't let your hearts be troubled or afraid" (John 14:27 NCV).

UNPLUGGED
a deeper look

With homework, hobbies, and all that teens have going on today, how can they stop and make time to be at peace with God? It's really easy to get too busy; that is something I have been working on. In fact, I don't know how to be anything but busy. However, God has been teaching me to just stop and smell the roses and listen to Him. Sometimes you need to teach yourself to take a deep breath and STOP. When you do, all of a sudden you realize that it feels good. That's when you can get in tune with God.

We, as humans, want to be in control of our own plans. As we are still, and at peace with our Lord, will He begin to show us His plans, and make a change inside of us? Yes, I believe so, maybe not all the time, but it certainly opens the door to be able to hear from Him. It's amazing to know that God wants to talk to us. It makes us more aware of His presence.

BACKSTAGE PASS
getting to know

Favorite Books: *Mere Christianity* by C.S. Lewis and *Blue Like Jazz* by Donald Miller

Musical Influences: Billy Joel, Marvin Gaye, Bob Dylan, and The Cardigans

What is God teaching you now? To be patient, and just how valuable my family is.

How has your family helped you in your walk with God? They keep me honest with them, as well as with God.

How do you plan to expand your ministry in the future?

I think everyday, everything that we do is ministry. I've learned to take one day at a time. When I try to foresee the future, I usually mess up.

Birthday:
October 15

Favorite Bible Verse:
2 Corinthians 12:9

Website:
www.jacivelasquez.com

Booking Agency:
William Morris Agency
615-963-3000
www.wmaccm.com

Fan Mail Address:
Jaci Fan Club
P.O. Box 3568
Brentwood, TN 37024

STAPLE

SING TO THE LORD

Darin Keim

"But I trust in your unfailing love; my heart rejoices in your salvation. I will sing to the LORD, for he has been good to me" (Psalm 13:5-6 NIV).

These verses, to me, seem to sum up the whole of what my relationship with God should be. There are so many people within the sphere of Christian living who are caught in the trap of surrounding themselves with a religion - adding rules and regulations to a lifestyle to somehow reach a standard of perfection - when all that is asked, or desired from us, is a relationship fueled by love between us and our Creator. I believe that the institution of religion has flip-flopped things around; put the end first and the means last. In a religious mentality, we think that making a list of "do's and don'ts" will somehow bring us closer with God, and His love is extended to us after we meet these "holiness requirements." In a genuine relationship, one that I have with a Creator who has indeed "been good to me," **I serve Him because I love Him** - He loved me first - and all of the "do's and don'ts" fall into place, because I want to live right for Him based off of the knowledge that I have about my God. So in reference to the Scripture, my point is this: We can face persecution, we can face deaths in the family, we can face sickness or injury, and still know that we can "trust in His unfailing love; my heart rejoices in His salvation." No matter what, if we've accepted Christ into our hearts, then we're aware of what God has done for us by sending His Son. He sent us a spotless sacrifice to die in place of all of our imperfections, and because of this we are redeemed and holy before God. *The only thing* God asks of us in our Christian walk is to remember that. And He only needs us to remember that, because He knows that when we grasp how amazing a concept that is, and how far and deep His love truly runs for us, we can't help but "sing to the Lord, for he has been good to me." All of a sudden, the means have brought about the end. God has reached down and touched me, and now I am holy. Therefore, I will live for Him.

UNPLUGGED
a deeper look

What are some ways that teens can come closer to grasping the vastness of how good God truly is to them? One way I've seen God's goodness is through seeing the world around me. We are definitely in Enemy-occupied territory, and the fact that someone took the time to be used by God and share His love to me is the biggest expression of goodness in my life. Even when times are hard and we struggle, God's goodness stands through it all.

Do you think teens should go "outside of the church walls" and gather the unsaved to bring a fresh spark to what Christianity is about, "a relationship fueled by love between us and our Creator?" This is one of the most important pieces of a Christian life, sharing Christ's influence through your life. If we are huddled in the corner keeping this influence and love to ourselves, how powerful could it really be? If this is a life-changing event in your life, make it known. Jesus was a minister to those that were unchurched and lonely; what better example do we need? He wants His creation to love Him and to reflect His love in their lives.

BACKSTAGE PASS
getting to know

How did the band meet and form? Darin and Brian met at a small Bible College in central Ohio. Music was one of the things that they loved, and it brought them together to write their own music and start a band. Israel was added to the band after he graduated from school. They have been together since 2001.

Do you feel God leading the band in a special direction? God has been the focus of our band since the very beginning. It is important for us to be following His lead no matter what position we're in, be it the band or personally. In the last few years, we as a band have seen that He truly knows what is best for us - even though, sometimes, His plans are not our plans.

How does the band plan to further its ministry in the future? We as a band can only do so much; it's God's strength and plans that will carry us anywhere else. We would like to get our songs to everyone that might be affected through them, so we plan to continue writing the best music we can and letting God work through the music and us.

Birthdays:
Israel: March 20
Darin: October 1
Brian: May 8

Favorite Bible Verses:
Israel: 1 Samuel 16:7
Darin: Psalm 13:5-6
Brian: Philippians 4:13

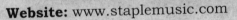

Website: www.staplemusic.com

Booking Agency:
Bridge Street Artist Agency
615-332-7990
www.bsaa.biz

Fan Mail Address:
Staple
5 1/2 S. Main St.
Mechanicsburg, OH 43044

Fan Email Address: stapleband@hotmail.com

Tree63

Standing Up

John Ellis

$\mathcal{I}$n early 2003, during one of my adventurous early morning prayer times with God up on the roof of my house in Durban, South Africa, I wrote a song called "I Stand For You." Early morning is an ideal time for devotions; it makes for healthy reflection and godly introspection, and the quietness of it is usually an occasion for God to reveal Himself.

That morning, I was thinking and praying about my life, my calling, and Tree63, and it occurred to me that, despite all the challenges and hardships that God had led us through, I was still deeply and quietly steadfast in my decision to follow Jesus and be counted as His friend.

I had managed to drag a guitar with me up that thin ladder to the roof, and I was just singing and worshipping up there, when the first few lines of the song became part of the prayer: *"Jesus, I stand for You"* - a declaration of intent, a flag in the ground, a fresh resolution.

Tree63 had recently been offered an opportunity to become part of the mainstream music industry in the U.S., something I felt very strongly that God purposed for us as a band. However, the offers were conditional: drop the Jesus stuff, cover up some of the overt and "offensive" references to your faith, and we'll consider you. The message was clear: Jesus' friends are not too welcome here. Ultimately, we were passed over, and it was heartbreaking. That episode was followed by a year or so of even stronger difficulty and challenge. So that quiet summer morning on my roof, taking the time to talk to God and hear His voice, I felt Him ask me, "Are you still mine, despite everything?"

Here's the reality: following Jesus through a dark, broken, unfriendly world is difficult. It takes immense courage; it calls for unwavering faith and confidence. The truth is, God will try our devotion. He will put our commitment to the test. **He wants our all, our everything.**

"Jesus, I stand for You." That's a badge we wear, and we simultaneously become a target for the cruelty of the world. But here's the challenge: how much worldly ridicule will we endure for the prize set before us? How long will we stand to be rejected and hurt by this world for professing our love for Jesus? It's a lot easier on the heart to just give in and play it the world's way. But that's the short term, the wide road. The narrow road is, *"Jesus, I stand for You, no matter what You lead me through; they will chase me out and close me down, but Jesus, I stand for You."* This amounts to Jesus' teaching that in order to live, we must die - to self, to the world we are a part of. Dead to self, alive in Christ. We need to choose whether we live for rewards now or rewards later. It's a hard test, but then, being known as a follower of Jesus is a hard road. The good news is, that road ends in heaven. In the meantime, we learn the value of standing up, and continuing to stand when all around us fails. We will not escape trials and tribulation, but Jesus has assured us, "Fear not, for I have overcome the world" (John 16:33 NIV).

Another Verse:
1 Corinthians 16:13

UNPLUGGED
a deeper look

How can we trust in God's promise to take care of us when we stand for our faith, when we face rejection, humiliation, and persecution? One way is for us to understand that we're trusting in a God who's made some radical promises. We're not trusting in some idea or a fellow human being. We're trusting in an Almighty God. We're trusting in the Creator of the universe, who's unable to make mistakes, who's incapable of taking back His promises. He's absolutely faithful and trustworthy. We can say, "Jesus, I stand for You," with utmost confidence, because Jesus is always there for us. He always follows through with tangible evidence of asking us to be faithful. Those are the things that encourage us and strengthen us on the way. If we say, "I stand for You," we're saying we stand for Somebody who's able to take His promise and do something with it. We're trusting His character and who He's promised He is, and that's all the difference.

If teens are questioning whether they are taking that stand for Jesus, what should they do next? And how can they again receive a fire that will last? One of the difficulties these days is that we're so overstimulated with things - media and culture, even in the church. Sometimes we miss the simplicity of the message. To continue standing for Jesus is to have a daily hour by hour, minute by minute personal relationship, and realize that He's with us all the time. The promise He made - I'll be with you till the end of the earth; I'll be with you always (Matthew 28:20). That's not just fancy-sounding, religious language. It's really true. Jesus loves you personally and couldn't love you more, and it's quite an astounding truth. The problem with some teens these days, is that they come out of families where their moms and dads don't love them that much. It's hard for them to have a picture of this God who loves unconditionally. The only way we can reach that understanding is to make sure we're maintaining a personal, actual, day-by-day relationship with Jesus, which means getting into a habit of prayer, getting into a habit of fasting regularly, if possible, and getting into the Word and learning what the Bible's all about.

BACKSTAGE PASS
getting to know

How did the band meet and form? The band started in December 1996, kind of by accident. I'd been a Christian for almost a year by that point. I had been a musician before that, but I stopped playing music when I found the Lord. The last thing I ever wanted to do was be in a band again. I'd written these songs about my newfound faith, and found some guys to play them with me. Suddenly we had this concert to be part of, so we went along and played, and broke up afterwards. We pursued it and broke up again and again. After a few years of trying to avoid God's call on the thing, I finally felt God say, "This is what I want you to do. This is what I've called you to do. I want you to use your gift of music to honor Me." So far it's Tree63.

Do you feel God leading the band in a special direction? There's definitely a calling in terms of what Tree63's about - Tree's more of a calling than a career, to offer something fresh and vital to a very jaded industry and Christian culture. We've uprooted our lives, our families, everything, just to be here, because we honestly believe that something that we carry can make a difference.

How does the band plan to further its ministry in the future? Because this is a calling rather than a career, there's no set career plan other than just to be obedient to God's call. Any second that goes by, it could end. We're trusting God that when He says, "Time's up," we'll be open to hear that and stop. We have dreams, but we don't have any five-year goals or ten-year goals. We try to be faithful and let God do it. At the end of the day, we'll be able to boast that God did it, and not us.

Birthdays:
John: July 6
Darryl: June 24
Daniel: May 1

Favorite Bible Verses:
John: John 3:30
Darryl: Hebrews 11:1
Daniel: Galatians 5:1

Booking Agency:
Jeff Roberts & Associates
615-859-7040
www.jeffroberts.com

Website: www.tree63.com

Fan Mail Address:
Tree63
2000 Mallory Lane, Ste. 130, #137
Franklin, TN 37067

Fan Email Address: treemail@tree63.com

SEVENTH DAY SLUMBER

STRENGTH FROM GOD

Joseph Rojas

The band members of Seventh Day Slumber often refer people to the Scripture of Philippians 4:13 (NKJV), "I can do all things through Christ who strengthens me." I always believed that I could do all things through Christ. Some of my friends who weren't Christians thought I was crazy, but I felt a change the day I gave my life to Jesus, and I knew He was real. I went from having a $400/day cocaine habit to becoming a husband and father of two children. God has surely changed my life. He looked beyond my faults and saw something beautiful in this broken building.

What we want you to know is that **your life is so worth living**. You have to leave your past in the past, and stop beating yourself up, and believe you are worth more than you give yourself credit for. What you see as not beautiful or not cool, God sees as a "perfect 10," and we see as a "work in progress." If you will be crazy enough to believe that you can do all things through Christ who strengthens you, I promise you that God will take you places you've never even dreamed were possible!

We in Seventh Day Slumber love all of you, and want you to know that we are proud of you. We believe in you, and if you trust God, we know you will do big things. We hope to see you on the road this year. Please come up and talk to us. We need as many friends as we can get. Love you guys!

UNPLUGGED
a deeper look

When we trust Jesus, and ask Him to save us from our sins, will there always be a miraculous conversion that others can see in our lives? It depends on what you consider miraculous. I believe that true repentance brings about a change in your life that is evident for people to see. However, some people have more work to do than others, and the change takes longer. For some people, God takes away a real problem, like drug addiction, in a second. For others, it takes longer, but everything God does is miraculous. If people choose to see Him, they will.

To us, our lives sometimes seem like broken buildings, but will God always see something beautiful in us? Absolutely! He created us and to Him, each of us is a masterpiece - a perfect 10!

If teenagers take the first step and trust that they can do all things through Christ, will the opportunities to do big things just come, or is further patience, persistence, prayer, and faith required on their part? For some, big things come right away, but it depends on the maturity level of the person. To whom much is given, much is required. For others, it takes longer, but one thing is absolutely true. You definitely need patience, because God's time is not our time.

BACKSTAGE PASS
getting to know

How did the band meet and form? Josh and I met at Bible College, Christ for the Nation. I met Jeremy later. He's my brother-in-law. Ray is our newest member; we met him through a nationwide search for a drummer.

Do you feel God leading the band in a special direction? I just think He tells us all to do a certain thing. Some people do it; some don't.

How does the band plan to further its ministry in the future? We just want to keep being real with our fans, open and honest, transparent, and somewhat vulnerable. We want God to do whatever He wants to do with us.

Birthdays:
Joseph: June 21
Jeremy: May 24
Ray: June 24
Josh: April 13

Favorite Bible Verses:
Joseph: Philippians 4:13
Jeremy: Joshua 24:15
Ray: John 3:16
Josh: 1 John 4:4

Website:
www.seventhdayslumber.com

Booking Agency:
Jeff Roberts & Associates
615-859-7040
www.jeffroberts.com

Fan Mail Address:
Seventh Day Slumber
P.O. Box 1710
Topanga, CA 90290

Fan Email Address: email@seventhdayslumber.com

Seventh Day Slumber Seventh Day

NEWSBOYS

STRONG TOWER

Peter Furler
(and Jim Laffoon)

Strong and mighty, Strong to save us, Like a fortress, Never failing ...
When the winds blow strong against us, You are steadfast; You are true.
When the ground beneath us trembles, Your foundation never moves. When the Enemy surrounds us, Closing in as darkness falls, Though his armies rage against us, They can never scale these walls.

Despite the fact that God has never failed to be my personal refuge, this has not been the case in the life of every believer that I have known. How many times have I wept, as I watched the life of someone I have loved and even served with in the ministry, blown off course by the violent winds of deception or illicit passion? Why are the lives of some Christians ransacked by the hordes of hell, but other believers stand strong against every foe? Is God fickle? Is He unfair? Obviously not! It is impossible for our perfect God to be fickle or unfair.

Why then are the lives of some Christians shattered? The answer is simple, yet profound. The promise of God to be our fortress and strong tower, like many other promises in Scripture, is conditional. God is a fortress and a high tower to those who take refuge in Him.

"As for God, his way is perfect; the word of the LORD is flawless. He is a shield for all who take refuge in him" (Psalm 18:30 NIV).

"He who fears the LORD has a secure fortress ..." (Proverbs 14:26 NIV).

"The name of the LORD is a strong tower, the righteous run to it and are safe" (Proverbs 18:10 NIV).

There are at least four doors through which we can experience the reality of God as our fortress and high tower: the promises of God, the people of God, the purity of God, and the person of Christ. As for the promises of God, it is clear from 2 Peter 1:4 that they are the doorway through which you and I can experience the divine nature of Christ. I have found that no matter what I am facing, there is a promise that corresponds to that need. Whether it is healing, protection, strength, joy, or deliverance, all of them can be appropriated as I place my faith in the promises of God.

It is clear from Scriptures like Hebrews 3:13 and James 5:16 that the people of God play a critical role in our lives. I cannot count the times that the fulfillment of God's promise to be my fortress and tower has come in the form of another Christian. I have voluntarily chosen to make my life transparent and accountable to the men that God has placed in my life. Never forget, whether it is your pastor, a leader in your church or ministry, or another mature Christian of the same gender, God wants to bring you into the joys and protection of transparency and accountability.

As for the purity of God, **it is vital that you and I never forget that Jesus came to be both our Savior and our Lord**. He demands that every area of our lives be brought under His authority. We must actively cooperate with the Holy Spirit's plan to change us. If we willingly live in habitual sin, it will create breaches in the walls of protection that surround our lives. Even though Judas had Jesus Christ as his pastor and was in the world's greatest cell group - the twelve apostles, his life was destroyed, because he refused to bring an area of financial uncleanness into the light and deal with it (John 12:6). His habitual thievery was the very door Satan walked through when he tempted him to sell Jesus for thirty pieces of silver.

Lastly, you and I must never forget the power of the person and work of Christ. According to John 10:7, Jesus is the door.

I have discovered that even in those moments when my faith is weak and I seem to be losing my battle against sin, I can run into the high tower of God's protection because of the person and work of His precious Son. Through His work on Calvary, I have access to every promise of God's provision and protection (2 Corinthians 1:20).

Do you see it now? Our God is strong and mighty. He will save us, but we must run into the fortress that His person and promises have built. No matter what you and I are facing today, this invincible fortress stands like a strong tower against the raging hordes of hell, and shines like a beacon in the midst of a seething sea of darkness.

UNPLUGGED
a deeper look

How can teens remember to call on the promises of the Word when they are experiencing difficult circumstances? First you have to know them, so you need to be in the Word consistently. One of the greatest promises of the Bible is concerning trials and tough situations, how we'll never be faced with any temptation beyond escape. We don't need to fear we don't know enough of the Bible to survive; we need to continually be learning, being fed, and being in the Word. On a practical note, I write the Scriptures down on little business cards. I have a bunch of blank ones that I put in my pocket, and I carry them around with me during the day. It's helped me out a lot. - Phil

Can people not only encourage, but also prevent us from taking refuge in God? Our primary place of refuge should be the Lord. That should be the place that we run to first, but unfortunately, we decide that we're gonna' run to our friends, or get on the phone, before we even take it to the Lord. The Lord wants us to take that all to Him, so He can work it out.

It's quite an important thing to say, "Lord, this is what's happening. Direct my path in regard to who I should seek counsel from" - to make sure we are getting counsel from the right people. The Lord will show us which people to ask. - Phil

BACKSTAGE PASS
getting to know

Do you feel God leading the band in a special direction? We're feeling a stronger calling than ever to the church, to solidify the body of Christ. We see all kinds of denominations and age groups come to our events, and socio-economic and racial differences are all left at the door. It's a very unique position that we've been put in, a very special situation that needs to be handled with care and with great responsibility. We really feel a call on the band to be a tool to the local church, to unify the body, so that the world would know that we are His disciples, by the way we love one another. We're just seeking the Lord and waiting on Him. - Phil

How does the band plan to further its ministry in the future? We have *lots* of plans, but the Lord has *one*. We don't want to be too quick to move, but at the same time, we don't want to squander the time that the Lord's given us. We're seeking the Lord, in regard to the band, our own personal ministry, and our corporate ministry. We also feel that the Lord needs to prepare our hearts to a greater degree in these days that are coming. God's leading us to a new and different territory, and we feel called to the nations. We're waiting to see how that unfolds. - Phil

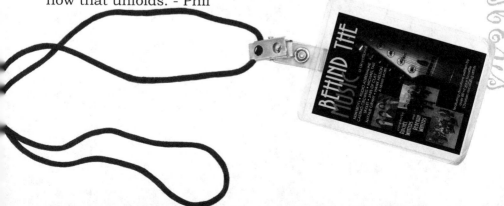

Newsboys Newsboys Newsboys

Birthdays:
Peter: September 8
Phil: January 5
Paul: August 22
Jeff: June 26
Duncan: March 3

Favorite Bible Verses:
Peter: Romans 8:28
Phil: James 4:8
Paul: Isaiah 53
Jeff: Isaiah 26:3
Duncan: Psalm 112

Website:
www.newsboys.com

Booking Agency:
H2O Artist Agency
770-736-5363
www.h2oartistagency.com

Fan Mail Address:
Newsboys Fan Mail
P.O. Box 681668
Franklin, TN 37068

Fan Email Address: newsboys@streetteam.inpop.com

KJ-52

SWEEPING UNDER THE RUG

*I*f you were anything like me growing up, you probably couldn't stand cleaning up your room. What I used to do was take all my mess, ball it up, and toss it underneath my bed. Unfortunately, that only worked for a little while, because sooner or later Mom would find out, and I got in big trouble. However, I've seen that we tend to treat our walk with God in the same manner. We take our sin and the areas that God isn't happy with, and we ball it up and push it to the side, and pretend like everything is okay. In Mark 4:22 (NIV) it says, "For whatever is hidden is meant to be disclosed, and whatever is concealed is meant to be brought out into the open."

This verse shows us that God doesn't want us to hide our sin from Him; after all, He knows it's there anyway! The Bible says in 1 John 1:9 (NIV), "If we confess our sin, he is faithful and just and will forgive us ..." God is calling us to bring those areas out in the open and not hide them. Think about it, hiding our sin really isn't worth it; we're just going to get in trouble, like I always did with my room! Bring it out in the open to God; **let Him forgive us and cleanse us**. It's not easy living with a hidden mess in our room, but it's even harder living for Christ with hidden sin in our lives.

1. What are some areas of sin that people hide in their lives?
2. What are some areas of sin that you hide?
3. Why do most people hide things in their lives?
4. What's the hardest thing about being open and honest with God?
5. What can we do to be more real with God?

UNPLUGGED
a deeper look

As you mentioned, God already knows our sins, so there's really no reason not to admit them. But why is it important to confess our sins to Him? God *does* know everything, so there's nothing "new under the sun" to Him, but I think there's power in confession. When you take that time to open up and say, "God, I messed up," it's a way of admitting it. The Bible says in Romans 10:9 (NIV), "... you confess with your mouth, you believe in your heart." If you're willing to go, "Hey, God, I really did this wrong," it's your way of saying, "I really mean business about what You mean business about."

Will God convict us, remind us, and possibly punish us, for refusing to confess our sins? If God is our Father, He's going to do the same thing as our parents would do. As a kid, sometimes I'd walk around like nothing was wrong when I knew I'd messed up, and my mom or my dad had to do certain things to get my attention, so to speak. So, yes, God will do what it takes to get our attention, not because He's a God who loves to punish us and He's angry with us, but He loves us enough not to want us to go down the wrong path and get into the wrong things. He definitely will convict us, and He will put us on the "hot seat" sometimes.

Will sin in our lives, especially hidden sin, diminish our effectiveness in living for Christ and being a witness for Him? There are times in the Bible where God used some very sinful people that were blatantly walking the wrong way. God's not limited by ourselves; but on the other hand, the Bible says to set ourselves apart, to be holy vessels - the deeper we go in Him, and the more we walk in righteousness, the more that He can use us. I think at the ultimate end of the day, God's gonna' do whatever it takes to get His purpose done. We should do whatever it takes to make sure He gets His purpose done in us.

BACKSTAGE PASS
getting to know

Favorite Books: *The Purpose Driven Life* by Rick Warren, *This Present Darkness* by Frank Peretti, and *Love & Respect - The Love She Most Desires, The Respect He Desperately Needs* by Dr. Emerson Eggerichs

Musical Influences: Pretty diverse there. Hip hop, late 80's to early 90's, U2, The Police, Switchfoot, and Mat Kearney.

What is God teaching you now? He's been teaching me just to push a little bit deeper. You get so used to doing one thing, you can stop relying on the Spirit of God. God's been showing me that with the blessing comes more responsibility, which means I have to make sure I'm that much more focused on my prayer time, that much more focused on still doing the basics. At the same time, God's been showing me that it's okay to enjoy His blessing. I've really been praying for God's favor in my life, not just in the big things, but even in the little things. Just praying, "God, give me a good seat on the airplane today," seeing Him working in even those little things, has been a big thing.

How has your family helped you in your walk with God? I don't come from a believer family. I can say my wife has. My family has always been the extended family of the church. That was really the only family that took me in. The Bible says, He sets the lonely in families ... (Psalm 68:6) Honestly, there were those times where He really did that.

How do you plan to expand your ministry in the future?
That's something I've been thinking about. It's been everything from trying to expand what He originally started to doing more speaking, books, or getting into TV ... doing more production, more making of the music, other things besides just playing and writing music. I'm starting to see those things come into reality.

Birthday:
June 26

Favorite Bible Verse:
Proverbs 18:24

Website:
www.kj52.com

Booking Agency:
Jeff Roberts & Associates
615-859-7040
www.jeffroberts.com

Fan Mail Address:
KJ-52
P.O. Box 150415
Cape Coral, FL 33915

Fan Email Address: kj@kj52.com

JADYN MARIA

TAKE A STAND

I can remember so many times from my childhood where my parents totally impacted me. I'll bring them up, and they honestly don't remember, but it influenced me enough that, ten years later, I still remember. They were being "watched" by me, and they didn't even realize it.

That's truly the reality of every Christian's life. It's easy to live however we want and forget that **we're being "watched" by others around us at all times - you never know who you may have the opportunity to influence**.

At times it's so tempting to ask, "I'm only one person in this amazingly huge world; is there any way that I could impact it enough to even make a small dent?" Yes, you can! I have a song called "One Girl," that I feel totally answers this question. Even in a crowd of people, if only one person decides to take a stand in what they believe, it will not go unnoticed; people will recognize that *one* person who stands up - and you don't even have to be in a crowd. If you influence one person and they, in turn, influence another, then you have a chain effect that, hopefully, will just keep going and going. I would really just like to encourage you to realize your influence, and use it to impact this generation in an enormous way.

My favorite verse for quite some time now has been 1 Timothy 4:12 (NIV), "Don't let anyone look down on you because you are young, but set an example for the believers in speech, in life, in love, in faith, and in purity." It doesn't matter how old we are - we have the power to be a positive impact. Ephesians 3:20 (NIV) says, "Now to him who is able to do immeasurably more than all we ask or imagine, according to his power that is at work within us, to him be glory in the church and in Christ Jesus throughout all generations, forever and ever! Amen." With God's help, we can do anything. Let's choose to do all we can to positively impact the world.

More verses:
Psalm 107:2
2 Timothy 3:12
Job 23:12

UNPLUGGED
a deeper look

How can teens understand the authority they're given and do their best to fulfill their duty as a Christian and a witness? How can they always reflect God and see the outcome of the biggest impact of all - bringing souls to Christ? Someone once said, "Your walk talks, your talk talks, but your walk talks louder than your talk talks." That's so true - actions speak louder than words, and sometimes they speak so loudly that people can't hear what we say. We need to realize that God commands us to be "salt and light" to the world around us. I am a firm believer in making the right choices. With every choice comes a consequence. What we do with the authority that God has given us is up to us. If we choose to go down the wrong road, we may not only hurt ourselves, but also hurt others. Let's make the right choice and do our best to be an example to the world.

If teens have influence over one life, could they have an impact on the world? I referenced my song 'One Girl," earlier and the reason I love and believe in that song so much is because it's so encouraging. It talks about how one girl in a huge crowd is enough to make a difference - ONE! Imagine if we all got together and worked toward the same goal, how amazing that would be! To influence our world I believe the following things are essential:

- Live an exemplary Christian testimony before others
- Verbally witness for Jesus
- Endure the difficult times gracefully

BACKSTAGE PASS
getting to know

Favorite Books: Right now, *Next Door Savior* by Max Lucado

Musical Influences: I grew up listening to the Gaithers, the Kingsmen, The Isaacs, the Cathedrals, and southern gospel, all the way.

What is God teaching you now? Right now, God is teaching me how to rely on Him in every area of my life.

How has your family helped you in your walk with God? My family is super supportive, and they keep me accountable.

How do you plan to expand your ministry in the future? I hope to touch as many people with my music as possible. I hope to use the stage that God has entrusted me with to inspire and encourage.

Birthday:
April 20

Favorite Bible Verse:
1 Timothy 4:12

Websites:
www.jadynmaria.com
www.jadyn.com

JARS OF CLAY

THE CYCLE OF WORSHIP

Dan Haseltine

How does taking care of the poor and the needy bring us into an experience of worship? Through the prophet, Isaiah, God speaks to His people. To all those who have been diligent with the sacrifice of animals, with the lighting of incense, and the act of presenting offerings to God in the temple, God shares the deeper heart of worship.

God calls us to a new kind of fast, or worship. The new worship is through the practice of relationships. Relationships are difficult; they are impossible on our own. All the things God tells His people to do as an act of worship are connected to relationships. Taking care of the sick, the homeless, the oppressed, the naked, the weary, the needy, the widows and the orphans, the afflicted, and the self-righteous are impossible tasks to accomplish without an authentic presence of compassion and mercy.

We cannot create compassion on our own. We cannot build a heart of mercy toward other people. **It is God alone who stirs our hearts and molds us into something useable** for the purpose of serving others.

When *we* try to accomplish the acts of mercy and compassion that God says are worship, we are painfully aware that only God can do this through us. As we come to the end of our own human abilities and emotions, we are brought to the cross of Jesus - the one merciful and compassionate act by which all other acts are compared and judged.

When we are at the cross, we see God begin to fill the places where mercy should be in our lives. We feel God fill the spaces where compassion should be, and we know without a doubt that we need God and His love to be who and what we strive to be.

And when we come to this place, we worship the one true God that is compassion and mercy, and has the touch that heals, and comforts, and releases, and shelters.

This is the kind of worship that comes by way of entering into messy, inconvenient, painful relationships. And this is the worship beyond the songs we sing, beyond the hands we raise on a Sunday morning, that God has held up as life changing, heart molding worship. This is worship through service, in love ... because of Jesus Christ and the gifts of mercy and compassion that we have been given. If we were made for worship, then this is the calling of every person who has been captured by the gospel. This is your calling.

Scripture:
Isaiah 58:6-12

UNPLUGGED
a deeper look

Will we automatically return to the cross when are at the "end of our rope" in human terms, or do we have to discipline ourselves to go to the cross? I don't think it's natural for us as individuals to go to the cross. The gospel is the story of God pursuing man and man running away. Even in our most extreme circumstances, when we are the most lonely, or have the most to pray for, we seek other things to handle the sense of restlessness. When we see what God has called us to, and come to the place where we recognize we can't fulfill that, even though we have a desire to - then the only place we have to go is to God, and that's the key.

Through this kind of worship, service, and love can teens win lost souls to Christ? I think that is by far the way transformation happens in the lives of students. We had lunch with a woman who takes students from America to Kenya. She said, "We're going on a mission trip, but here's the thing: We're not going over there to share Christ with these people." As Americans, we think we're going to do that, but in Africa, they have a much deeper, stronger, well-rooted sense of who God and Jesus are than we do. They experience God in the midst of real suffering. When we go to serve these people, we have to walk humbly into these situations because most times, they have a greater spiritual life than we do. When you go on a mission trip to experience God, you're going to experience God in a way that you never have.

BACKSTAGE PASS
getting to know

How did the band meet and form? We were all music students at Greenville College in Illinois, and we started there. We just started writing songs, and describing things, and we thought we knew everything. Now, the end of the world looks much more confusing and difficult, yet there's so much more to write about than there ever was.

Do you feel God leading the band in a special direction? As a band, we've been struck by this idea of community - that allows us to be honest and real, to live weakness to weakness. God reorients our hearts to the gospel when we're in community with people. We've been in a band for almost thirteen years, and we're just now getting to a place where we feel like if Jars of Clay as a musical entity were to dissolve, we would have some amazing friendships intact. It takes a lot of courage. It takes people in your life that really know you, that know the deepest parts and darkest secrets you have to give. That's what we're learning as a band.

How does the band plan to further its ministry in the future? As songwriters, we just hope to improve and be better communicators. When we look at the world, we want to be able to describe it with more of a vivid capacity. We're really investing our hearts in the lives of people in Africa - the work that we get to do, the relationships that we're building, the communities that we get to be a part of - and that may actually have a greater longevity than our music.

0202402

Birthdays:
Dan: January 12
Steve: July 8
Matt: January 25
Charlie: October 21

0202401

Favorite Bible Verses:
Dan: Isaiah 58:6-12
Steve: Hebrews 10:23
Matt: Philippians 1:21
Charlie: Micah 6:8

Post Card

Booking Agency:
Creative Artists Agency
615-383-8787
www.caaccm.com

Fan Email Address:
www.myspace.com/jarsofclay

Website: www.jarsofclay.com

FUSEBOX

THE LITTLE THINGS

A DEVOTION ON BLESSINGS AND BEING THANKFUL

Billy Buchanan

*L*ast night when I was driving home, I actually took the time to look at the beautiful scenery in my neighborhood. I hardly ever do that. Usually, I'm moving so fast I just "don't have time." As I stood in awe of my neighbors' yards, the mountains in the distance, and the numerous trees all around, I couldn't help but say, "Thank You, Lord." Of course, once I started thinking about all that God had given us through creation, I started thinking about all the other blessings in my life. I pulled into the driveway of my gorgeous new home. "Thank You, Lord." I walked through my front door, into the kitchen, and there was my wife cooking. "Thank You, Lord." I continued into the living room, and there were my son and daughter playing on the living room floor. "Thank You, Lord." I continued into my office, and there was my assistant working hard to keep my businesses in order. "Thank You, Lord."

What have I done to deserve so much? I didn't grow up with a lot of material possessions. My dad was never around, and my mom had to work two jobs just to pay the bills. There were many nights when the lights were turned off, the heat was off, and there was no food in the refrigerator. It's funny. When you don't know any better, you think that is just the way it's supposed to be. My mom taught my brothers and me, at a very early age, to be thankful for "the little things." I think when she said little things she was talking about food, a roof over our heads, clothing, family, and friends. Well, those things aren't little at all. They're huge! In Matthew 6:31-33 (NKJV) Jesus said, "Therefore do not worry, saying,

'What shall we eat?' or 'What shall we drink?' or 'What shall we wear?' For after all these things the Gentiles seek. For your heavenly Father knows that you need all these things. But seek first the kingdom of God and His righteousness, and all these things shall be added to you." Before I was a believer, I spent so many years trying to gain worldly success and possessions. It wasn't until I took these verses to heart that I truly understood God's way. **When we chase after God and His righteousness, He'll take care of the rest.** That doesn't mean that we won't have to work hard to get the things we need. It does mean that God will open the doors, and bring the opportunities our way. God has blessed me enormously. I have an amazing family, a really nice home, a great career, and a basketball goal in my backyard. I am so thankful for all these things. But more importantly, I'm thankful for the One who gave it all to me. I will continue to seek first the Kingdom of God and His righteousness.

UNPLUGGED
a deeper look

Sometimes it's hard to find the money and time to give to those in need. Are we as Christians created to "share" our blessings? Definitely. Jesus taught us that it is better to give than to receive. The Lord blesses us with material possessions so that we can give to others. There is something that happens to us spiritually when we give ourselves away.

Are you able to thank God even during bad days and hard times? Is that the time we need Him most? Because I was raised in a very poor home, I learned to do this at a very young age. God has shown me over and over again the "blessing of hardship." We become completely dependent on Him during these times.

How can teens understand that God wants to shower believers with blessings, if we will only accept them? All they have to do is try Him. He's faithful to not only meet our daily needs, but He loves blessing us with so much more than we deserve.

BACKSTAGE PASS
getting to know

Favorite Book: *Mere Christianity* by C.S. Lewis

Musical Influences: Stevie Wonder, Tears For Fears, King's X, U2, Sade, and Anita Baker

What is God teaching you now? How to love my wife as He loves the church!

How has your family helped you in your walk with God? My wife and kids are everything to me. They've taught me how to love.

How do you plan to expand your ministry in the future? I have a heart for independent Christian artists. Before I was signed, I spent many years touring as an independent artist. Because of that, I know the unique struggles they face. I own a company called Vision 1st Music (Vision1stmusic.com) that specializes in helping independent Christian artists grow as ministers, songwriters, performers, and recording artists.

Birthday:
June 6

Favorite Bible Verse:
1 John 3:1

Booking Agency:
Jeff Roberts & Associates
615-859-7040
www.jeffroberts.com

Fan Email Address:
Fusebox@Fuseboxmusic.com

Website: www.Fuseboxmusic.com

Thousand Foot Krutch

The Sky's The Limit

Trevor McNevan

When we choose to step out into something that we feel God's called us to do, we need to watch the way we live - make sure we mean what we say. A lot of people often think, "Wow! Who would look up to me?" That is our attitude. We don't understand it, but we have to pay attention to it and be responsible for it.

After the show, we love to hang out for as long as we can, because that's the time when we get to connect and talk to kids one-on-one. That's when they get to see that we are just normal guys who actually care and want to listen to them - and vice versa. We're encouraged and blessed by these people. That's what keeps us going. We hear some very serious things, like tendencies of suicide, and we always feel so privileged that someone would feel comfortable enough to talk to us about something like that. We feel very blessed to even be in this place. We pray, "God, give us the words to say," before we go out, because we're not pros at life.

I'd be lying if I said life isn't difficult sometimes, so it's absolutely key to have at least one person that you feel comfortable talking to about things that you wouldn't want to talk to anybody else about - someone who has the experience of life in general, who's lived through it. You can talk to them about anything in life - look up to them, learn from them, and take from them the wisdom that God's given them. Without that person, things can get confusing and get way out of hand.

To seek out a positive role model is very important and

Thousand Foot Krutch Thousand Foot

beneficial. Ideally, a good role model would be someone who can live what they talk, who can lead by example, someone who can be real about life. A Bible study or group where people get together and talk about things that go on can be so helpful, because you're realizing that everybody deals with the same stuff. If you're someone who doesn't want to let people in - because you don't want to let people know how you really are - it would be a good thing to keep those doors open. This is the world that we all live in. **If we let go and let God work, the sky's the limit.**

"For the LORD gives wisdom, and from his mouth come knowledge and understanding" (Proverbs 2:6 NIV).

UNPLUGGED
a deeper look

Is it difficult when people at concerts tend to put you on a pedestal because of your music? You don't want to put people on pedestals. Our heart as a band is never to be like, "This is right, and this is wrong, and those people are wrong, and we're right" ... we definitely don't have all the answers. Often, everyone who comes to shows feels like they connect with you from listening to your record, and you don't really know them. But it's an incredible opportunity, and we're very excited to be able to make music.

Does listening to positive, Christian music help to focus us in our walk with Christ? When I was growing up, anything to do with Christian music - or just positive music in general - and the church, was twenty years behind the times, and there were probably five bands that anyone had ever heard of. Now, it's such a different world. God's really opened the doors in so many ways, and there are hundreds of great bands. It just broadens that whole horizon.

BACKSTAGE PASS
getting to know

How did the band meet and form? I started the band back in high school, and we had several different members back then.

We've had a handful of changes through the years. I met the current guys through different musical circles and bands in our area, and God just brought together a great group of guys. I couldn't ask for better people to be able to play with.

Do you feel God leading the band in a special direction? Our hearts have always been for the kids both inside and outside of the church, but as a writer, my heart connects with the cry of those youth outside of the church. God's really been opening a lot of doors in the general market side of things, so we'll see what's in store.

How does the band plan to further its ministry in the future? There's so much on the horizon, and it's just a day to day thing. Everything is in God's timing. I spend a lot of time working with other acts; that's what I love and enjoy. We all have our own side-projects that we enjoy doing, and there's a lot going on with the music right now, too.

Favorite Bible Verses:
Trevor: 2 Corinthians 5:12
Steve: 1 Corinthians 12:4-6
Joel: Isaiah 40:8
Jamie: Proverbs 3:5-6

Fan Email Address:
tfk@thousandfootkrutch.com

Booking Agency:
Third Coast Artists Agency
615-297-2021
www.tcaa.biz

Birthdays:
Trevor: July 17
Steve: March 26
Joel: February 2
Jamie: October 28

Fan Mail Address:
Thousand Foot Krutch
c/o Dryve Artist Management, LLC
P.O. Box 682546
Franklin, TN 37067

Website: www.thousandfootkrutch.com

SARA GROVES

THIS JOURNEY IS MY OWN

My mom is a good balance of hopeful idealist and down-to-earth realist. She has the rare gift of knowing when to comfort me and when to get in my face. One of the things that she exposes in me over and over again is a victim mentality. I'm not talking about someone who is a true victim of abuse; I'm talking about our tendency as a society to shift blame for all our actions, as if we are not accountable for anything. Blame-shifting is something I am determined to work out of my life. There is something so gross about a person whose first instinct is to start naming everyone else's faults when she gets in trouble. She claims that she would have never acted in such a way if so-and-so hadn't done this other horrible thing. I am completely guilty of this. Whenever I am in a bad mood, I will say the rudest things, be short with my kids or husband, and then instead of apologizing, I will claim that it's their fault that I am in a bad mood in the first place. Nice.

There is something so noble about a person who admits her error without blame, who apologizes without getting in that last zinger, who takes responsibility for herself. I am not that noble person, but I would like to be, and one of the thoughts that helps me get there is that **everything I do, I do it as unto the Lord**. Blame-shifting is a symptom of trying to impress the people around me. It is a compulsion to clear my name, even at someone else's expense. But ultimately, this journey is my own journey, and at the end of it, my actions are my own actions. Regardless of how others respond to me, I am responsible for how I respond to them. And this is how the Kingdom of God comes into my home, car, the grocery store, or restaurant - I ask God to change my heart, so that instead of responding the way I want to, with blame-shifting and accusations, I respond with what is noble, lovely, excellent, and true.

More Verses:
1 Corinthians 4:3-4

Prayer

Lord, help me to always remember that this journey through life is my own journey. At the end of my life, I am responsible for myself. So, come shine in me all Your good traits. Help me be gentle, kind, and compassionate. Fill me with Your love for people. Amen.

UNPLUGGED
a deeper look

How would you describe "walking with God?" There are so many metaphors in the Bible to explain to us how our relationship with God is supposed to work: the shepherd and the sheep, the potter and the clay, the father and the prodigal, but I think the most personal and applicable to my life is a marriage. I try to approach my walk with God like I do my marriage, always trying to communicate, love, and serve, always fighting my pride, independence, and selfishness.

Can you give us an example of searching to find your next step on your faith journey? Early on in my music career, Troy and I were approached by a label. I was teaching at the time, and thought this was a dream come true. I had a strong sense that God was making a way for me to share the music I had been writing for years. I asked for a year-leave to pursue music, emailed my family that we were going to sign with the label, and waited for the contract to come. My hand was in the cookie jar and at the last minute God said (clearly), "No." I can't explain how I heard Him - there was no other sign or feeling of assurance that another opportunity would come. I will never forget that night, or that season in our lives. Troy and I cried and prayed and decided to go ahead and take the year off to try music on our own. It was hard and humbling work. During that time I wrote the songs "Hello, Lord," "Cave of Adullum," and "He's Always Been Faithful." The chorus of that song was written in the future tense, because at the time that I wrote it, I was facing a seemingly immovable mountain. I had been praying about my next step, but could not see it. In my anxiety God asked me one question, "Can you name a time of trial in your life, or in your family's life that I did not resolve in my time?" I couldn't think of one time that God was not faithful. "Then I will be faithful again." The day after I wrote it, Troy and I received news that our next project, <u>Conversations</u> (our breakthrough album) would be fully funded by private investors.

If we are walking in the Lord's will, should we ever doubt the actions we take? I doubt myself all the time, but I can't be anxious about it. God may or may not care if you eat a bagel or a donut for breakfast (exaggerated example), but He has left us broader "precepts" and those are always right and true. Paul says if you change your thoughts to think about the world the way God thinks about the world, then you will always be in tune with His will whenever you have to make a decision (Romans 12). God says His thoughts are not far away up in heaven or hidden away for mankind so that we have to search for them, but they are right in our own hearts if we will just pay attention.

BACKSTAGE PASS
getting to know

Favorite Books: Favorite authors - C.S. Lewis and Madeleine L'Engle

Musical Influences: I grew up on Amy Grant, Michael W. Smith, Andre Crouch, and Keith Green. In high school I lived on Sting, Peter Gabriel, and Billy Joel. But the people who influenced my music and the way I write the most have to be my folks. I grew up listening to my mom write and play music every night. She has written some choral music, but mostly plays for her own enjoyment. She played and wrote because it helped her work through things. My dad teaches Old Testament at a Christian Liberal Arts college. He was always challenging me to think about my world-view, to integrate my faith and my life. My music reflects their influence the most. I write because it is therapeutic.

What is God teaching you now? Gratitude. You can't get to joy without gratitude.

How has your family helped you in your walk with God? It's easier to do everything when I know I am loved, and my family gives me that assurance.

How do you plan to expand your ministry in the future? We are just taking each opportunity as it comes.

Birthday:
September 10

Favorite Bible Verse:
Isaiah 41:9-10

0202401

00004

Booking Agency:
Creative Artists Agency
615-383-8787
www.caaccm.com

Website: www.saragroves.com

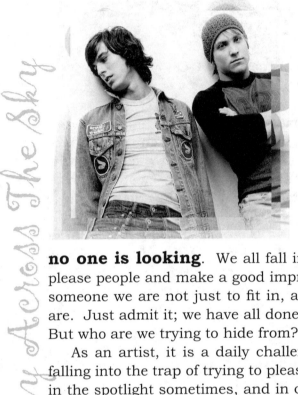

ACROSS THE SKY

TRUE CHARACTER

Justin Unger

*I*t has been said that **true character is who you are when no one is looking**. We all fall into the trap of wanting to please people and make a good impression. We pretend to be someone we are not just to fit in, and we hide who we really are. Just admit it; we have all done it at one time or another. But who are we trying to hide from?

As an artist, it is a daily challenge to guard myself from falling into the trap of trying to please others. My job puts me in the spotlight sometimes, and in contact with many people. It is a challenge to keep my mind focused, not on what others think of me, but on what Christ thinks. I think it is critical for me to be the same person onstage as I am offstage. My grandfather always told me that he was praying that my heart would stay close to the Lord and that I would not become a "performer." Over the past few years, I have learned what he meant by that. God wants us to be real as He is real!

As Christians we should be most concerned with pleasing the One who is always watching. 2 Chronicles 16:9 (NASB) says, "For the eyes of the Lord move to and fro throughout the earth that he may strongly support those whose hearts are completely his." When we give our hearts fully to the Lord, He is the One who works in us and strengthens us to be more like Him. I think it is important for us to strive to live a life full of Christ's character. When we allow Him to live His life through us, He will honor and bless us. Colossians 3:23-24 (NIV) says, "Whatever you do, work at it with all your heart, as working for the Lord, not for men, since you know that you will receive an inheritance from the Lord as a reward. It is the Lord Christ you are serving." We must continue to remind ourselves that we cannot find this godly character on our own. True character is only found in Christ. Stop hiding and let Christ's character live through you.

UNPLUGGED
a deeper look

How would you describe "character?" Jesus Christ.

What are some key elements that you think are essential to a Christian's character? Having a manifestation of Christ's life shining through. Also examining the fruit that we bear. Jesus said, you will know them by what they do, not what they say.

What are some ways for teens to develop a Christlike character? I think the best way is to search through the Scriptures and examine Christ's character. How badly do you want to be like Christ? Ask the Lord to mold you into the character He wants you to have, not what you want. A person's character affects his witness to others.

BACKSTAGE PASS
getting to know

How did the two of you meet and begin performing together? Ben and I met in Nashville. We were both working on our solo careers and learning more about the music industry. We were introduced in the hallway of our record label. We started writing songs together and we hit it off. Within one year we became as close as brothers. We call it our divine appointment, set up by the Lord many years ago.

Do you feel God leading your musical career in a special direction? Greatly. Ben and I have learned so many things in our Christian music ministry. Most of all, we are learning who we are as one unit in Christ. We don't want to base our songs and concerts on what feels good to us, but on what the Lord wants. It has been so awesome to see the Lord take hold of our records. I can't wait to see what He will do this year and in the years to come.

How do you plan to further your ministry in the future?
However the Lord leads. We are excited to walk through the doors that He opens for us.

Birthdays:
Ben: August 24
Justin: February 4

0202402

Favorite Bible Verses:
Ben: Psalm 139:23-24
Justin: John 17:3 and
         Jeremiah 10:23

0202401

Website:
www.justinunger.com

Fan Mail Address:
Across The Sky
430 Keen Street
Prescott, AZ 86305

Fan Email Address: theband@acrossthesky.com

MICHAEL PASSONS

TRUST GAMES

*H*ave you ever been to youth camp and played those "trust games?" You know, the ones where you are blindfolded and then led around by a friend that you supposedly "trust?" Well, I have! At the time, I really didn't get the life application as well as I do now. I kept thinking, "Why do I have to fall backwards blindfolded, hoping this person will catch me?" As I have lived a little and hopefully learned a little, I have realized that this seemingly pointless recreational activity indeed had great significance.

Many years have passed since youth camp, and my life has had many twists and turns. Such it is with us all. Sometimes life is great and the road ahead seems in plain view, but there are those other times when life just hits you like a brick wall. For me it was like somebody turned out the lights, and I was left just fumbling around with no sense of direction or purpose.

Flashback! One day during this seemingly endless walk in the dark, I remembered that trust game. It suddenly all became clear. Now - when I can't see my hand in front of my face, when I have no idea which direction to go, when I can't fathom what good can possibly come from any of my circumstances - *Now* is the time to let my Friend lead me, to fall backwards in blind trust and let Him catch me! **Nothing makes God happier than when we trust Him.** He knows we can't see very far ahead - whether it's a decision about schools, or that perfect person, or careers, or our life's purpose - He knows that sometimes it's like fumbling around in the dark! That's why God wants us to trust Him and take His hand, and let Him lead us through these twists and turns of life. Remember that Jesus lived life! He knows the joys and also the confusion of it all. Trust Him to lead you down a road that He has walked before.

More Verses:
Proverbs 3:5-6

Prayer

God, whenever I feel lost or lonely, and when I can't see which way to go, let me know that You're near even though I can't see You. Give me the faith to trust You blindly even when it's hard to understand why I am so in the dark.

UNPLUGGED
a deeper look

If even a friend will catch us, how much more can we rely on the heavenly Father? Jesus said He would be with us always, that He would be our refuge and strength. No person can match that promise, as hard as he would try. Only Jesus can live up to our highest expectations.

Through trusting God and remembering "trust games," can we begin to see what good can come from our troubling circumstances? Only if we look through different eyes than we may be used to. God's answers to our prayers and His loving way of building our character, courage, and strength can easily be overlooked or construed as something else … like a hardship or even His absence.

How can we trust and depend on Jesus in the "good times," too? Trusting Jesus is just one of many things in the Christian life that needs time to cultivate. As we see evidence that He is indeed faithful and cares for us so intimately, then our resolve to trust Him more can turn into a fortress of faith … even in the good times.

BACKSTAGE PASS
getting to know

Favorite Books: *How the Grinch Stole Christmas* by Dr. Seuss and *Wild at Heart* by John Eldredge

Musical Influences: Amy Grant, Russ Taff, Lionel Richie, and Don Henley

What is God teaching you now? To wait on Him - to wait and trust even when I can't see Him moving.

How has your family helped you in your walk with God? First of all, by giving me a foundation of faith since I was a child. They led by example and showed me how to live a godly life. Even now, after living a long life, my mom is still very faithful and as committed to Christ as the day she accepted Him as a child.

How do you plan to expand your ministry in the future? I really just walk in faith with this one ... I know the doors I will walk through, that will change my course of direction or expand my ministry, will be opened by God in His time. Perhaps more writing.

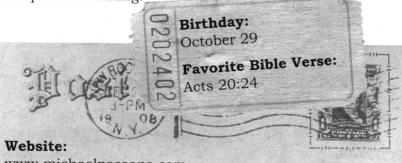

Birthday: October 29

Favorite Bible Verse: Acts 20:24

Website: www.michaelpassons.com

Booking Agency: The Breen Agency
615-777-2227
www.thebreenagency.com

Fan Mail Address: Michael Passons
P.O. Box 158561
Nashville, TN 37215

Fan Email Address: michael@michaelpassons.com

BARLOWGIRL

TRUSTING GOD

*T*rust ... a scary word, but one that God has continued to bring to our daily lives. Being in a band was the last thing that we girls wanted to do. Each of us had been making her own plans for many years. Becca's included starting her own coffee/hair-cutting/ mechanics shop, Lauren was hoping to further her dreams of training dolphins at Sea World, while Alyssa was counting down the days when she could finally fulfill her dreams on the stages of Broadway. However, five years ago, God began tugging at our hearts and asking us if we'd be willing to find out what *HIS* dreams for us were. We were all pretty scared. Asking God what He had for us meant being willing to give up control of our own destiny. To open our hands meant that they might have to be emptied before He could fill them. So many questions ran through our minds. "Is it worth it?" "Could we give it all up for Him?" And the biggest, "Is He trustworthy?" Those same questions were brought up again when He asked us to surrender our dating years to Him. He asked if we'd be willing to give up having dating relationships, so that we could use our time to fully seek Him and His love for us, and to also trust that in His right timing He would reveal our future spouses to us. "Could we trust Him to meet all of our needs and fill us up in these single years? Is our God faithful to fulfill all of His promises?" We have been on this journey that we could have missed, had God not required us to trust Him with our destiny. We don't regret one day giving up our dreams or never having dated anyone, because we are seeing now that our God really is trustworthy. We have been amazed to see such a small sacrifice, that once seemed so huge, open a door for blessings above and beyond what we could have ever hoped for. Have you stopped to ask God what *His* dreams are for your life? Do you know that **He has plans for you that are greater than anything you could ever dream up on your own**? Let's be people that don't hold anything back from Him, but do everything to let go and watch Him direct our steps.

More Verses:
Jeremiah 29:11
Proverbs 3:5-6 and 16:9

UNPLUGGED
a deeper look

Do you consider the blessings you've received by surrender and trusting God a reward? We feel that God asks us to trust Him and obey Him in all He asks us to do. His Word is clear that He does reward us for our obedience - far beyond what we gave up, and far beyond what we could have ever dreamed. It is like tithing; it is a supernatural blessing that comes when we obey Him and give our tithe. He then promises to bless our finances. It's just proof that God is a trustworthy God. We do believe that all of the blessings in our lives come from God and not from our works.

How can we deal with waiting and trusting that God will answer us in His time? Without faith it is impossible to please God. There is nothing He desires more than for us to trust Him and surrender our lives to Him. When there are dry times of waiting, we believe those are the times to draw closer to God and love Him alone - no matter what our circumstances.

Is giving up dating to God something everyone should consider, or are certain people convicted? We believe that dating is not a biblical model for God's plan of connecting

us with our future spouses. We're going to boyfriends and girlfriends to try to define us, and it's getting us into trouble. We think God's just trying to pull back the reins, and say, "I have a calling on your lives, and you're going to miss it if you're chasing guys and girls 24 hours a day." The mentality of recreational dating is a distraction from what God is trying to do in our lives. The point of male/female relationships is to move towards marriage. God's plan for our lives does include marriage, and we believe it includes the one person God created for us. Why would we go and try out other people's spouses, instead of just waiting for our own - for God to open our eyes to who that person is? Our hearts are called to be in love with Christ, and we are called to strive after God. We challenge everyone to honestly consider God's Word and what it says about dating and marriage. Our generation is getting more and more empty, and what it boils down to is, we don't know our self-worth. We encourage everyone to question the world's way and compare it to God's way, so it's a call that we try to put out to everybody.

As you discovered, sometimes God's plan for our lives is different than our own dreams and desires. How can teens handle that change (or disappointment) and continue trusting Him? We have found that there is no better place to be on earth than in the center of God's will for our lives. 1 John talks about the love of this world, and how it keeps us from loving God with all of our hearts. If we fall in love with God, and trust that He desires to bless us and give us life to the fullest, we will be able to surrender all to Him.

BACKSTAGE PASS
getting to know

How did the band meet and form? Well, we are sisters so we never officially "met." Music has always been a huge part of our lives. We traveled around the country for two and a half years as our dad's backup band, doing his music at family services. About four years ago, we began writing our own songs, and

God began to reveal to us that He had a plan for us to begin singing and speaking what He was placing in our hearts. Dad and Mom were more than excited to begin to support us in our music, and we now continue to travel as a family.

Do you feel God leading the band in a special direction?
To be able to lift God's name and standards of purity over this nation. To challenge people to trust God with their lives.

How does the band plan to further its ministry in the future?
Our biggest desire is to follow God with all our hearts and to watch and join Him in His plans to further our ministry.

0202402

Birthdays:
Rebecca: November 24
Alyssa: January 4
Lauren: July 29

0202401

Favorite Bible Verses:
Rebecca: Isaiah 62
Alyssa: Isaiah 49:1-4
Lauren: Psalm 73

Post Card

Booking Agency:
GOA, Inc.
615-790-5540
www.goa-inc.com

Fan Email Address:
contactus@Barlowgirl.com

Website: www.barlowgirl.com

SHAUN GROVES

TWILIGHT - THE STORY BEHIND THE SONG

Confusion crossed her face. My daughter scanned the sky, waiting for the exact moment the sun "turned off." It was our routine to play together in the front yard every afternoon until she exclaimed, "The sun's off!" But this day was different from the others. For the first time ever, she saw the sun and moon together in the sky.

This wasn't right - she must have thought. It had to be one or the other, but not both. She began feverishly explaining to me in two-year-old gibberish how the sky was supposed to look - first the sun turns off and then the moon comes on.

And as I explained to her new little mind what twilight is, I realized that this unusual time of day was the metaphor I'd been searching for. I'd just finished reading a book by Dwight Edwards, *Revolution Within,* that had for the first time, made Romans 7 and the source of so much struggle in my life clear to me. I was eager to tell everyone about what I'd just learned, but hadn't found a way to boil it down to a three-minute pop song. I was missing a metaphor.

Until, there in my front yard, when I least expected it, the answer came from my little girl's bewilderment. We, too - like children looking at a twilight sky for the first time - are often puzzled by the state of our life - torn, it seems, between two opposites: the person we want to be and the person we are. It seems that we're neither sinners nor saints, but instead caught somewhere between the two, unsure which to claim as our true identity. We wonder if everyone's sky is as confused as ours and whether the dawn will ever come.

But I know now that this overlapping of night and day is

only temporary. The scene is slowly changing and the sun will outlast the night. This life change is possible because of the solution, one primary weapon in this great effort, found in Paul's words:

"What a wretched man I am! Who will rescue me from this body of death? Thanks be to God - through Jesus Christ our Lord! ..." (Romans 7:24-25 NIV).

He is slowly bringing up the sun, **increasing our hunger for Himself** and killing off the old longings still distracting us from being who we already are at heart. We are living in twilight, but we hold tightly to the hope of knowing that, because God is still powerful and working, the sun will come up. Someday.

UNPLUGGED
a deeper look

Do you believe God can use our "twilight" time to increase our knowledge of Him? I think our whole life is twilight time. From the moment I entered into a relationship with God (and His Spirit came to live in me, and caused me to desire what He desires), to the time that I see God face to face, is twilight. So I hope He can use this time, the whole rest of my life, to make me over into who I'm supposed to be.

Is this the time when we can totally humble ourselves before Him and listen for his voice, waiting for Him to rescue us as Paul says? Yeah. Dealing with the twilight time, we have one of two choices - we can either be ignorant about it and say, "There's grace, and there's mercy, and there's love. I know that I want to do what's right, but I'm going to do what's wrong, because what's the consequence? What's the big deal?" Or we can go to the other side and humble ourselves before God, and say, "Look, I know I could technically get by

with this, but I know that there's something greater than 'what I can get by with' for me to live for. I want to be part of Your plan to make Yourself known. For people to know who You are, I need to be more like You, so that they understand more of You. I'm humbly coming to You as a guy with a guitar, or a teacher in front of a blackboard, or a student in a desk, and just saying, 'I don't have much to offer, but I want to do things *Your* way, even when I also want to do things *my* way, so use me.'" That, to me, is the humility that's required. The apostle Paul says it's mixed up; we want two things, *God's way* and *my way*. I think it's important that he doesn't say, "*What* will save me from this?" He says, "*Who* will save me from this?" There's a *Who* involved; He comes in and guides us through the twilight time, reminds us what we're supposed to do, and gives us the power to do it. That person is Christ, in the form of His Holy Spirit in our lives.

BACKSTAGE PASS
getting to know

Favorite Books: *Resident Aliens* by Stanley Hauerwas and William Willimon, *The Cost of Discipleship* by Dietrich Bonhoeffer, and *The Celebration of Discipline* by Richard Foster

Musical Influences: Buddy Holly, Elvis, Kenny Rogers on "Coward of the County," Billy Joel, and in college years, Caedmon's Call, Jars of Clay, and Matchbox Twenty.

What is God teaching you now? That I should focus more of my time on being faithful instead of being successful - to focus on cultivating attributes in my life like being obedient to God and being faithful to His character. Following Jesus, "taking up our cross," means that we're taking up our instrument of death, we're taking up something that could kill us, something that could leave us abandoned, and lonely, and unpopular ... with a *linoleum* record instead of a *platinum* record. So that's just the challenge to me - that sometimes being obedient to God isn't going to result in success the way we measure it, but it could have a tragic and unsuccessful end.

How has your family helped you in your walk with God?
Well, going back, Mom and Dad. My mom was my first Sunday School teacher. She's the one I'd ask questions like, "What happens when I die?" My dad also taught me. We'd go camping together and look up at the stars and talk about God, and things that I was worried about or wondered about. He was great at being patient and answering all my questions. I think my kids teach me a lot about God because I understand more the father side of God, and how He can "not like" what I do, but still love *me*. That makes a lot of sense to me, and how that love can't be revoked. No matter what my kids do, my worst nightmare could come true, and I would still love them. I get that now; that's how God loves me. My wife is just the person that knows me better than anybody. She doesn't let me believe that I'm better than I actually am, and she lovingly keeps me humble.

What are your plans to expand your ministry in the future?
We're hopefully going to do more band shows and fewer solo shows. We'll continue to play the colleges, but also do a better job of embracing all of the other generations in the church, and do lots of touring, not just here, but in other parts of the world.

Website:
www.shaungroves.com

Fan Email Address:
shaungrovesfanmail@charter.net

Birthday:
December 27

Favorite Bible Verse:
Isaiah 26:8

Booking Agency:
The Hummingbird Agency
thehummingbirdagency@charter.net

KIDS IN THE WAY

WE ARE THE CHURCH

*T*he world has a picture of Christianity, and for a lot of people, it's a joke. We give them an opportunity to turn their backs, to laugh, and scoff at us. People who call themselves Christians need to realize what that really means - following Christ, and following in His footsteps. Why did God send His Son, Jesus, to the earth to die? It wasn't for religion. It wasn't for the Catholics, or the Presbyterians, or the Baptists, or the Methodists, or the non-denominational Christians. It wasn't for the Democrats or the Republicans. It wasn't for a certain country, or culture, or race. It was for a world of lost people, and it was all in the name of love.

The church is a body of people unified in their relationship with Jesus, not necessarily a building - where we have to be, in order to be comfortable to worship. The focus of the church right now is growing more inward than outward. It's starting to become "the building," and "the programs," and "making worship amazing." It's important for the church to realize that it's okay to have a nice facility, but if it's causing people on the outside to question our motives, to look at the church as just another business that's trying to make more money and grow, it's a bad thing.

What if we could get back to the way it was when Jesus and Paul started churches in the New Testament - cities and communities coming together as a church, not focused on a building, or programs, or spectacular youth nights? Those things are good, but is that our motivation? Is our motivation to run a successful business, to have successful members, and a successful income, or **is our motive to share the love,**

and the acceptance, and the grace of Jesus?

We want to reach lost souls and spread the message of Jesus, but we can't *make* somebody believe something. All we can do is live our lives and pray that the Holy Spirit will introduce Himself to them. It's more than going to a building, going through the motions of worship, and being entertained. We want people to think about what it means to really follow Jesus.

UNPLUGGED
a deeper look

To the kids in the church right now, how would you suggest that they take the news of Jesus' sacrifice for them to the world? Prove it - that you have accepted that sacrifice, and you want to deny yourself. Love people. Love is the key; it's the whole theme of the Bible. It speaks volumes if you can love people that don't love you. If you show someone love, they're going to want to get to know you. In that situation, build a relationship. Then you can share - "Well, this is why I love you. This is why my life is different than yours." - Nathan

What would you say to an unsaved youth who may be reading this? Life is a journey, and we all choose to take certain roads and paths. There's one path that will always lead you to where you want to be and where you need to be. It has all the answers. It has all the truths. It has all the love, promises, and blessings that you could ever hope to get from any other path you might take. I've found it true in my life, and I know lots of people who have found it true in their lives. I can't think of one case where somebody has found it true, then been able to deny it later. It's a 100% guarantee. It's fail-proof. Try this path; you've tried all the other ones. You've found yourself at dead-ends - because that's where they all lead. Try Jesus. Get to know Him. Pick up a Bible, find a church, and talk to somebody that knows Jesus. Find out what He can do for your life, because He's the Answer that we all need. - Dave

BACKSTAGE PASS
getting to know

How did the band meet and form? Three of us met in high school - Dave, Eric, and myself. About four years ago, Austin joined. He was in other bands growing up, and we've always known each other. Our bassist just started playing with us, and that's how we met. - Nathan

Do you feel God leading the band in a special direction? He's called us to spread our music and the message that's in our lives to the people that are lost and to the church. In the past couple of years, we've really felt a desire and a passion in our hearts to try to encourage, and empower, and inspire the church to take a look at itself and try and figure out what it means to really follow Jesus. Being a Christian is having a relationship with Jesus. - Dave

How does the band plan to further its ministry in the future? We are starting to work with an organization called Hands and Feet. Mark Stuart of Audio Adrenaline started it, and his parents are running an orphanage in Haiti right now. As a band, we've always felt that we're playing our music, and we're spreading the gospel, but there's always something more we can do. - Austin

Favorite Bible Verses & Books:
Dave: Psalm 116
Nathan: James
Austin: Romans
Eric: Psalms

Birthdays:
Dave: July 2
Nathan: January 8
Austin: November 4
Eric: May 8

Booking Agency:
Jeff Roberts & Associates
615-859-7040
www.jeffroberts.com

Website: www.kidsintheway.com

Kids in the Way Kids in the Way Kids in the Way

KAINOS

WHY GOD IS BETTER THAN PAXIL

Ben: I can talk about Paxil® and every other anti-depressant out there, because I have taken them all at some point in my life. This is really not about Paxil®, at all - but hopefully it caught your attention. I do want to talk about something that I think affects all of us at some point. I am talking about depression.

I have tried to blame it on rainy days, pop quizzes, friends, parents, and even Hannah. There are some days that I just feel worthless. I honestly believe that the thought of the ceiling falling on me would not move me. In fact, I think I would welcome it. When I feel down, I find it easy to put things off until tomorrow. Suddenly, my thoughts become polluted by sin that I would normally find offensive, but that now doesn't seem so bad. Emotionally, I become numb and if anyone comments on how I am doing, I snap at them and become extremely defensive. Actually, after reading this, even *I* don't want to be around me when I am depressed.

For years I treated my depression as a cold or a virus, something that happened by random chance and that my body was just reacting to. Unlike a cold, though, depression *can* be prevented and you can even predict when it is going to happen. To avoid depression you have to know what causes it.

Usually, it hits me like a ton of bricks after I have been sitting watching the Smurfs marathon on Cartoon Network all day. I realize that I haven't been reading my Bible ... you know, I haven't even talked to God in three days!!! No wonder I feel so crummy!!! It all makes sense now. I have been disconnected from the Source of my life, the Giver of my purpose and worth.

Hannah: I would like to add that the process of becoming disconnected from God always starts when I begin thinking more about what I want and what pleases me (and others around me), than what God wants and what pleases Him. Galatians 1:10 (NIV) says, "Am I now trying to win the approval of men, or of God? Or am I trying to please men? If I were still trying to please men, I would not be a servant of Christ." I must **start out looking to God first, and allow Him to be in every thought and action**, so that I may be filled with joy and patient love for others. If we remain in Christ, then He will remain in us (John 15:4). When I truly seek to be a servant of Christ and look to please Him, not myself and those around me, depression isn't an option.

Ben: Don't let the Devil or your flesh keep you depressed ... shut them down by living in the Spirit (Galatians 5:16). In John 5:10-11 (NIV), Jesus prescribes the ultimate solution to depression when He says, "If you obey my commands, you will remain in my love, just as I have obeyed my Father's commands and remain in his love. I have told you this so that my joy may be in you and that your joy may be complete." We are lacking nothing when we obey God, for He supplies everything we need. Our joy is complete and no, Paxil® can't even come close to promising us that.

Prayer

My dear Father and Savior, thank You so much for Your love. Please help me to look to You each morning and seek Your will for my life, rather than my will or the will of those around me. Help me to stay focused on You throughout this day. Please keep me from drowning in my pride that can lead to depression. Father, I thank You for the gift of grace. I want to abide in You. Amen.

UNPLUGGED
a deeper look

If teens are struggling with depression, and aren't plugged in to the Source of Life, how can they become reconnected? Getting reconnected can seem a bit overwhelming, especially if we are depressed. That is why it is important that we not try to do it alone. There are others like us who have been through similar issues, and that is why the body of Christ is so important. The Bible says in James 5:16 (NLT), "Confess your sins to each other and pray for each other so that you may be healed ..." This tells us that we are to seek help and further counsel from someone like our Youth Pastor, Senior Pastor, or someone within whom the Spirit of God is evident. Establish an accountability core within your youth group and let them know the symptoms of your depression. The most important thing to remember is that you have to be honest with yourself and with God. 1 John 1:9 (NLT) says, "But if we confess our sins to him, he is faithful and just to forgive us and to cleanse us from every wrong." If we will search ourselves we can see that at the root of our depression there is sin, and that sin has separated us from God. If we confess it, God will forgive it and we can begin to grow and fellowship again. I needed help from mentors to help me look at the root of my depression, and they helped me to bring it to the Father. You can do it - just ask God to help you. Get on the phone and call someone; tell your parents, your friends, anyone who will listen to what your plan of action is, so that they can hold you accountable and help you. - Ben

How can kids avoid Satan's traps and stay focused on their joy found in Christ? "So I advise you to live according to your new life in the Holy Spirit. Then you won't be doing what your sinful nature craves" (Galatians 5:16 NLT). I find it easy to fall right into Satan's traps when I am not living in the Spirit. As

a believer, I can feel it when I start to stray away from God's path. It starts when I neglect to read my Bible. Soon I am not praying, and before you know it, I am making excuses not to go to church. It's very much like a snowball effect. One action leads to another, and to another, until it reaches a consequence. In this case, the consequence would be the traps Satan has set for us. In order to be full of joy, we have to recognize the formula. It only takes a spark to get a fire going, and it only takes one choice to send us in a downward spiral of sin. Read God's Word, talk to Him as much as possible, fellowship with friends at church, and pay attention to that feeling in your gut when you are faced with a choice. That still, small voice is the Holy Spirit, and He will guide you in the right path. - Ben

Do you feel God leading the band in a special direction?
Yes. We feel our calling is to challenge our generation to truly seek God and live in His truth - not man's truth. Our mission is based on Colossians 2:6-8. Growing up in the church, we have found it easy to just get into the groove of religion and to lose focus of why we are here in the first place. We don't want to sit on the sidelines of life, and we pray that our generation will join us in making our faith in Christ loud. - Ben

BACKSTAGE PASS
getting to know

How did the two of you meet and begin performing together?
We met through a mutual friend my junior year of high school. After a few weeks, Ben left and lived in Mississippi until the beginning of my senior year. I saw him again at the fair, and we exchanged numbers and started hanging out. Within the first month we had written our first song, and we felt that God would use us in music together. We started a garage band a few months later, and then got married the summer after I graduated high school. - Hannah

How do you plan to further your ministry in the future?
We are open to wherever God will take us, and we trust that

He will show us what steps to take next. We are involved with Gospel For Asia and Food For The Hungry. At the heart of our ministry is missions, in whatever field God leads us. - Ben

Birthdays:
Ben: April 21
Hannah: June 10
Micah: July 20
Christian: March 5
Brandon: November 9

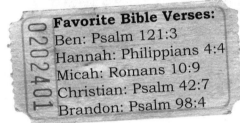

Favorite Bible Verses:
Ben: Psalm 121:3
Hannah: Philippians 4:4
Micah: Romans 10:9
Christian: Psalm 42:7
Brandon: Psalm 98:4

Booking Agency:
Pure Zone Artist Agency
bskaggs@purezoneagency.com

Fan Email Address:
kainos@kainosmusic.com

Websites:
www.kainosmusic.com
www.myspace.com/kainosband

Ever Stays Red

Witnessing "In Spirit And In Truth"

Dustin Carlson

*F*or decades the church has been faced with the obstacle of trying to reach a lost and dying world. Fear of conformity has caused many Christians to take the sideline in many of the avenues that so heavily influence popular culture. In the name of righteousness, Christians have boycotted Hollywood, abandoned politics, and written off rock 'n' roll as a device of the Devil. For the greater part of its existence, the church has allowed self-imposed rules and regulations to construct a wall between Christ's message of love and a world that is starving for it. Fortunately, times have changed. The stage has been set, the time is now, and we are the ones to break that wall and take the light within us, and let it be a light unto all men. Okay, but how?

I have often found inspiration in the story of Jesus and His encounter with the Samaritan woman at the well, depicted in the fourth chapter of John. Historical context shows that for a Jewish Rabbi to have any contact whatsoever with a Samaritan was considered an unclean act against God. Jesus Christ, weary from a long journey, forgets His own discomfort, He sets aside the opinions of His disciples and the religious authorities of His day, and He reaches out to this woman in love. The parallel to our own lives is clear: How often do we, weary from the everyday grind of life, fail to extend ourselves for the sake of love? How often do we fail to sacrifice our own comforts, or put aside the opinions of others, in order to show someone in need the love of Christ? In the story, the disciples return to find their Lord in this religious predicament and are astonished at the sight. How could this man, whom they had given up everything to follow, whom they had trusted to be the promised Messiah, degrade Himself by speaking with this woman? In verse 35 (NKJV), Jesus addresses the disciples saying, "Do you not say 'There are still four months and *then* comes the harvest?' Behold I say to you, lift up your eyes and look at the fields, for they are already white for the harvest!"

As Christians living in a hurting world, do we not continually say, "There are still four months and then comes the harvest?" Do we not read the Word, read these stories of Jesus sacrificing Himself for the sake of love, and yet when presented with the opportunity to do the same, we make excuses? We say things like, "It's not my time," or "I'm too shy," or "My friends will laugh at me." We make excuses as to why we can't, while **Jesus longs for someone who will**. Let us lift up our eyes and look at the fields. Let us lift up our eyes and truly see this world - our friends and relatives, the people we work with, the people we sit next to in class, the nameless faces that serve us food or pass us on the street. Let us lift up our eyes and see the people that surround us every day of our lives, just as Jesus sees them - "already white for the harvest." For just as the harvest sits ready and waiting to be gathered, so the world sits, ready and waiting to experience the love of Jesus Christ. It is on us to stretch ourselves to show it to them.

More Verses:
John 4:5-35
Philippians 2:3 and 2:5-7
Hebrews 10

UNPLUGGED
a deeper look

How can teens overcome the fears of witnessing: that their friends might laugh at them, that they don't want to be seen talking to the "unpopular kid," that they're too shy, and rise up to be who Christ has called them to be? The best way I have found is simply by confessing the Word of God over our circumstances. When confronted with the fear of reaching out to someone, confess 2 Timothy 1:7-8 (NKJV), "For God has not given us a spirit of fear but of power and of love and of a sound mind. Therefore do not be ashamed of the testimony of our Lord ..." Confess it over and over again until you get to the point that you actually believe it deep down. Remember, the idea is to display the love of Jesus Christ throughout the course of our daily lives. It is amazing how far a single considerate act can go.

When an opportunity to witness arises, should we always take it, or are there times when we could push people away from Jesus rather than bringing them to Him? How can teens know if God is leading them to witness, or if their own fears are pulling them away? I cannot think of a time in which Christ did not try to impact someone He came in contact with in a real way. There were certainly times when people did not understand the significance of His message. Every day he looked for opportunities to serve other people in love, with lowliness of mind, esteeming others better than himself (Philippians 2:3). The mind-set that existed in Christ always sought to serve other people. I think if our intent is to serve others, to esteem others better than we esteem ourselves, the Spirit will guide us in a way that will not cause those around us to take offense.

BACKSTAGE PASS
getting to know

How did the band meet and form? Dustin, the singer, and Erik, the bass player, were involved in a worship band together at a local church. Josh, the drummer, and Zach, the guitar player, were playing basketball at a Christian college together. Josh and Dustin have been brothers since birth, creating the common link among all four members.

Do you feel God leading the band in a special direction? Ever Stays Red has always made promoting the message of God the primary focus of its ministry. It seems as if the more we promote God, the more He opens doors. We are working to put out our next album and hope to have more opportunities to travel and spread that message.

How does the band plan to further its ministry in the future? We have been overseas on two different occasions and spent two weeks playing shows in Brazil. That was a very rewarding experience for the band. There are so many kids living on the streets in Brazil that are very into rock music. There is nothing like bringing a message of hope to those kids in a format they are open to. Our hope is that the opportunity to get back to Brazil will present itself again.

Birthdays:
Dustin: November 25
Zach: March 25
Erik: May 13
Josh: April 26

Favorite Bible Verses:
Dustin: Psalm 5:11-12
Zach: Psalm 27:1
Erik: Nahum 2:5
Josh: Philippians 1:6

Booking:
booking@everstaysred.com

Fan Email Address:
erik@everstaysred.com
dustin@everstaysred.com
josh@everstaysred.com
zach@everstaysred.com

Website: www.everstaysred.com

Get Involved

Many of the artists included in this book support organizations that allow them to put their faith into action. Check out the websites listed below to see how you can get involved, too!

Blood:Water Mission
www.bloodwatermission.org

Compassion International
www.compassion.com

Food For The Hungry
www.fh.org

Gospel For Asia
www.gfa.org

Hands & Feet Project
www.handsandfeetproject.org

Jump Start Resources
www.jumpstartresources.com

Redeem The Vote
www.redeemthevote.com

The Home Foundation
www.thehomefoundation.org

World Vision
www.worldvision.org

Youth For Christ
www.yfc.net

Photo Credits

Concert photo page, p. 12: photos by Tracy Winters

Kutless, p. 14: photo courtesy BEC Recordings

Out of Eden, p. 18: photo courtesy Gotee Records

Supertones, p. 22: photo courtesy Tooth & Nail Records

Jason Morant, p. 26: photo by Jeremy Cowart courtesy Integrity Media

Jill Phillips, p. 30: photo by Mark Nicholas

Krystal Meyers, p. 33: photo by Justin Stephens courtesy Essential Records

John Reuben, p. 36: photo courtesy Gotee Records

Natalie Grant, p. 39: photo by Dominick Guillemot courtesy Curb Records

Kimberly Perry, p. 43: photo by Marie Perry

BDA, p. 48: photo by Jimmy Abegg courtesy Creative Trust Workshop www.jimmyabegg.com www.tslcreative.com

Nate Sallie, p. 52: photo courtesy Cider Mountain Recorders

Tim Hughes, p. 55: photo by Jimmy Abegg www.jimmyabegg.com www.tslcreative.com

Monk & Neagle, p. 60: photo by Jeremy Cowart courtesy Flicker Records

Charlie Hall, p. 64: photo by Katherine Bomboy courtesy sixstepsrecords

Scott Krippayne, p. 68: photo by David Johnson courtesy Spring Hill Music Group

Denver Bierman, p. 72: photo courtesy Reel Loud Records

Paul Colman, p. 76: photo courtesy Inpop Records

Pillar, p. 80: photo by Lee Webb courtesy Flicker Records

Casting Crowns, p. 84: photo courtesy Provident Label Group

Palisade, p. 88: photo by Kristin Barlowe courtesy Fervent Records

Sanctus Real, p. 92: photo courtesy Sparrow Records

Detour180, p. 96: photo by Sarah Scarlet

Jeff Anderson, p. 100: photo courtesy Gotee Records

The Darins, p. 105: photo by Sandy Campbell

Todd Agnew, p. 110: photo courtesy Ardent Records

Donnie Lewis, p. 115: photo courtesy Paradigm Management Group

James Clay, p. 119: photo courtesy Inpop Records

Warren Barfield, p. 122: photo by Jeremy Cowart courtesy Essential Records

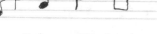

Photo Credits Photo Credits Photo Credits Photo

Alathea, p. 127: photo courtesy
Rocketown Records

The Myriad, p. 131: photo courtesy
Floodgate Records

Avalon, p. 135: photo by Robert Ascroft

Michael Tait, p. 140: photo courtesy
True Artist Management

Starfield, p. 144: photo by Rob Campbell
www.robscampbell.ca

The Elms, p. 148: photo by Michael Wilson
courtesy Universal South Records

ZOEgirl, Chrissy Conway, p. 152: photo by
Michelle Spurr

Bethany Dillon, p. 157: photo by
Robert Deutschman

Hawk Nelson, p. 162: photo courtesy
Tooth & Nail Records

Audio Adrenaline, p. 166: photo by
Kerri Stuart

Russ Lee, p. 169: photo courtesy
Vertical Vibe Records

Daniel's Window, p. 173: photo by
Dan Machnik

Darlene Zschech, p. 177: photo by
Tony Mott

Silers Bald, p. 181: photo by Kristin
Barlowe courtesy Essential Records

Building 429, p. 185: photo by
Aaron Rapoport courtesy Word Records

Forever Changed, p. 190: photo courtesy
Floodgate Records

Carried Away, p. 194: photo by
Kristin Barlowe

Skillet, p. 199: photo courtesy
Ardent Records

Tammy Trent, p. 203: photo courtesy
Michael Gomez Photography

Jeff Deyo, p. 207: photo courtesy
Gotee Records

Day of Fire, p. 212: photo by Reisig &
Taylor courtesy Essential Records

Everyday Sunday, p. 217: photo by Jeremy
Cowart courtesy Flicker Records

John David Webster, p. 220: photo
courtesy BHT Records

Erin O'Donnell, p. 223: photo courtesy
Inpop Records

ZOEgirl, Kristin Swinford, p. 226: photo by
Michelle Spurr

FFH, p. 230: photo by Robert Ascroft
courtesy Essential Records

Rachael Lampa, p. 234: photo by Kristin
Barlowe courtesy Word Records

Brad Miles, p. 238: photo by Bill Welch
bwstudios.com

Crystal Lewis, p. 242: photo by
James Allen

NewSong, p. 247 and 249: photo by
Jimmy Abegg courtesy Van-Liere Wilcox
Management / www.jimmyabegg.com
www.tslcreative.com

Everlife, p. 253: photo by Allen Clark
courtesy Crowne Music Group

Overflow, p. 257: photo by Kristin Barlowe
courtesy Essential Records

Sarah Kelly, p. 261: photo courtesy
Gotee Records

Whisper Loud, p. 265 - 267: photo by
Rita Blumer

Philmore, p. 271: photo by
Brett Schoneman

Shawn McDonald, p. 274: photo by
Joel Flory

Joel Engle, p. 277: photo courtesy
Joel Engle Ministries

Kent Bottenfield, p. 280: photo by
Robert Stewart

Jaci Velasquez, p. 283: photo by Kristin
Barlowe courtesy Word Records

Staple, p. 286: photo by Drew Reynolds
courtesy Flicker Records

Tree63, p. 289: photo courtesy
Inpop Records

Seventh Day Slumber, p. 293: photo
courtesy BEC Recordings

Newsboys, p. 296: photo courtesy
Inpop Records

KJ-52, p. 301: photo courtesy
Uprok Records

Jadyn Maria, p. 305: photo by Chad Hiner

Jars of Clay, p. 308: photo from
Redemption Songs by David Dobson
courtesy Essential Records

Fusebox, p. 312: photo by Melissa Dilley

Thousand Foot Krutch, p. 315: photo
courtesy Tooth & Nail Records

Sara Groves, p. 318: photo courtesy
INO Records

Across The Sky, p. 322: photo by Kristin
Barlowe courtesy Word Records

Michael Passons, p. 325: photo by
Matthew Barnes

BarlowGirl, p. 328: photo by Kristin
Barlowe courtesy Fervent Records

Shaun Groves, p. 332: photo courtesy
Rocketown Records

Kids in the Way, p. 336: photo by Frank
Mullen courtesy Flicker Records

Kainos, p. 339: photo by Carla Porch

Ever Stays Red, p. 344: photo courtesy
Wrinkle Free Records

Rachel and Rebekah Winters, p. 350:
photos by Artistic Photography,
Greensburg, IN 812-662-7888

About The Authors

Rachel Winters attends online high school, which allowed her more time to complete this book. In her spare time, she enjoys playing keyboards, graphic design, writing, attending

Christian concerts and festivals, and spending time with her family and friends. She is active in her church youth group and plays keyboards for the youth praise team. After college, she plans on a career in the Christian music industry, and hopes to continue with her writing.

Rebekah Winters attends Greensburg Community High School, where she participates in speech team, academic team, art club, and is on the yearbook staff. She loves music and NFL football (especially the Colts). After attending college, she hopes to work in the music industry. She is active in her church youth group, is a computer tech for Sunday worship services, and plays guitar for the youth praise team. While at Christian concerts and festivals, she enjoys meeting new people.

About The Authors About The Authors About The Authors

Index Of Artists

Postlude · A Last Note Postlude · A

Would You Like To Become A Christian?

If you have read these devotions and made the decision to ask Jesus to be your Savior, you can pray the following prayer:

"Dear Lord Jesus, I know that I am a sinner. I believe that You died for me on the cross, rose again, and through Your blood I am saved. Please forgive me of my sins and come into my heart. Change my life, Lord, bless me with a giving spirit, and help me live for You. In Your holy name I pray, Amen."

Now you know without question that you will spend eternity with God in heaven. Find a good Bible-believing church and begin to surround yourself with Christian friends. Read and study the Bible everyday. Be sure to spend time in prayer.

Comments And Additional Copies

Did a devotion encourage or challenge you?
Were you inspired to take a stand for your faith?

We would love to hear your comments, stories, and feedback!

Please contact us at:

btmdevotional@hotmail.com or
info@behindthemusicdevotional.com

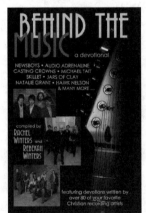

BEHIND THE MUSIC

P.O. Box 501
Greensburg, IN 47240

Visit us at our website:
www.behindthemusicdevotional.com

For the latest news and to interact with other
Christian music fans, go to:
www.myspace.com/behindthemusicdevotional

For additional copies, order online or call 800-457-3230.